THE ALCHEMIST'S ALMANACH

T H E
ALCHEMIST'S
ALMANACH

Reweaving the Tapestry of Time

Harlan Margold

BEAR & COMPANY
P U B L I S H I N G
SANTA FE, NEW MEXICO

LIBRARY OF CONGRESS CATALOGING-IN-PUBLICATION DATA
Margold, Harlan, 1941-
    The alchemist's almanach : reweaving the tapestry of time /
by Harlan Margold.
        p.   cm.
    ISBN 0-939680-74-2
    1. New Age movement. 2. Spiritual life. 3. Religions—
History. 4. Civilization. I. Title.
BP605.N48M34 1991
299′ .93—dc20   90-47080
                                                                CIP

Text & illustration copyright © 1991 by Harlan Margold

Bear & Company, Inc.
Santa Fe, NM 87504-2860

Cover illustration: Suzanne de Veuve © 1991, courtesy of
Floating Lotus Gallery, San Francisco
Interior illustration: Harlan Margold
Cover and interior design: Angela C. Werneke
Editing: Barbara Doern Drew
Typography: Casa Sin Nombre, Ltd.
Printed in the United States of America By R.R. Donnelley

9 8 7 6 5 4 3 2 1

To my family

And with special thanks
to Barbara Hand Clow for her astral and editorial guidance;
to Mark Lerner for giving me graffiti space
in his monthly magazine, *Welcome to Planet Earth*;
to Barbara Doern Drew for her fine-tune editing;
and to three unusual teachers:
Charles F. Thompson, Linda Joyce, and Julie Alsobrooks.

C O N T E N T S

Foreword by Bob Longacre............................xiii

Prologue: An Introduction to the Modern Art of Alchemy.....xv

Part One: The Alchemy of Storytelling

Chapter 1: Explaining the Unexplainable 1
Circles & Spirals. Our Bodies, Our Selves. In-Car-Nations.
Body & Soul. Who Are We?

Part Two: The Alchemy of Self-Healing

Chapter 2: Learning Our Unconscious Powers...............11
Our Psychic Centers. The Seven E-Zones. Auras. Cords.

Chapter 3: Taking Our Unconscious Powers.................23
Seven E-Zone Meditation. Grounding. Grounding
Technique. Mediums. Palm and Foot E-Zones. Running
Energy. Running Energy Exercise. Running Energy through
the E-Zones. Cleansing Your Aura. Breaking Cords. Ending
Your Meditation.

Chapter 4: Using Our Unconscious Powers.................33
Transforming Holograms. Transforming Holograms
Meditation. Imagination Meditation. Past Lives & the
Akashic Records. Healing Meditations. Your Perfection.
Healing through the E-Zones. Totality.

Chapter 5: Reincarceration 49
Parents. Planet of Choice. Bodies. Bodiless Souls.
Relationships. Higher & Lower Selves. Suicide. Spiraling
Circles.

Part Three: The Sacred Heart of Time

Chapter 6: Genesis......................................61
The Organized Sacred World. Light & Darkness. Rhythm
of Sevens. The Mortal World. The Birth of the Earth. First
Civilization—The Mental Plane. Second Civilization—The

Astral Plane. The Duality of the Sexes. Third Civilization—
The Etheric Plane. Mu. Lilith & Adam & Eve. Heaven,
Earth & Hell. Humanity Descends. Back to the Drawing
Board.

Chapter 7: Exodus 88
Third Civilization to Fourth Civilization. Magnus Magus &
Lemuria. Atlantis. Cain & Abel. Fratricidal Love. Semites &
Aryans. Noah.

Chapter 8: Numbers. 103
Fifth Civilization. The Rise of Ego. The Great Mother & the
Horned God Meet the Sky Gods. Death. The Return of the
Semite Storytellers. Children of Abraham. YaHWeH.
Moses. Prophets.

Chapter 9: Chronicles 122
Zoroaster & Mithras. Israel's Duality. Egyptian Trinity.
Amenhotep, Part IV. Osiris, Isis & Horus. Greco-Roman
Multiplicity. Apollo & Dionysus. The Grecian Mysteries.
Roman Multiplicity. Roman Collegia. Outer Religion.
Essenes, Sadducees & Pharisees. The Deliverer.

Chapter 10: The Gospel According to Melchizedek 145

Chapter 11: Revelations 167
Judas. The Inner Temple. John the Diviner. Crucifixion &
Cruci-Fictions. The Grail.

Part Four: The Profaned Heart of Time

Chapter 12: Age of Light/Age of Darkness, 0-1000 A.Z. 183
Sacred Librarians. The Christ & the Antichrist. Two Israels.
Holy Whores. Saint Paul. Hierarchies & Heretics. Gnostics,
Dualists & Arians. Two Romes. Monasticism. Justinian.
Allah: The Third Face of the One God. The Age of
Fragmentation. The Knight & the Lady. Rhythms of
Civilization. Doomsday.

Chapter 13: The Muddled Ages, 500-1500 A.Z. 209
Sorcerer Ethics. Cabala & Capitalism. The Necrocracy.
Zero. The Crusades. Orders of the Cross. Troubadours,
Builders & Templars. The Age of Heavy Metal. The
Renaissance. The Old World Meets the New World.

Chapter 14: The Age of Information, Reformation &
            Transformation, 1500-1800 A.Z. 228
            The Reformation. Communities of God. Protester
            Hierarchies. The Empire Strikes Back: The Counter-
            Reformation. Rosicrucians. The Messiah Returns. The
            Law of the Grave. Age of Enlightenment. Revolutions of
            Time & Space. The French Revolution, Part I.

Chapter 15: The Age of Fragmented Unities, 1800-1900 A.Z. 246
            Napoleon Bonaparte. A Revolution Named Industrial. The
            Insect World. The First of the Marx Brothers. Sisterhood
            Emerges. The Nineteenth Century, Part II. Darwin of the
            Apes. The Mechanical Eye of Humanity Opens. The
            Roman Empire Never Died. The Overworld, the
            Underworld & Free Enterprise. The World of the Dead.

Chapter 16: The Age of Relativity, 1900-1990 A.Z. 266
            The War-to-End-All-Wars, Part I. The French Revolution,
            Part II. The Heaviest Marx Brother of Them All.
            Sisterhood, Part II. Einstein & Frankenstein. Return of the
            Holy Roller Empire. Hello, Hitler. The War-to-End-All-Wars,
            the Sequel. The Birth of the Antichrist Child. The
            Disunited Nations. Israel Rises Anew. The Twentieth
            Century, Part II. The Cold War. Outer Space & Inner Space.
            The French Revolution, Part III. Doomsday, Part II.

Chapter 17: The Age of America 295
            Human Color-Worlds. Christian Israel. Comes the
            Revolution. The Primary Residency. The Experiment Takes
            Hold. Latter-day Saints. Union & Disunion. The Astral
            Comes Down to Earth. Materialism Depressingly
            Rampant. The Underworld Rises. Enter the Nuclear Age.
            The World Goes 2-D. Sex, Drugs & Rock 'n' Roll. Sects,
            Rugs & Rocky Road Ice Cream. More Revolutions. Enter
            the Dreammaster. Endings & Beginnings.

Epilogue. 333

About the Author 335

F O R E W O R D

Whenever Earth's Tree of Life is threatened, out from their homes deep under its roots come the usually shy gnomes. They begin to move amongst us, mending the tears in the tapestry with the clarity and gaiety of their wisdom. Their immense perspective is gained from quietly living under the roots and listening (through the tree) to the cosmos. However, openly sharing this understanding with us is usually at great personal distress and sacrifice. Gnomes, you see, are reclusive because humans have abused the environment and the other kingdoms of life—unforgivable to a gnome.

Harlan Margold is one of these shy gnomes, surfacing to tell us stories in *The Alchemist's Almanach* of what *was*, what *is*, and what *can be* in this "circular, cyclical world where . . . we always have choice as to beginnings and endings and the in-betweens that take us from one to the other." In classical gnome tradition, high humor abounds, and the tale of humanity takes on the flavor of Tolkien's Bilbo Baggins bumbling through a series of Gary Larson cartoons.

The Age of Metal becomes the age of loud machinery: the Age of Heavy Metal, which leads to the "revolution named Industrial." Harlan portrays this potentially depressing era with imaginative wit: "The inventiveness of humanity throughout its dual metal ages has always reflected the forms and brittleness of the insect world, with the tool-makers among us creating mechanical creatures that superficially mimic those odd biological beings that swarm and sting and crawl in outrageous numbers over the humid and temperate zones of Earth."

Being extremely clever and full of innate love of this silly, cyclical hologram called "life on planet Earth," gnomes can have us laughing at the grimmest cycles of "conquest, supremacy, warfare, death, and destruction" that we humans have always lived and died for. This self-described "science friction" writer gnome deftly deals with such taboo subjects as Christian myth, spinning and weaving his golden words so lovingly as to offend no one. The message of the Christ thus becomes: "Acting out of a high-hearted mischief, the Master performed his farewell trick with just a magical cup and the slightest of sleights of hand to give his disciples their final unheard message: that instead of searching for the illusions behind his truths, they should have been looking for the truth behind his illusions, for therein lay his true Word."

If, while you are reading these tales, you hear a gentle rustle nearby, whisper, "Harlan, Harlan," and you will probably hear a giggle. And before long, you will be giggling, too, because we are all gnomes when we listen.

Bob Longacre
Walpole, New Hampshire
January 1991

Bob Longacre is a woods' gnome, a writer about the world's magical kingdoms, and co-publisher of Sweet Fern, *a magazine about self-empowerment and information to aid us in walking what we talk.*

P R O L O G U E

An Introduction to the Modern Art of Alchemy

Alchemy is the art of transforming idea into actuality. In medieval times, this much misunderstood process was associated with transmuting base metals into gold. But true alchemy has a far deeper and richer meaning than that, for it lies at the very core of our imaginative existence upon the Earth. Whenever we turn thoughts into realities, we are performing alchemy or making something into something else entirely.

Because we exist on a living world that throbs to the erosive rhythms of time, we, too, are all continually evolving, changing, and testing our abilities at manifestation here. Thus, each of us is a practicing alchemist within the framework of our lives, whether we choose to call ourselves that or not.

The people who know how to directly spin the threads of their dreams into the gold of real experience are intuitively operating on a very high alchemical level. This is an innate skill that all of us possess to varying degree, and those who can tap into it the most successfully usually wind up leading the most satisfying and fulfilling lives. This seems to be one of the primary reasons we are all in physical bodies on this physical world—to learn how to get in touch with our alchemist within and allow that magical being to make each of our manifested existences as rich and complete as possible.

THE ALCHEMIST'S ALMANACH

The Alchemist's Almanach was written to help enhance that process, on both an individual and a larger collective level. It reweaves tapestries of time and personal space together to create a new and, hopefully, more golden way of looking at the long story of humanity's presence upon the Earth, while exploring the various dimensions of our own bodies and the many pathways toward growth that they represent.

To help facilitate that goal, *The Alchemist's Almanach* is divided into four parts. The first part deals with the alchemy of storytelling, and briefly explains the seeming unexplainability of what we are all doing here on this curious planet, where nothing is ever quite what it seems to be.

The second part goes into the alchemy of self-healing. It shows the reader how to use his or her body and its hidden energy centers as a gateway into the realm of the unconscious, and how that unconscious can be an extraordinarily valuable tool in opening up each of us to the full breadth of our being.

The third and fourth parts deal with the larger body of humanity, tracing the spirituality of our presence here from primeval times on up through the sacred and profane stories of present Western civilization, in order to explain many of the seeming contradictions and conflicts of our modern world. These two sections are purposely biblical in their structure, for the tradition of magical storytelling that the Bible represents has long been with us as a means of stretching our limited worldly minds to embrace the possibility of otherworldly presences here as well.

Like any almanach, this is a work that is dense with story and fact. It can be casually browsed or intensely read straight through, since it was written under the precepts of alchemy and is meant to combine with each of its readers differently.

A WORD FROM THE AUTHOR

I consider myself a "science friction" writer. Science friction rubs up against reality. Perhaps its content is true. Perhaps it isn't. It's meant to bridge the world of the imagination with the world of accepted reality, and it asks its readership to try to do the same. Science friction also pays deep homage to the magic of language: the texture and subtle play of words and phrases, and how they knit together into the larger cloth of intricate idea.

Finally, sci-fri is a highly mischievous form, for it deals with breaking boundaries and questioning the questions that have long held the hypnotizing answers of acceptability. Our world seems to have been conceived in high good humor, and yet its recorded human presence has long shown a remarkably consistent fascination with the grimmest aspects possible of dwelling here in its endless pursuits of conquest, supremacy, warfare, death, and destruction.

I wrote *The Alchemist's Almanach* in the spirit that civilization doesn't have to be a continuous collective downer. Ours is a world of many worlds—deeply joyous, raucously entertaining, enchantingly magical, rapaciously carnal, innocently ascetic, violently exciting, violently stupifying, numbingly sorrowful, and dully routine. Each of us is presented with constant choice on how to proceed through all that, and in our choices we have the power to create many realities here, which, once again, is the very basis of alchemy.

So, welcome, reader, to the wonder-filled realm of storytelling alchemy. May it open you up to the magic within that each of us so deeply and dearly carries here.

T H E
ALCHEMY OF
STORYTELLING

Part One

Explaining the Unexplainable

There is one gift that all of humanity shares: the gift of storytelling. We are all storytellers, even if we never entertain an audience larger than ourselves. Stories are one of the basic currencies of life. They define us. They define the many worlds in which we live. They make this fleeting place a little more understandable. They seem to be a key to the greater mysteries of who we really are and what we are all doing here—if, indeed, we are doing anything here at all, other than hanging out in chaotic uncertainty until our inevitable disappearance into the unknown. The "un-ness" of life—its uncertainty, its unpredictability, its unknowingness—has fed heavily into the stories we have created around our reason for being here. The stories seem to be the one thing that really give us continuity, a sense of design, and even meaning in an otherwise chaotic universe.

We have marked our stay on planet Earth through imaginative and scientific tales and legends and fables and romances of what we feel is the true nature of this multidimensional world. The stories that have touched us the most have become our enduring myths, our explanations of the unexplainable. Many have been given abiding spirit and have passed beyond myth into rock-hard belief, creating realities far deeper than life itself.

CIRCLES & SPIRALS

All of us are connected to this planet through disposable bodies. That is the heart and soul of our story here: trying to explain and accept the frustrations and fears of our own frail mortality. We have been taught in Western culture that we and our bodies are one. Once the body goes, we are either at the mercy of divine judgment, or we are absolutely nothing at all. Where we come from before earth life nobody knows. But where we go afterward has inspired an endless spate of stories to ease the fear behind that awesome question. Perhaps the two are the same place.

We live on a gravity-defined planet that is part of a solar system that lies in the outer reaches of its greater galaxy. Earth is an outpost on the frontier of our visible universe, isolated and self-sufficient, and seemingly all alone in a vast heaven. It seems to house the only sign of life around. Maybe, then, some of its mysteries can be seen through its very life signs.

Every twenty-four-hour period of our lives, we spend, on the average, up to a third of that time in a state of unconscious sleep. Each day, we go through the ritual of resurrection, returning from the dead of sleep into the waking world. Each night our conscious mind disconnects, and each morning, it returns through the act of reawakening. This daily death and rebirth that all of us continually experience here has somehow eluded our greater sense of the dynamics of our four-dimensional sphere. It seems to be poignant reminder that our minds and bodies may not be *one*, but rather a temporary marriage of elements which need separation and restful sustenance in order to coordinate effectively. If we do experience a symbolic death each night through sleep, could we not also experience a larger shift of bodies and minds from lifetime to lifetime, much in the same manner?

The rhythms of nature—with the birth of spring, the ripening of summer, the harvesting of fall, and the death of winter—are all stages in the story of human life as well. Somehow the inevitable fact that winter always leads into spring has escaped Western humanity's view of the greater universe, so insistent is it that this round world is governed by straight-line rules.

The cyclical reappearance of spring every year after winter's death—and day after each night's darkness—would seem to indicate that we, too, might come and go from this planet in a similar manner, living in the same circular pattern as our larger host. The straight-line, three-dimensional story of birth, life, and death that is at the base of Western culture does not really fit in with the physical model we have of our immediate universe: a round globe spinning in steady circles around an even larger round burning ball, the sun, the very symbol of life itself.

On a macrocosmic level, we seem to be governed by the rhythms and laws of circles—that is how our physical world is shaped. That is the pattern of Earth's heavenly wanderings. That is the form that most of its deep space companions take. In the circle of our days and seasons and lives, darkness breeds light, winter breeds spring, life breeds death. And more than likely, death breeds life, in this world where the eternality of life is discontinuous but, nevertheless, is always there in one form or another.

Since we are ruled by gravity and the laws of the grave, everything is drawn strongly downward here. This wearing process eventually does all bodies in, but somehow new ones always appear to replace them, to give continuity to the continually interrupted rhythm of existence here: sleeping/waking; winter/spring; dark/light; death/life.

On a microcosmic level, all of us are composed of billions of cells, and inside each living cell are components that dictate the dimensions and the characteristics of the larger creature they compose. One of the basic shapes the transmitters of this information takes is the spiral, as in the dual-spiraled double helix contained in all DNA, the shaper and mover of life. Macrocosmic circles and microcosmic spirals complement one another. The spiral is a circle that does not wish to end where it began, but pushes upward and downward in a circular motion to find its true nature. Could this be the ongoing story of continuous human life as well, spiraling up and down through the orderly circles of time to discover its true essence?

OUR BODIES, OUR SELVES

Since our physical plane of existence is defined by time and space, all we ever have available to us is the eternal present. Anything that we project on either the past or the future or greater worlds than this one always comes from that highly limited perspective. This strange world is also compounded by the irony that the people who are the most uninformed about its ultimate workings are the ones who are usually the most aggressive in foisting their energetic ignorance on everyone else. Many of us spend our lives doing incessant battle with the twisted tales these distortions create. When you live on a sphere that is partially explained by science and partially by mystery, you are left with a lot of questions unanswered by both.

Perhaps the answer to some of the greater mysteries can be found in the smaller workings of our own lives, since spirals, even those that are partially invisible, constantly reflect themselves in their ongoing patterns. Maybe, by looking at some of our many separated parts, a different, much larger whole can emerge than the one we have collectively concocted so far. Our grave-bound bodies and the interrupted immortality we experience through them are probably humanity's greatest collective frustration. And yet these bodies are the vehicles that allow us to touch the earth as well as to give expression to life. They seem to be easily entered and exited through sleep and wakefulness, and, sometimes, they seem to have horrifying self-destructive wills all their own.

IN-CAR-NATIONS

Consider, then, the automobile. Cars are metallic bodies that have been designed with projected life spans for highly specific biospheres, or life-supporting environments. They are incarnations unto themselves, rolling, roaring insectlike creatures that can run at high speeds and carry great loads but which must conform to very restrictive physical laws to do so. Otherwise they find themselves permanently off the road—just like humans.

When a driver steps into a car, it is very much like someone stepping into a physical body. Here is a highly complex machine that takes a wide range of skills to acquire, navigate, and maintain. All car owners make a conscious choice about how they relate to cars. They can run them down, knowing they'll just get another one, or they can maintain them in top running order, assuming this is the only one they'll ever have. Some cars spend their earth time under the ownership of a single driver and last for decades. Others come and go in startling and tragic fashion. Some are the property of families or groups who share in their ownership as well as their use. Some get stolen quite easily and are made the prey of parasite drivers, who abandon or wreck them. Some are inordinately accident prone. Some are costly beyond belief. Some never pick up a scratch. And some seem to go on and on forever.

BODY & SOUL

All the above are appropriate metaphors for the way we operate human bodies. The standard rule would seem to be one being per body, but the actuality is probably far more complicated than that. Bodies, like cars, seem to have their own lives. In much the same manner that cars can be sold or given over from one driver to the next, a body does not necessarily have to end its existence with the same driver it had at its beginning. Many times humans go through such profound life changes that their present selves are hardly recognizable relative to their pasts. What really might have happened is that the body changed drivers in midjourney or accepted a more-or-less advanced version of the driver to assume responsibility for it. So, despite the fact that your body may be the same car rolling down the four-dimensional "timepike" that you have always called your life, there is no guarantee just who exactly is sitting behind the wheel. What you think of as your physical "I" may be the result of a host of navigators sharing in your various specialities or just one continuous chauffeur intent on maintaining the unbroken continuity of your existence.

One driver can also own a whole fleet of cars and run many of them at once if she or he is so disposed—the combination of drivers and cars is as plentiful as there are bodies and souls. Those who have developed the greatest skills at manifestation are probably the ones who are allowed to run the most interesting bodies. Just as a powerful car can be overwhelming for a driver without the ability to control it, so can a powerful body prove far too dangerous for an equally inexperienced or inept novice to operate. In the same way, a body that has too many different drivers telling it to go in too many different directions at once usually winds up never going anywhere at all. In order to be effective, then, bodies and souls have to somehow mesh, to reflect one another. Otherwise they are going to be constantly reminded about their disconnections as they lurch down life's roads unsteadily together.

If all that is confusing, it is only meant to show that there all sorts of possibilities here and there are endless combinations of bodies and souls. Most of us are probably one soul linked to one body, with that soul trying to find its way back home. That may be why we came to this sacred world where the blatant and the mysterious live side by side. This is a place for great masters as well as people who can barely survive—a world of many worlds and of many different levels of existence.

WHO ARE WE?

If we are not our bodies, but only their disembodied drivers—or maybe really neither—who or what are we?

This is a planet that attracts a great variety of life forms to it. Many worlds seem to feed into Earth, all with different laws and rules: the animal world, the insect world, the vegetable world, the mineral world, the oceanic world, the lighter-than-air world. Perhaps there are laws and rules applied to the membership of each of these worlds. And perhaps they, too, are part of the higher circles of existence here.

In the spiral of time through the seasonal circles of Earth, there is a continuing, evolving, changing story to the natural world, and all the creatures who have ever lived here have been participants in it. In the ongoing story of planetary life here, what do the plants and animals get out of it? They operate directly in the rhythms of the planet. They change their environments only through the subtlest of means. They live lives based largely on their physical skills. They are either totally in the moment or fast asleep. There is an intensity to their wakeful activity that seems to say that all creatures who dwell here, great and small, use the spirals of this world for their learning, growing, or self-destructive purposes.

This is a continuous world of predator and prey. Do animal souls get to switch roles? Is this a way for them to learn to operate larger and more dangerous bodies? Are the different levels of predator actually degrees of mastery for their particular level of existence? Are the different levels of prey equally engaged in a hierarchical learning process? Can ten thousand rabbit lives be one of the prerequisites for becoming a cheetah? In a world as competitive and as cannibalistic as this one, the animal world would seem to offer far more interesting challenges than its surface appearance might indicate—particularly if animal souls use their spiral to create their own multibodied stories as well, allowing everything to experience being everything else here: hunter and hunted, herd-bound and solitary, domesticated and wild. This is a rich world for both the warriors and burghers of animaldom to act out an extraordinary range of circumstances, so this is probably an equally special and confounding place to them as well. They very well might use it much in the manner of humans, to see themselves through the millions of disguises available here to anyone who wishes to touch the physical earth.

Plants and minerals, which operate out of a different reality, may have their own incarnational bylaws as well, based on serving and surviving, as might the planet itself. Earth is probably a unique spot in the universe, where a host of alien creatures have come to see if they can live together on two worlds that do not visibly meet, but somehow seem to spiral around one another: a world of the living and a world of the dead. Perhaps the physical Earth has been set up in order for each of us to take a spiraling ride through the convoluted chronicles of humanity in as many ways as we possibly can, so that we can see and experience and feel and then try to heal the many aspects of ourselves—and in so doing, live far more in the light of our own love and the love of others around us.

The glue that holds humanity's spiral to the larger circles of nature does seem to be love. On a planet as predatory as this one, love is the singularly redeeming and binding emotion between creatures, but it is stretched to its limits by the very un-ness of our existence. Perhaps that is precisely why this world spirals through the forgetfulness of death before it allows life to return, so that each new life can continually search for love in an unloving world with an innocent heart—and, perhaps, see where its weaknesses and unlovingness lie. And then, perhaps, ride on the upward spiral of things here to heal those imperfections. Or get stuck on a lower spiral and reexperience that unlovingness even deeper.

Who are we, then? We seem to be imperfect love, using the vehicles of physical bodies and physical laws to spiral our way through a circular world of remembrance and forgetfulness that was designed to allow us to deal with our many aspects and flaws in the innocence and ignorance of our true selves. Though this all may be part of a much larger process of advancing and declining through worlds far more complicated than our own, it seems to be the pathway that has brought most of us to this planet, from wherever or whatever we were before we came here.

Who are we, then? We are ageless aliens living on a planet that takes many lifetimes and many forms to truly understand, because being alive in a physical body on a world where the stakes are always for life and death is not a phenomenon that is easily mastered. We are also energy, that mysterious essence that can neither be created nor destroyed. As eternal energy, then, each of us has agreed to enter the pathway of this circular world and accept its tenets of life and death, of wisdom and ignorance, of creation and destruction to see just who we really are.

Perhaps by chasing this continuously interrupted spiral of our isolated parts, we can somehow ultimately draw them all together. Then, perhaps, we can finally feel ourselves as love. And from that point, we can move on to far more loving worlds, including other levels of this one, for we will at last be ready for them.

○

THE
ALCHEMY OF
SELF-HEALING

Part Two

Learning Our Unconscious Powers

In order to see our true selves more clearly, it is first necessary to look at our many separated parts. Inside all of us is a hidden connection to our drivers called the unconscious. Just because it is called the unconscious, this doesn't mean we have to be unconscious of its existence. Most of us manage to use it all the time without realizing it. Whenever we have premonitions or hunches or flashes of intuition, we are tapping into its vast and virtually limitless reservoir—our true driver's mind. People we call psychic have direct access to their unconscious and can perceive all sorts of odd truths, as well as distortions, through their familiarity with its shimmering realities. Each and every one of us has the potential to do the same.

OUR PSYCHIC CENTERS

Whether we realize it or not, each of us has a good deal more power at our disposal than we have been led to believe. All over our bodies are invisible eyes and ears that are constantly drawing in both visual and auditory information and giving us subtle direction through that information. All these stimuli are constantly being processed and fed into both our conscious and unconscious minds for us to act upon. Many times this information manifests as intuitive feelings, seemingly based on nothing more than a superficial assessment of a person or a situation, and yet often these assessments are surprisingly accurate.

This is because the human body houses a complex series of invisible energy centers up and down its spine and in its palms and feet. These energy zones, or "e-zones," are little interconnected minds operating in the same way the larger mind does, but without all the nervous chatter. They represent "wisdom of the body," or *irrational wisdom*, in contrast to the rational, conscious way we as Westerners are used to perceiving the realities around us. They can be pictured as camera lenses, constantly dilating and expanding with the continual barrage of sense information to which life on planet Earth is subject.

Each of our e-zones is filled with both the individual information that we gather from our personal experience and the general information we all share as fellow beings on this planet. They are always taking in data and storing it or relaying it to the rest of our physical corpus, depending on what is asked of them. Since we cannot consciously trigger them, save through the discipline of meditation, e-zones work somewhat differently from the way our central minds do, for we have far less rational control over them.

Since we also cannot consciously control what is in our e-zones, often the information we hold there can be quite erroneous. Many of us spend a lot of our time trying to separate this misinformation from what truly serves us, a seemingly never-ending process that continues all our lives. This misinformation can come from well-meaning sources like teachers, parents, and friends, and may serve them quite well, but if it doesn't work for us, then it acts only as a hindrance to our own personal growth. Most of us, when reflecting backward, can see this process quite clearly through the wisdom of hindsight.

It is a lot more difficult, however, to view the present from the same clear, lofty perspective. That is where a knowledge of energy centers can prove to be quite useful. You can quite literally cleanse your entire body of its accumulated anxieties, worries, and distresses through the mere exercise of thought and, in the process, create a much healthier and happier sense of yourself, as well as far more interesting pathways for you to trod with that greater sense of self.

Sit down and close your eyes for a moment, and let your attention run over your body. Become aware of your various body parts, and see if some of them trigger immediate associations. If you happened to injure your elbow last week, for example, and you look at it through closed eyes, the dynamics of the circumstances of that injury suddenly leap forward. You remember the pain, the distress, and what you might have done to avoid that injury. In the same way, you can free associate up and down your body, and suddenly all sorts of stories loom into view—the time you did this, the time you did that. Your body carries a lot of memories, and those memories can be used to serve you through the discipline of active meditation, after you first familiarize yourself with the many hidden tools you hold within. Let us begin with the seven spinal energy zones.

THE SEVEN E-ZONES

First E-Zone

The first e-zone is located at the base of the spine and contains all the information we need to know about our own survival. Under normal circumstances, it is relatively closed down, but under life-threatening situations it opens up to its fullest, taking in and giving out as much data as it possibly can in order to help us.

For example, if you suddenly find yourself tumbling off a cliff, your first e-zone would start rattling off all the possibilities to you— "branch over to your left—grab it" . . . "slim ledge ten feet down— aim your legs toward it" . . . or, if nothing looms as a possibility, "been nice knowing youuuuuuuuuuuuuu"—all delivered at a lightning speed far faster than your conscious mind could calculate. If you've ever miraculously survived an accident or some other threat to life and limb, you can credit your first e-zone with telling you what you needed to know at the precise moment you needed to know it. Most of us who can generate food, clothing, and shelter for ourselves have reasonably well-developed first e-zones and are working more on other informational centers in our bodies. But those who have to constantly scuffle around for a place to sleep on a day-to-day basis, while barely taking care of essential nutritional needs, live what might be called "first e-zone existences."

Viewed from a middle-class perspective, those people who lead first e-zone existences seem to be total failures, but seen from the standpoint of e-zone development, they may be looked at in a variety of ways. They may be reprogramming themselves from the bottom up; have totally faulty first e-zones; or have such well-developed survival skills that they can do as they please, and this is what pleases them the most. So, before we judge the existences of others, it is important to note that each and every one of us who exists in a body on this planet is working out something different. We each do what serves our spiritual development at the moment, whether it is living in luxury, living in poverty, or living somewhere in between.

Soldiers on the battlefield keep their first e-zones wide open if they wish to fight another day, as do animals that live in the wild. The more life-threatening our existence is, the more information we need direct access to in order to survive.

Anyone who is about to die has a first e-zone that is almost totally closed down. If it could be seen in terms of color, it would be either dark gray or black. In contrast, a person in good health would manifest much brighter colors. So, the first e-zone is an indication of one's general state of being and the information and skills needed to maintain existence on this planet. The cleaner and clearer it operates, the more strongly a person sits here.

Second E-Zone

The second e-zone is located in the area of the sexual organs and contains all the information we need to know about sexuality and our abilities to procreate. Since there are widely divergent views on the nature of human sexuality in Western culture, each of us is a storehouse of information based on our heritages as well as our own personal experiences. A person brought up in a puritanical environment where sex is viewed totally in terms of procreation would have a far different second e-zone from someone brought up with the idea that sex is primarily a source of recreation. If our beliefs are in tune with our heritages, then we will have no problem with the information we have been given here, but if they are in opposition, a lifetime of strong struggles in this area is indicated.

Because the nature of human sexuality is so open to interpretation, and because mores and morals are constantly changing, sometimes from decade to decade, there is no element in our makeup that causes more confusion than this one. Lest we judge anyone here, it is important to remember that each of us chooses a sexual orientation in accordance with our own spiritual development, be it hetero, homo, promiscuous, or celibate. Then we act accordingly within the framework of the public laws and private norms available to us. What serves one person can be absolutely repugnant to another, and yet, both people may be absolutely right in their beliefs—for themselves.

The second e-zone, then, is not composed of a standard of absolutes handed down from the heavens on tablets of stone, but rather it acts as a guideline for each individual's development. This is an area that is particularly vulnerable to abuse, for those who burn especially brightly with their sexuality draw all sorts of unwanted energy to them, while those who prize lust over love constantly suffer the consequences of their illusionary conquests.

A healthy second e-zone holds information that is in accord with the beliefs and actions of the person it serves. An unhealthy second e-zone is filled with conflicting misinformation that causes erratic and sometimes criminal behavior, as well as a great deal of obsessive unhappiness, for unresolved problems here usually emerge in a very explosive manner, when they at last rise grimly to the surface.

Third E-Zone

The third e-zone is located in the solar plexus and contains all the information we need to know about our own sense of power and how we stand in relationship to the rest of the world. Here is a human dimension that is highly open to personal interpretation. Some of us are filled with an exaggerated sense of our own self-worth, while most of us have a lot of difficulty in asserting ourselves, feeling that we are inferior and unworthy of the love and respect of others.

This lack of a true sense of self makes the third e-zone another area that is ripe for manipulation through misinformation. It is easy for us to belittle people in order to make ourselves feel more important. And it is just as easy for us to make ourselves unimportant by believing that we are less than what we truly are.

The third e-zone, then, is where we define ourselves through our relationship with the outside world and the people we know in it. Whether we have a realistic sense of our own personal power or not is all a product of this particular energy center and how we use the information stored there.

It is easy to remember the first three e-zones if you think of the words *survival*, *sex*, and *power*. These are the three areas that cater to humanity's baser instincts, and in order to touch on our higher sense of self, they must be integrated into who we feel we really are, not who everyone else tells us they think we should be.

The four upper e-zones represent our loftier aspects. They show us where we have the potential to open up our own loving, creative energies, and how we can be better beings for it.

Fourth E-Zone

The fourth e-zone is located in the chest and contains all the information we need to know about that most complex of earthly commodities, love. Of all the elements that constitute our earthly reality, it is love that is the most difficult to define, capture, and harness, for it is as elusive as the breath of a butterfly and yet strong enough to tear down entire civilizations. Nothing can exist here long without it.

Despite all its ephemeral, intangible qualities, love is the primary reason all of us are on this planet. It is a universal puzzle to everyone, and very few of us can truly say we understand it. Since it cannot be measured by any standard (does one mother's worth equal ten friends' worth?), it cannot be put to scale like rational wisdom, so it falls over onto the irrational, unmeasurable side of human knowledge.

Irrational concepts have always made much of Western culture nervous, and though a lot of lip service is paid to love, it is rather low on our collective priority list, despite its importance to our lives. Until we learn how to love both ourselves and the people whose lives we touch, we are going to be mired in a world that constantly threatens itself with self-destruction, for without love there is no real purpose for existence.

Like the culture of which we are a part, some of us are horribly blocked and underdeveloped when it comes to love. Others are absolutely shredded and uncontrolled in this area, for it is subject to more abuse than any other e-zone save the second. Those who wind up exiting this plane through severe damage to their heart and/or lungs usually have problems in accepting or expressing love for themselves. The more blocked the chest is, the more susceptible it is to life-ending "dis-ease." People with well-developed fourth e-zones can breeze through life, for they understand that the basic currency on planet Earth always has been and always will be "love . . . love . . . love," despite what we read in the newspapers. For the rest of us, love involves a lot of painful lessons, until we learn how to properly protect our hearts from those who do not wish us well and open up that same organ to those who do, as well as to be able to tell the difference between the two.

Fifth E-Zone

The fifth e-zone is located in the throat and holds all the information we need to know about communication. This area includes all the skills we have in expressing ourselves to others, from speaking to singing to playing instruments to writing to acting to whatever it is we each do to make ourselves recognized as self-expressive beings. As we develop our higher skills, we also learn how to express ourselves to greater effect, which leads some of us toward discovering the artist within, be it through language, acting, music, or painting, and others toward finding the teacher without, through the same diverse media.

The throat, which is home to the fifth e-zone, is a highly vulnerable area. Those who make their exit from the Earth via a disability in this region usually have problems of self-expression. Sometimes this disability comes after the wellsprings of a creative life have dried up, and sometimes from an overfondness for substance abuse.

The fifth e-zone, then, gives us the ability to teach and to give expression to our creativity. Those of us with some special gift in either of those areas usually spend our lives with our focus centered around this e-zone.

Sixth E-Zone

The sixth e-zone is located in the middle of the forehead and is the entryway to the imagination. The term *third eye* refers to this area, for the sixth e-zone sits right on the pineal gland, that magical part of our physical bodies that enables us to see way beyond the four-dimensional limits of reality.

Most of us only have occasional indirect glimpses into what lies here. Opening the third eye is a long, slow process, since it has been collectively shut down in our bodies ever since the material world became our prime focus and definition of reality.

We can think of the imagination as a bridge between our lower physical selves and our higher spiritual selves, our drivers. The imagination is unrestricted by the bonds that bind the machinery of our bodies to the planet, so we can soar as high as we want with it, providing, of course, we know how to get back into our bodies when we return.

There is a large difference between our conscious and unconscious minds. The conscious mind is actually a trash heap of sorts, filtering out all sorts of crazy thoughts so that they don't have to be verbalized or acted upon. In contrast, the unconscious is a repository of all sorts of hidden information that comes to us sometimes in fantasy, sometimes in meditation, and sometimes in dreams, but only the highly trained have direct access to it. For the rest of us, it is an indirect vehicle for thought, as mysterious as our conscious mind is blatant, yet it is just as much a part of our thought processes as the ability to rationalize.

Seventh E-Zone

The seventh e-zone is located at the crown of the head and is the completion of our being. It is also called the crown e-zone and may be considered our direct plug into the spiritual realms. It represents what humanity may be destined ultimately to become: a collection of divine beings with a deitylike understanding of life, love, and death. This e-zone contains the sum total of everything there is to know about us, and can be considered a personal manual that we carry above our heads with total memory of everything we have ever seen, done, or learned.

Little children usually maintain a connection between themselves and their parents through an invisible "cord" that attaches their seventh e-zones to their parents' seventh e-zones. By the time a child has reached the age of seven, this cord is supposed to wither, but many times it continues much longer, often to the detriment of both parent and offspring. When we give up our seventh e-zones to someone else, we are, in effect, giving up our whole being to someone else's domination.

Many authoritarian religious leaders take total control of their disciples by running invisible cords to their seventh e-zones and then dictating behavior to them. The people who give up their personal power in this way are desperately in need of some outer guidance, because they don't trust their inner beings. But few of them truly realize how much they are giving away in order to have the false stability of someone else taking responsibility for them. The phenomenon of reprogramming people who have been part of authoritarian cults is actually the painful process of cutting seventh e-zone cords and returning them to their rightful owners.

The seven e-zones, then, can be divided into two groups: the lower three of survival, sex, and power and the upper four of love, communication, imagination, and totality. The first trio helps us to be functioning, physical beings with both feet firmly planted on the planet, while the latter quartet allows us to transcend the physicality of this sphere and touch upon the divine that is both within and above us. People who are able to integrate those two into their existences find themselves leading rich, full lives. They have the best of both worlds, the physical and the spiritual, while those who dwell too much in either sphere do so at a cost to their fullest possible development.

A thorough knowledge of e-zones is extremely important, for they tell us how well we are attuned to the realities that make up our lives. There are many ways we can utilize them in helping to improve our existence so that we can realize our greater potential here.

Before continuing with the e-zones, it is important to understand two concepts, *auras* and *cords*, that allow us to work on our e-zones, even if we can't see them and even if we are not even sure they exist.

AURAS

Everyone who exists in physical form on this planet has a body. In fact, we probably have several bodies, but only one is visible to the naked eye: our physical machine, which is subject to all the laws of time and decay. It is the only body we feel with our five senses, so, naturally, we assume it is the only body we have.

Those who have begun to develop their third eyes are able to see a number of bodies surrounding the basic human physical shape, one of which is called the "auric," or "etheric," body. It is a body made up entirely of energy and color, and it frames our four-dimensional forms with an extra coat of light.

Those people who claim to see auras are actually looking at the auric bodies that surround all life-forms on this planet. If you have ever seen something oddly lit so that it reflected a rainbow of color around itself, you have some idea of what an aura looks like.

Everybody's aura has a different color, different parts of the same aura can be colored differently, and auras also can change in color from moment to moment. A person who is very angry can turn a scarlet red and then, when the anger is past, slip back into a contrite dull yellow. Many times the colors people wear in their clothing reflect their aura. So, if you have a predilection for a certain outer color, like blue, that could be a dominant color in your aura.

Generally, the brighter the colors are in an aura, the more vibrant the energy is. Even if you can't see your own aura or anyone else's, you can start watching what colors people close to you wear and how the colors reflect their moods. You can also experiment by observing if wearing certain colors lifts you up or wearing others drains you.

Many times people say all sorts of revealing things about themselves by the colors they wear. If their upper half is warmly colored and their lower half is not, they may be far more open spiritually than physically at that particular time. In the same way, if a certain e-zone is highlighted by bright colors, there can be an emphasis there.

Once you familiarize yourself with the various meanings that colors can have, then you can begin to *read* things, for, as you will find, everything can be read, if only you learn the proper language. So, even if you can't see auras, you can learn to look at the colors with which people surround themselves, and this can key you into some of the hidden things they are saying about themselves.

An aura, then, is an energy field that surrounds a person's basic physical machine. It can be different colors at different times, and it can be different colors all at once. Whatever is happening in the physical body is also reflected in the aura, so it is another means for detecting a condition of health or dis-ease upon the four-dimensional human form.

CORDS

As its name suggests, a "cord" is a long, thin attachment that generally goes from one or more e-zones on one person to one or more on another. They can be attached to any part of the body, both in front and in the back, and they have to be agreed upon by both parties in order to happen, although this agreement is always carried out on a subconscious level. Because cords are invisible, they are not restrained by space and can go all the way around the world if need be, so that we don't have to be in anybody's proximity to be corded by them.

Up until the time people are around seven years of age, they usually cord themselves to a parent. This process helps relay a lot of nonverbal information from parent to child, since cords act as transmitters from one body to another. After that age, there is no real need to cord ourselves to anybody or to allow anyone to cord themselves to us. Yet most of us wind up corded to and corded by a host of people throughout our lives. Because this is an invisible process, much like reading auras, it is difficult to know when it is happening, since cords can be seen only by people specifically trained to see them.

They are, however, much easier to feel on our own bodies, since they usually are attached to points of stress. So any continuing pain often can be caused by someone throwing a cord at us and hooking into a bodily vulnerability. There are several methods for breaking cords, but first they must be recognized and understood before they can be properly dealt with.

We can be corded by both people we love and those we hate, but mostly it happens when others want to control at least a part of us or when we want to do the same to them. An unfulfilling romance, then, can leave us with cords coming out of our fourth e-zones and plunging into the dissatisfied fourth e-zones of our partners, allowing us to pump negativity into each other long after the physical connection has been broken.

In the same way, we can carry a parent or two around with us into adult life through cords, even after they have departed from this plane, for cords respect neither space nor time. Because of this characteristic, it is important to know of their existence. Even if we can't see them, we can feel them either through bodily pain or obsessive thought about someone.

Once you familiarize yourself with the concepts of auras, e-zones, and cords, you are ready for the next step: learning how to recognize them in yourself and, then, how to recognize them in others. In the process, you will also move into the realm of self-healing and the deep, untapped world of your interior.

○

CHAPTER THREE

Taking Our Unconscious Powers

When most Westerners think of meditating, they conjure up pictures of turbaned people in uncomfortable cross-legged postures, contemplating the nature of their navels. This may be the way some people choose to sit and ruminate upon life, but there are as many different ways to meditate as there are to think, and no one singular way is superior to any other.

Anytime we have ever sat down and closed our eyes in search of momentary peace, we have meditated. Anytime we have let our thoughts carry us temporarily away from the reality of the moment, we have also meditated. So, most of us are closet meditators without even realizing it, for meditation is a fairly universal human process that all of us do to some degree during the course of each day.

Fantasies, daydreams, and wishes are all a form of meditation. *Anytime we let our minds take over our physical reality, we are practicing a form of meditation.* Most of us, whether we realize it or not, spend a good deal of our time wandering in an undisciplined manner through our minds, so that even if you've never meditated before, you'll soon find it as natural as daydreaming or fantasizing. Despite the seeming passivity of meditation, it can be a very active way of altering our lives, for our minds are another vehicle that travels roadways just as real and treacherous as our physical bodies.

SEVEN E-ZONE MEDITATION

The Seven E-Zone Meditation is an interior bath that helps clean out our physical and auric bodies, and enables us to take a far closer look at ourselves than our rational minds ever could.

Grounding

Whenever you do psychic or mental work, it is very important that you stay rooted or *grounded* to where you are. Being grounded is being attached to the planet, not floating around in inner space. This may sound simpler than it actually is, for most of us spend a great deal of time outside our bodies without realizing it. Just because you are mentally conscious of yourself at the moment, you cannot assume you are physically conscious of yourself as well. As you are reading this, notice what you have done to your body. Is it draped over a chair, or slung upon a bed, or slumped down over a desk? Has it been placed in a comfortable, healthful position, or has it been momentarily abandoned as your mind pursues other interests? Very few of us are conscious of what we do with our bodies when our minds are intensely interested in other stimuli, and generally we just drop them into the nearest appropriate receptacle in order to concentrate on whatever it is we wish to mentally pursue. If someone has ever startled you, or if you have ever awakened suddenly and experienced a momentary loss of where you were, then you know what it is like to be temporarily out of your body and trying to get back in.

Once you begin noticing how often people or outside stimuli bring you back into your body, you'll begin to realize how much time you spend outside of it. You can also start noticing how you reenter your body upon being startled. Is it through the throat? The heart? The solar plexus? You'll feel a little nervous tingle in the area through which you reenter. If it is the same area all the time, it might be where you exit as well, which tells you that that is an area of vulnerability. The proper place to exit is through the crown e-zone, which is atop the head and represents your total being. Anywhere else that you subconsciously exit through indicates a hole in that area, which leaves it susceptible to both injury and dis-ease. So, even if you can't see your own aura, if you begin to sense when and through where you leave your body, and when and through where you return, then you can begin to get a psychic feel for yourself.

Drugs, alcohol, tobacco, caffeine, and most other stimulants and depressants are an easy way to leave your body, so it is best to stay as clean as possible if you want to be an effective reader of yourself, for the people who can see the clearest are always the ones who can consciously stay grounded in their bodies while doing so. The concept of being *grounded*, or physically attached to the earth, is an extremely important one, and there is a very simple visualization technique you can use to insure this state.

Grounding Technique: Find yourself a comfortable seat and sit down. Make sure your back is as straight as possible. Place both feet firmly on the floor; it is best that they are spread slightly apart and are not touching one another. Put your open hands on top of your thighs, then turn them palms up, so that your open palms are parallel with the ground, but facing skyward.

Close your eyes. Sit as erect as you can, but also as comfortably as you can, so that your body isn't under any kind of physical strain. Imagine two lines inside your head, one going from ear to ear and one going from your forehead to the back of your skull. Both are parallel to the ground and both intersect in the exact middle of your head. Find that spot and then concentrate on being there. That is your center, where you will reside while you are meditating or reading or driving or simply being.

Once you have found your center, imagine an anchor dropping from the base of your spine down into the ground, going all the way to the center of the Earth, where it hooks into the very core of the planet. This technique connects you to the greater processes that surround you and leaves your body plugged into its basic life-support system while you root around in your head. Whenever you feel yourself slipping away, repeat the above process. The more you discover about psychic phenomena, the more you will see that it is of the utmost importance to keep yourself as grounded as you possibly can.

Finally, place yourself in present time. You can do this by saying the current date to yourself and telling yourself that is exactly where you are at the moment. As you are doing this, also concentrate on your breathing. You should be drawing breath in through your nose, where it can be filtered and cleansed through your nostril hairs. Draw it into your body and then exhale through your mouth. If you inhale through your mouth, you wind up bringing in a lot more impurities than you do through your nose. You will notice this difference immediately when you are sitting quietly, concentrating on the workings of your inner self.

Mediums

Some people have the ability to let other entities come through them. Sometimes the "channelers" speak in voices other than their own, and sometimes their features change appreciably as they approximate the facial mask of someone else entirely. These people are called "mediums" and they have the facility for totally vacating their bodies and letting other beings reside inside them. Unless you know precisely what you are doing, being a medium can be extremely hazardous. There are all sorts of strange entities hanging around this planet looking for convenient vehicles in which to do mischief, and if you innocently offer up your corpus, you are, in effect, stepping into the back seat of a driverless car.

This is a difficult concept for most Westerners to accept, since "beings without bodies" can neither be tasted, smelt, felt, touched, or seen. Therefore, according to Western canon, they cannot possibly exist. But if you've ever known people who change their behavior radically under the influence of drink or drug, then you've experienced uncontrolled mediumship by individuals who like to make glassy-eyed exits from their bodies so that other entities can use their vacated premises for their own purposes. When these "chemical and alcohol mediums" return to their bodies upon sobering up they then can deny responsibility for their actions (and memory of them as well) because of their intoxicated states. Just because you see a familiar body in front of you, don't always assume that a being who is familiar to you is inside it!

If you do have the gift of mediumship, learn how to protect yourself before you use it, since it can be most demanding on your body and can leave it open to all sorts of ghastly and ghostly invasions. If you are doing any kind of meditative exercise, remember to always protect yourself through the simple expedient of grounding.

Palm & Foot E-Zones

Once you have grounded yourself and placed your feet firmly on the floor and your open hands with the palm facing upward on your upper thighs, which are parallel and apart, you can concentrate on the four other e-zones in your body: the ones in the center of each of your feet and the ones in each of your hands. These e-zones are basically for taking in information, and you use them that way a lot more than you realize. Anytime you shake hands with someone, you are drawing in information through your palm, as is the other person. Since those of us who dwell in concrete civilization keep our feet covered most of the time, these two e-zones are used less directly than the ones in our palms, but they are just as important. If you can think of these four e-zones as energy orifices, or openings, then you can use them to draw energy into your body, both from the earth below and the sky above.

Running Energy Exercise: As you sit with your back erect, your eyes closed, your feet firmly planted on the ground, and your palms facing upward, imagine that you are opening up two holes in the center of your feet, and drawing in the rich brown energy of the earth through them. Let this energy rise up through your legs and clean them out, as if water were rushing geyserlike through your system, with its source at the base of your feet. At the same time, imagine golden light coming down from the heavens and entering your body through your palms, before flowing through your arms and down your spine to meet the brown earth energy coming up through your legs to the base of your spine. This is called "running energy," since you are drawing the earth's primal force into your body from beneath and pulling the heaven's glowing light from above so that the two can meet inside you.

Practice doing this, and see what kind of interior feeling it elicits. Can you see the colors that you are summoning? Can you feel them? Do you feel any other sort of sensations? For those of you with little experience in meditating or visualizing, this exercise offers a good opportunity to reinforce your own abilities at conjuring things. If you can elicit some sort of sensation with the techniques described so far, then you are well on your way to seeing far more than you initially thought you were capable of. For those of you who are having difficulty in feeling anything, you might be trying too hard. The important thing is to relax and let your mind carry you once your body has been firmly anchored in place.

Running Energy through the E-Zones

After you have successfully grounded yourself, placed your feet firmly on the floor, opened your palms face upward on your thighs, closed your eyes, and drawn the earth's rich full rays up through your feet and the heaven's golden light down through your palms, you are ready to run energy through the rest of your body.

Beginning with your first e-zone, your survival center, let the earth's light and the heaven's light meet and intermix at the base of your spine, washing out and cleansing everything that is sitting in there. Once that feels properly bathed, move up to the second e-zone, your sexual center, and do the same thing, cleansing out the area above your genitalia. As you proceed upward through your seven e-zones, clean out each one, so that you wind up giving yourself an internal shower, flushing yourself out from beneath with earth energy and from above with heavenly light.

If you can feel something happening inside, like a little tingle, all the better, but even if you feel nothing, you are still plugging into two of the basic energy sources of this plane, the earth and the sky. Concentrate until you can feel each of your e-zones, and if nothing happens, relax and try again. When dealing with meditative and mental phenomena, you are basically conjuring up your own realities, so it is good to continually check on what you feel is happening, since you are now learning to trust your own intuition. There is no one except yourself who can tell you what is happening and what isn't along your mysterious interior.

Moving upward to your solar plexus, clean out your third e-zone, your power center, while you continue to run energy through e-zones numbers one and two. When you are ready, move up to your heart, and clean out your fourth e-zone, your love center, and then let your double fountain of energy within rise to cleanse your throat, your fifth e-zone and your communication center. Once that has been properly bathed, you may enter your forehead and sixth e-zone, your imagination center, and let your energy waters rise to there, before allowing all of it to run through the crown of your head, your seventh e-zone, your totality, and gush upward like a huge geyser.

You now have two "fountains" running through you from opposite directions. One, composed of rich, brown earth energy, enters through your feet, rises up through your legs, climbs your spine, and exits out through your arms and palms, as well as continues on up through your head and your crown e-zone. The other, composed of the golden light of the heavens, enters through your palms, courses through your arms, and then simultaneously rises and lowers itself through your body, so that it also exits through your crown e-zone, in addition to running down the whole length of your spine and splashing over your legs before finally flushing itself out through your feet.

The more often you do this meditative exercise, the more easily it will come to you, and you will soon find that it is an excellent way to overcome temporarily debilitating moods, as well as unpleasant feelings. It helps you put both feet on terra firma and look more resolutely at your problems. It also helps you to "be there in the moment," instead of floating around inside your mind, as most of us do much of the time. Once you learn how to *really be where you are*, you will notice that other people take more notice of you, because you are now much more of a physical presence.

Once you see yourself as more in the here and now, you will begin to see who among the people you know are really "present" and who aren't. People who have a tendency to talk a great deal are often unconsciously using their excess verbosity to camouflage the fact that they really aren't present in any way except in voice. Their constant barrage of words is a grounding technique that makes other people participate in the process of keeping them on the planet, by forcing others to acknowledge their presence by listening to their drivel. If you have ever been pinned down by a boring drunk, then you've experienced a gross exaggeration of this phenomenon; however, it also happens quite often in our day-to-day exchanges, and once you begin to notice it, you will discover that most people are not really present a surprising amount of the time. This will come as quite a shock initially, since we have been taught to assume that if someone's body is present, surely some *one* is there as well.

Unfortunately, most of us spend far too much time in places other than where we physically are, in irrational chaotic meditation—fantasizing, worrying, plotting, scheming, feeling depressed, "future tripping," and dancing down memory lane—doing everything, in fact, but being grounded in the present moment. So, by learning the Seven E-Zone Meditation, you can begin to make your presence felt far more, as well as imbue that presence with a strong sense of self and self-awareness.

Cleansing Your Aura

While you clean out your e-zones, it is good to cleanse your aura as well, for that is the energy field that both surrounds and reflects the general state of your physical body. To do this, all you have to do is extend the range of the two fountains gushing through you so that they include your auric body in their onrush of energy.

Imagine an energy field that fits all around your body and under your feet like a snug pair of child's zip-up pajamas. This is your auric body, and it bends and flexes everywhere you do. Take the light that is cascading in huge geyserlike gushes out of your crown e-zone and flush it down through your aura, so that you are covered in both gold and brown. If you should tire of those colors, blue and green are excellent healing hues and may be easily substituted. Any color you like may be used to wash your interior e-zones and cleanse your aura, but it would be preferable not to use black or white, since both of them represent all of the shades of the rainbow combined and do not necessarily have good healing properties. Cleansing your aura is exactly the same as cleansing your e-zones. Just imagine a watery flow of energy washing through the energy field that surrounds you and flushing out through the same openings as in your physical body, your auric palms and feet, and your auric crown e-zone.

Once you sense what it feels like to run energy through your physical and auric bodies, you can learn to do it without thinking through each step. Until you do, however, it is a good idea to totally familiarize yourself with the process first, so that it becomes a helpful way for you to both relax and be in the moment at the same time.

Breaking Cords

Once you have your two "fountains of energy" running through your physical and auric bodies, you can begin to do things with yourself on a psychic level, even if you can't really see what is happening. If you have little areas of pain in your body, or if you've been thinking obsessively about someone, there is a fair chance that someone is throwing a cord at you and that you're letting it happen for some self-punishing reason. There are several ways of breaking cords, but the process has to be used again and again until you feel either the pain or the obsession go away. If you are suffering both at the same time, there is a good chance they are coming from the same source.

To break a cord, first see if the pain resides in one of your e-zones. If it does, is it relative to the person or relationship or thing about which you are obsessed? Is someone giving you a sharp pain in the back of the neck? Or do you have chest pains over a relationship that turned out badly? Or is your stomach sinking heavily over some poor choice you've recently made? If you have felt a strong heart connection with another person, but that connection has become muddied and you can't get rid of your resentments, more than likely you are still cording one another.

The easiest way to get rid of cords is to imagine you are pulling them out while you are running energy through your body. Just yank them out with your mind and quickly fill in the holes that creates with color and light. This process can become a part of your meditation.

You can also achieve the same effect through physical movement. Place yourself in a meditative state, run energy, and then put your hands on the part of your body where you feel pain. Either touch the offending area and gently rub it or make a scissor cut with your fingers over it and imagine the cord broken in that manner. After you finish pulling out or cutting all the cords you can find, stretch out your aura so that it fills up all your visual space.

Ending Your Meditation

When at last you feel you have cleansed both your e-zones and your auric body, and you have run enough energy through your body to feel quite revitalized, it is time to complete your meditation. Because of the amount of energy you have generated from those two flowing fountains that are gushing through your system, it is important to dump off the excess, so that you have a comfortable amount of psychic energy running through you when you emerge from your meditative state.

This can be done quite simply by tilting your head forward, so that the amount of energy coming out of your crown e-zone levels off. Then, shake your hands as if you were drying them off, so that your palm e-zones also are drained of their excess. Once this has been accomplished, sit up straight and open your eyes, and see how readily this simple mental exercise has affected you. Is there a perceptible difference in the way your mind and body feel? Were you able to lose some of your anxieties and negative thoughts? If you are not sure, keep practicing until you do feel some effect from this exercise, for its effectiveness can be measured only by your own interior sense of well-being.

Some people have too many mental blocks to make self-meditation a useful tool in their arsenal for dealing with the world. If you are one of them, there is not too much this method can offer you other than to confirm your difficulties and urge you to try to overcome them. For everyone else, however, once you feel comfortable with this simple technique of visualization, then the wondrous world of your deeper multidimensional self awaits you.

○

Using Our Unconscious Powers

Once you begin to trust yourself around the release points of your body's many minds and eyes, you can begin looking into yourself using those same eyes to see what secret stories lie within you and what hidden memories you may have of your larger self. One of the major tools you have for this is your imagination.

Our imaginations are windows and doorways and mirrors that we carry around to remind us that we live in more places than the physical world. In our imaginations, anything at all is possible, everything and nothing are true, and everything is permitted. Some imaginations are extraordinarily attuned to the workings of the physical world and can make the magic of their conjurations happen at will. Most of us, however, live separate from our imaginations, dwelling in one realm or the other, but rarely bringing them both electrically together.

One of the prime ways our imaginations serve us is to give us vehicles in which we can act out a lot of our thoughts and feelings before committing them to the indelible workings of time. So, we can boldly confront our greatest fears, blow up half the planet in a fit of power-crazed pique, or be declared "Emperor of the Known World," all in the flick of a thought, with nary a drop of blood spilled in the process or a voice raised in righteous protest.

TRANSFORMING HOLOGRAMS

This process of dealing with outrage and other volatile internal feelings is actually an active meditation known as "transforming holograms." Holograms are images that can be projected three-dimensionally, so that they are pictures we can walk through and look at from all sides.

All of us, whether we realize it or not, carry a lot of visual baggage on our physical bodies that can be seen by people who look at things with all their body's eyes. These shimmering holographic images often are pictures of the pain, sadness, wounds, and loss we carry around with us. If someone feels they have a lot of responsibilities and burdens to bear, they can be carrying around a picture of themselves shouldering the whole world like the Greek god Atlas. An unblinking third eye, taking one glance at their slumped shoulders and upper back, would immediately start to pick up this hologram. Once unburdened of that burdensome picture, that person would actually feel as if a great weight were lifted off him or her. Many times a noticeable injury, like a limp or the disuse or total disappearance of a limb, is also accompanied by an appropriately debilitating picture. Some of these pictures are easy to see and some are totally internalized, but all can be treated via the special skills we hold in our imaginations.

Even if your psychic abilities are still at the undeveloped stages, see if you don't have particular associations with certain people, pictures of them doing things that seem to stick out more than any other memories you have of them. Maybe your mother was always saying "No!" to you, so that after awhile, you began to carry around a holographic picture of an adult authority figure who denied you things you felt that you deserved. So, sometimes when you think of Mom, there she is with "No!" written all over her. When you think of doing something for yourself, there you are bringing up that same picture and telling yourself "No!" So, even though the hologram you are carrying around does not serve you in the slightest, nor is it a full reflection of how you see your mother, still it is so basic to your nature that it is almost impossible for you to break its predictable pattern. If, however, you can make that into an image, such as your mother negatively shaking her head, then you've created a hologram with which you can do something.

Transforming Holograms Meditation

Before performing any meditations, it is important to ground yourself. After you've grounded yourself, run energy through your e-zones and your aura, and take possession of the time and the space that surrounds you.

Once you feel that you are strongly in the present moment, imagine the hologram you would like to get rid of. Then surround it with a huge red heart and slowly let the heart consume the hologram, until there is no trace of it left. It now has been transformed back into love, and you can release it. Let the heart fade back into the larger heart of the universe. If you can, thank the picture for its lessons, and, perhaps you will begin to more fully understand those lessons, so that you won't have to invoke that hologram again.

If you have a picture of a mother shaking her head "No!" and you surround it with a heart, watch as it melts and disappears, and then see how easy or how hard it is for you to let it go. It is your choice whether that hologram comes back or not, for it is now a part of your internal reality. If for some reason you continue to carry it around, you will at least be well aware of it, and you will have begun the process of ridding yourself of an ingrained response that no longer serves you. Even if you do not successfully get rid of a holographic picture, by recognizing it you become conscious of it each time it comes up, and that will enable you to deal with it differently and perhaps some day overcome it. When you transform holograms concerning specific people, you are destroying only certain aspects of them, not the whole person. So, destroying a picture of Mom saying "No" does not destroy Mom, only that negative aspect of her, leaving her free now to say "Yes," or whatever it is that you would prefer to hear from her.

Once you've finished, clean out your e-zones and aura, and then bend forward and dump off the excess energy you've created. Now open your eyes and return to the "real" world, where you are once again back in your body-machine but hopefully minus a few of its rusty dents.

Imagination Meditation

Most of us who have quaffed from the cup of Western culture have been taught to shun our creative, more irrational side as something slithering and hairy that is best left undisturbed lest it consume us. It is not surprising, then, that we have come to associate the more nightmarish aspects of our interior selves with imaginative and creative excess. If we look at virtually any popular entertainment form that deals with mystery or the world of the imagination, we will find that humanity is presented as being tinged in darkness and fear and madness, and that our hidden reaches are areas where no conscious being should trespass. The unknown is always what we make of it, and if we choose to live in fear of it, that is our choice, but it is important to realize that it is not necessarily the only reality open to us.

The sixth e-zone, which is the gateway to the imagination, holds a lot more in it than you could ever possibly use, so your creative capabilities with it are virtually limitless. Like everything else connected with the body, your imagination has to be exercised to be effective. Don't be afraid to take it out on long runs. Just remember to ground yourself and put yourself in present time and space when coming from your interior world back to the four-dimensional physical sphere. By being conscious of where you are, you have the possibility of opening yourself up to all sorts of different realms. If you carry a projection of a large heart with you for transforming fear, you really have nothing to fear, for everything has the potential to be turned into love.

Your mind is your singular sacred province, and you can do as you wish with it, as long as you are able to make the distinction between what is happening on the inside of it, which is under your control, and what is happening on the outside, which is not. Here is a place where you can put your outrage and anger, as well as your good feelings, without having to suffer the consequences of letting loose a barrage of uncontrolled negative emotions on someone else.

Once having expressed yourself in the confines of your own interior self, a lot of times you can find much more constructive ways of venting your displeasure on the ultimate recipient of your bad feelings, particularly after those feelings have built up for awhile. If you can manage to put bad feelings inside a holographic heart and let them go so that the lessons inside are opened to you, you will begin to see that a lot of the anger you vent is around things that actually reflect you and no one else. Other people wind up acting out stories to show you parts of yourself. And perhaps you serve as a similar mirror in the larger design of your friends and relations, acting out their wishes and dread desires. If you permit yourself, you might begin to see some of the patterns to all this—how the people in your surrounding reality reflect you, who your figures of love are and who your nightmares are, and who, if any, embody both. Perhaps there is less randomness in the stories that comprise your life than you thought. Perhaps some of them feel vaguely familiar, as if you could clothe them in other times and places or through other tension-filled dynamics.

PAST LIVES & THE AKASHIC RECORDS

In this world of the eternal present, where the distinct possibility exists that many of us have walked the Earth many times, it is possible that many stories contribute to the totality of who we are. Since we are all comprised of several different elements—a self, a body, and a name—all of those elements would have pasts as well, for we are a unique combination of a whole variety of flowing elements. In addition, in this world of the eternal present, any conjuration of the past is also a re-creation of it, since it no longer exists. So anything you feel you have been before immediately becomes so, unless your feelings change. Past lives, then, live in a multitude of guises and would seem to be irrelevant, unless we know the larger patterns they fit inside. Yet one of the main keys to the larger pattern is seeing our own patterns. And one of the keys to seeing ourselves is learning how to heal ourselves, to make ourselves more whole, so that we are truer reflections of our larger and more complete beings.

There is a prevailing myth here that all activity on planet Earth has been written down in a huge text called the "Akashic Records." *Akasha* is a Sanskrit word meaning "dust," or "ether." Whether these records do, indeed, exist and whether we have access to them or not are yet more questions of the imagination. What does seem to exist, however, are our own records that we carry around with us as part of the secret informational storehouse of our own bodies. These records may contain minute chronicles of the planet, or they may be just a narrow overview of ourselves. Whatever they are, we do seem to have access to them through meditative techniques, and, more than likely, these records change and grow and diminish with each of our lives. Whether or not they conform to a larger set of records which may or may not exist, they are another useful tool in our arsenal of weapons against the seeming ignorance and helplessness of being a spiraling immortal trapped in a mortal body.

Like past lives, the Akashic Records can be just as much a creation of the moment as they can be a reality. Whether they exist or not is not that important. If they exist for you, they give you an imaginary framework for an endless "library of life," with all of the answers and all of the questions that have ever been asked here. Figuring out a pathway to get there has more to do with trusting your intuition than anything else. The more you prove to yourself that the information you draw forth from your interior is valid and real, the more you begin to trust your skills, and this process of trust helps them become an accepted part of you. For some people this is a long, slow process, and for others it is immediate. Intuition is another of the gifts that all of us have but few of us really trust. It is another cerebral muscle that must be exercised and experimented with, before it can truly work for us.

HEALING MEDITATIONS

By using the earlier described meditative techniques of grounding and running energy through the seven e-zones and the auric body, we can go inside ourselves and start working on the areas of our bodies that are causing us the most distress. All of us have some skills at self-healing. You can test your abilities against minor things, like headaches, small pains, and the like, to see if you can deal with your body before you tackle some of its deeper out-of-balance aspects. Healing is a natural part of being human, and some people have been able to reverse seemingly irreversible conditions through the power of their own minds, so you always have the potential to heal yourself, if you really need to, although this is a multilevel skill that takes a long time to truly learn.

Whenever your body is dis-eased it is telling you that you are out of balance with yourself. If this dis-ease is life threatening, you are forced to look at your life through totally different vision, the eyes of mortality, and your story takes on a completely different tenor, since its ending suddenly hoves frighteningly into view. The AIDS epidemic that entered with the 1980s is a terrible teacher of the fragility of life, and somehow its sufferers have had to invoke that message on themselves, either to do robust battle to disprove it or to sink passively into its inevitability. By bringing the dying process into the prime years of its victims' lives, AIDS is a high-speed version of normal aging, a "time" dis-ease. By invoking time's future corruptions on a relatively young body, the mind attached to that body is forced to spiral through several ages at once, to grow old without being old. Is it possible to slow this process considerably through meditation? Or even to understand why some of us have been forced to speed up our stay here?

We seem to be on the planet to learn about ourselves and our deficiencies. Our mortality sets up a progression of youth, maturity, and old age in order to do so. When that progression is radically altered, the lessons become all the more intense. This intensification happens, perhaps, to help us appreciate life more when we are given it again on our inevitable spirals and, perhaps, as a test of our own strong desires to continue, to confront our own mortality and suspend it for years, as some people have been able to do. No matter what our afflictions are, they are there to teach us about ourselves, to widen our spirals, to give us new, far more vulnerable eyes for looking at ourselves and heightening our stories.

If we have invoked all this upon ourselves to truly bring out our healers, then the healing is a major part of that story, and if not, at least we can begin that process and make it more of a part of our future selves. Conscious dying is a very valuable lesson in conscious living, and sometimes we need the one before we can fully appreciate the other. All of us are slowly or quickly dying here, and all of us can use whatever help in the process we can give ourselves. If we can begin to see ourselves as part of a much larger spiral, then our disabilities also fit into a larger perspective; and until we learn the lessons they symbolize, they will probably stay with us in one form or another. In that spirit, here are some healings you can do on yourself.

Your Perfection

After you've grounded yourself and run energy, pause for a moment and try to imagine yourself as perfect—if you were exactly the way you always wanted to be, full of love and loved by all. This image could very well be a reality awaiting you when you are ready to leave this plane permanently for the higher dimensions, so somewhere out there, in some time zone, that state exists for you. If you can find it with your imagination, then you've taken a giant step toward getting there, claiming it, and bringing it down to your current physical world.

When you find your perfection, sit in it for a while, bask and glory in it, feel what it is like to be perfect and pain free and full of love. Even if you can't feel the full blast of it, feel its shadow or feel its light breath, and know that it is out there for you, if you want it.

Once you have felt your perfection, allow it to sit like a warm blanket all around you, and let your present physical body attune to it. Pull that perfect physical you into any of your pains and dis-eases, and let your body feel its radiant glow, bathing you in a light that lets you know you're *alive*. Feel what it is like to be full of life and love. Feel your juiciness, your vitality, your electric presence. This is a state to which you will always have access now, and once having found it, each time you return you can go deeper and deeper into it. It is a simple healing tool for you, and it is there at the mere blink of a thought.

Now that you have felt your perfection, allow yourself once again to feel your imperfections: your flaws, your pain, your sadness, the lack of love in your life, your failures, your unlovingness. Instead of feeling sorry for yourself, however, look at these many wounds as pathways you have to cross over to reach the other side of yourself. What is stopping you from crossing them? Do you understand the special lessons that each of your wounds represent? Can you see the possibility that if you are strongly afflicted this lifetime, it just might be because you are supposed to work harder at being alive to compensate for times when you did not?

Try to make your story connect up with a larger story, so that you are part of a larger flow that honors and praises your courage for being who you are and asks only that you be as loving as you can be toward yourself and your fellow equally wounded mortals. Understand that you are one among many who are clumsily trying to heal themselves and that your pace depends entirely on you—you are not in a race with anyone else. You have an endless circular reality here to play in and experiment with, and if the future should suddenly disappear, you still have the past to come back through to change the story, for all stories here are never ending in this spiraling, rotating universe. Understand that, and perhaps you will be able to release yourself from some of your longtime bonds and restrictions.

When you sit in your wholeness and completeness, see what cracks first appear in the mold of your perfect you, as you begin to come back down into your imperfect self. Play with those very first images of incompletion, for they are the most graphic pathways that you can conjure in giving you an opening into your wounds. Try associating as freely as you can with these images, and see where your associations take you. In a sense, these are waking dreams over which you have absolute control, and they can serve as clear keys into your deeper self. As you uncover your scars, wrap them in love, and don't be afraid to ask for pathways and people to come to you who will help you heal them. This is a planet that constantly demands that you make a special effort to stay alive to yourself; otherwise you will sink into the circular repetition of routine here, and the creative, healing, growing parts of you will die. This is a challenge all who come here continually face, for this is a world of the wounded and the constantly dying, and yet within that curious dynamic lies the potential for healing our larger immortal souls.

HEALING THROUGH THE E-ZONES

When you ground yourself and run energy through your auric body and your e-zones, you also can look at yourself through those special energy centers. Just focus in on a particular area, relax, and see what you draw forth. See what colors or pictures or feelings or holograms or stories it holds. The more associative you allow yourself to be, the more you will be able to bring out of yourself. Even if what emerges is only a color or a vague feeling, that is enough of a start to open up your body to your imagination.

First E-Zone

The first e-zone, around the tailbone, is our survival mind. See what holograms and pictures come forth when you look in here. Are you living way below your material needs? Here is where you can be carrying holograms of poverty, ineptitude, inability to manifest what you want—a whole host of images that limit you in who you are and what you can do. If you can touch on a hologram, transform it and free yourself of it. If you can touch on a story, try retelling it. The more concrete you make it, the more you can play around with it.

Fill up your first e-zone with your competence and your power to make things happen. Enrich the colors you find there. This is the area of your basic being, your "creature," and the better it feels about itself down here, the better your entire being will feel. All of us seem to be part creature in our survival skills, while the higher aspects of our personalities reflect our humanity and the divinity we seek. So, honor your creature. It is a special part of you. See if you can see its story. Perhaps it takes beast or bird form. Is there any form of life here, other than human, with which you have always secretly identified? That is your creature. Know that its skills are your skills. Even if you can't see yourself as anything other than human, know that you exist in many guises. Accepting your creature is a strong step in seeing your greater self, for that self exists on all levels in this multidimensional universe.

Second E-Zone

The second e-zone, the genital area, is our sexual mind. This is an area of much confusion for most of us. Once again, our creatures dwell here strongly with strong urges; however, the conventions of organized civilization have given us many rules and laws and behavorial restrictions on what we may do with our sexual energy, for it is a force of orgiastic proportions and does not seem to fit in with our other social interactions. Our sexuality would not be so electric if it were here as a tool solely of procreation: the body doesn't have to be raised to an intense level of excitation to follow its biological urges to procreate—it would do that naturally. Something else has to be going on here as well.

Our larger spiraling selves probably reflect both sexes, but our physical bodies, save in rare cases, always choose one of two forms available. It would seem we are here in different sexual guises to learn cooperation, for there has to be a whole other set of realities governing an act designed to penetrate the polite bounds of social intercourse and achieve a momentary melding of two people into a much larger body. In the alchemy of sex, there is a certain element of the divine, a release from being just human that enables us to experience the ecstasy of being ever so briefly on fire. Sexuality is one of the easiest pathways we have to ecstasy although it, too, is subject to the circular gravitational draw of repetition and dull animal urge that can make it just as much a part of the dead world here, where nothing grows and nothing is created save for another ring round the repetitious circle.

This pull toward union with the missing parts of ourselves and the stories we create around it form the crux of our sexuality. All of us on some level long to touch the divine, and here is the first place in our lower bodies that we can do so. Look deeply into your second e-zone. A lot of fantasies and images and wishes lie there. This is an easy area in which to practice storytelling. Look at your fantasies. Do they draw you into union? Or do they separate you? Are you forever watching yourself—a cool eye that cannot electrify itself? Or are you always on fire down here, never truly satisfied? Your second e-zone can be a prison made out of pictures you have carried for centuries and millennia. Like our imaginations, our sexuality is another world of interior power that can be expressed and released in many ways.

In your meditations, fill this area with love whenever you look into it. Put your perfection in here, and let it heal you of any and all disabuse you still carry here. Feel your beauty, feel your aroused self, feel your power, your electricity. Ask to be honored here. Look at your completions here, your manifest partners. Their pictures of you sit strongly within you. Is that how you see yourself? Are you caught in someone else's distortion of yourself? If you are not connected with anyone at the moment, look at your wished-for mate. Does he or she represent parts of you that you feel too lazy to develop? Do you need someone to give you more than you have to offer? Ask yourself hard questions here, for this is one of your electric areas, where your various truths may be buried the deepest.

Third E-Zone

The third e-zone, the solar plexus, is where our power lies. This is where our creature and our human begin to combine. There are two basic uses to power on this plane: it can be used to control and to dominate, or it can be used to release and free. People who need to control others rarely rise above themselves, for they are not open to learning from others, only regulating them. Look at the way you use your power. Do you control people around you, or do you like to empower them? Are you in an environment where you feel empowered, or are you stuck under the control of others? What is stopping you from acting out who you feel you really are? Why are you holding yourself back here?

As we move beyond the questions of mortality of the first e-zone and the desire to unite with the divine of the second, the third draws us into our projected essence and raises questions of how we and other people define ourselves. Look at your body here. Is it amply protected in flesh? Is it muscular? Is it soft? Is your power constantly being contained? Do you give it away? Is this an area where you are easily upset—ulcers, stomach problems? Play with the stories and pictures in here. Feel your power as a light that attracts other people rather than oppresses them. True power never has to be announced or forcibly acted out; it is there, a part of your presence, and if you are truly in touch with your power, you are always able to empower others and have them in turn empower you.

Fourth E-Zone

The fourth e-zone, the heart area, is love, pure and simple. Our hearts lie at the center of our seven e-zones, for all our worlds seem to emanate from the pulsing organ that dictates the very beat of life within us. Here we link our divinity, our humanity, and our creature together in the second of our bodily areas that allows us union with those other than ourselves. Our heart is our greatest vulnerability, for not only is it central to life but also to love as well, and without the latter the former is only empty ritual. This is the symbol of the very reason we are here: to learn to love not only ourselves and those whose lives we touch, but also, if possible, all things great and small upon this planet. The core of all life here is the universal linkage of love, and even though we are each separate and unique, we are also part of one another and part of a divine oneness that draws all the circles and spirals of existence together.

When you sit in your fourth e-zone, try to feel your larger connections in this area. Understand that the many wounds we suffer here are from the unfeeling ignorance of many equally wounded beings. Do not take the wounds of others in here, for they will only become yours. Learn how to protect your heart, without smothering it or turning it into an unfeeling organ. Bathe your heart in warm colors—blues, greens, and golds. Let it touch the hearts of those you love. Don't be afraid to draw sustenance from those who love you, for you will always be able to give it back in return. Honor the giving and receiving circles of love you have with your special friends. Build on what you have rather than wishing for what you don't have. When hearts connect, it is because they reflect aspects of one another. What is your heart reflecting in the circle of life and love around you? Look at your fourth e-zone stories carefully, for they will probably tell you more clearly than anywhere else what you are doing on planet Earth this lifetime.

Fifth E-Zone

The fifth e-zone, the throat area, is our communication mind. This is where we give expression to our humanity as it rises up to try to touch on the divine. All of the art forms—music, poetry, painting, and so on—are available to us here, for this is where we give expression to our special artistry. Here is where much of our power resides, for how we express ourselves depends a good deal on what we think of ourselves. Here is where a lot of our higher human worth lies as well, for this is where special gifts are both richly rewarded and savagely rejected by society at large and where most of us have at least some incipient talent that we are developing.

This area complements our third power e-zones, but it is a higher spiral of that same energy, for here is where our more developed aspects lie: our teachers, our healers, our artists, our music-makers. If they are not as they should be, what has stopped them from coming forth? Is your fifth e-zone closed to your greater powers? Are you struggling to bring them in, but still cannot touch on them?

Feel your throat and all its vulnerabilities. Concentrate on your breathing. Draw your breath in through your nose all the way into your body, down your spine and then back up along your front. Exhale through your mouth. Your fifth e-zone is where you transform oxygen into life and life into expression. It is your most alchemical area, and the one most easily subject to distortion, for it is how we link up with everyone, intimate and stranger alike. Look at your constrictions here—your fears, your power, and your powerlessness. Do you give yourself freedom of speech here, or are you always controlled? Do you use this area to overwhelm people with your empty words so that they cannot reach you? A lot of our fear sits in the third, fourth, and fifth e-zones, and the throat area is a good point of release for all of it, for here you can give voice to your rage and grief and anger. Try screaming into a pillow or bellowing in the shower or hollering on the freeways. The more you can release here without doing injury to anyone, including yourself, the more you can allow your gifts to come to the fore and transmute that outraged emotion into a teaching or a healing or a work of art.

Sixth E-Zone

The sixth e-zone, the forehead area, is our imagination. This is the third area that allows us union with forces greater than ourselves. This is the one bodily mind where we have had considerable practice in playing with our stories. It is a teacher for our other e-zone minds. Keep it filled with the vibrant colors of wishes, dreams, ideas, thoughts, and never-ending stories, and it will always serve you in kind. Learn how to make its potential abundance manifest upon the physical plane, and join the secret alchemists among us, who know how to make their own little worlds on this planet magical places to be.

Seventh E-Zone

The seventh, or crown, e-zone, the crown of the head, is our completed essence. This is where our creature, our humanity, and our divinity reside. This is the gateway to the higher aspects of the self. When you look at it, see if there are any limiting holograms here, plugging you into realities that keep you stuck. As in all the e-zones, you have the alchemical powers of transformation here. Your seventh e-zone is your spiraling stepping-stone out of here, and the cleaner you keep it while you are here, the easier your voyage out probably will be.

TOTALITY

Our sexuality (second), our hearts (fourth) and our imaginations (sixth) allow us union on a creature, human, and divine level with our surrounding universe. Our power (third) and our communication (fifth) abilities create the necessary links with our parallel worlds. Our survival (first) and our crown (seventh) e-zones hook us up with the world below and the world above. All seven make us a vital part of the energy vortex behind all life here, and they are the conduits to make this world whatever we need it to be for ourselves. Whenever you end a meditation, remember to get rid of the extra energy by tipping your head forward and shaking it and then loosely shaking off your hands before taking a moment or two to put yourself back in present place and present time.

Once you have familiarized yourself with these meditative routines, have created variations on them, or have blended them in with other techniques, you can go in and out of yourself anytime you want. You don't have to limit yourself to your e-zones. Your entire body is now your province to roam and look at with your liberated imagination. And once you can comfortably read yourself, you also can start to look at other people and the world around you, as well as the greater stories and themes of humanity, and begin to see the mystery that was there for the viewing all along.

○

Reincarceration

If, indeed, we are spiraling beings who inhabit a running stream of bodies up and down the curved timepikes of a round world that is constantly moving in circles, then a model of how all this works might go something like this. If there is a cold, clear logic behind the madness and mayhem of earthly existence, then all of us who enter this plane and agree to abide by the tenets of physical and temporal law do so for a very specific purpose, and that purpose is to heal ourselves, to make ourselves whole. By experiencing our many parts over and over through all sorts of bodies and all sorts of lives, we can continually deal with our problems and imperfections until we find the right combination that lets us finally overcome them.

"Reincarceration," or repetitive imprisonment in physical bodies on the physical sphere, seems to work on two levels, societal and individual, collective and self-centered, where both a civilization and all its members conform to a certain timetable of development in accordance with the unfolding of agreed-upon principles presented to them. Since the Earth has always been a repository for a wide variety of civilizations in totally different stages of development, this planet has also offered its citizenry a wide variety of verities and choice, so that you can continually be in the vanguard of the most advanced societies available or stay forever "primitive" amidst the anthropological splendor of the profusion of tribal life that has always been available here as well.

PARENTS

Each of us probably makes contact before we come onto the planet with the figure or figures we need to be our parents, since once we are off this plane, we need a biological way of getting back on. What goes on in these dialogues, brief as they may be, is probably most extraordinary. Are promises made? Is love exchanged? Is anger expressed? Or is it all arranged like a feudal marriage, where bride and groom never see one another until their wedding day?

Whatever happens, a contract is made, a union is consummated, and a child is born. That child could have little or no connection to its earthly parental figures and their paths could separate quickly, or it could be so deeply entwined with them that that relationship forms the basic crux of its entire life. If a lot of us have been on the planet many, many times in a whole host of guises, our relationships with our parents can be extremely convoluted, for in the past they could have been lovers or siblings or enemies or friends or even our own children, thus dictating complexities beyond measure that are totally hidden to our conscious minds.

Some people, then, can be ideal parents and teachers to us, while others can be filled with a host of unresolved rage from lifetimes long past that need to be acted out anew in order for us to heal our wounded psyches and move on to more ennobling things. Other parents can have absolutely no interest in us at all, acting as mere genetic conductors to get us on the planet, and once we are here, we are totally on our own, orphans of our own storms to be both parent and child in one to ourselves. This agreement between mother and/or father and child is far too crucial to be random. Everything rides on it: what your springboard into life will be; what you look like; how reality is first presented to you. Who you come in with is the most important choice that you make or that is made for you in your entire life.

If everyone was given free choice, the vast majority of us would opt for strong, beautiful bodies and loving, nurturing parents, but this does not seem to be the way the planet operates. Perhaps beauty and strength and love and nurturance are special rewards. Or perhaps they are on everyone's cycle, and sometimes you get them and sometimes you don't.

PLANET OF CHOICE

Whatever the actual process is, an overwhelming number of choices are made for us in the little double helix spirals in all our cells. Just how much of that is made up of elements that we directly chose? Is it possible we choose everything about our coming in for the specific purpose of healing ourselves? Is all of this our choice, even though some or a lot of it can be unbearably painful? If so, then we must take responsibility for exactly who we are. Unfortunately, many of us do not, particularly when incarnating into less-than-ideal circumstances with less-than-ideal progenitors and turning out to be less-than-ideal citizens of this planet.

In this realm of choice, we have constant choice of whether we want to continue on this planet or not, for death is a continual option wherever there is life. If we always have that awesome choice before us, is there also a good possibility that we have many other choices in who we are and how we came to be? It doesn't make sense that we can choose to terminate ourselves, if we also were not party to some of the choices in creating ourselves. Something makes most of us stay here as long as we can, and it isn't just fear of the unknown.

BODIES

In the same way we choose our parents, so do we choose our bodies, for whether we are athletic or crippled, obese or emaciated, that corpus is a total reflection of what we are working out in the present and what we have done in previous lives to get to where we are now. Although we discard the bodies of our completed existences each time we transcend this plane through death, the experience of that corpus stays with us through our body memories. All of us carry our old wounds until somehow we can get rid of them, for they are indication of areas where we need specific healing.

Many times the area of the body that finally does us in is the one that we have been working on that particular lifetime, so that attacks of the heart can come from unlovingness, stomach cancers from abuses of power, and so on. Our bodies, then, become instruments of not only the present but the past as well. Like our parents, from whom they came, they are instruments of choice and are our total responsibility, even if they are defective, since that is what we chose in this ongoing healing (and self-destructive) process called continuous life.

BODILESS SOULS

Although the planet is currently filled to overflowing with human bodies—more than five billion worth—many more beings are here in spirit shape as well, choosing not to exist in four-dimensional form either because they are awaiting the right circumstances in which to incarnate or because their mode of healing precludes conventional earthly existence. These spirits are representative of both the forces of darkness and light, and many attach themselves to those already in body.

Although each of us upon this sphere who can be visibly recognized inhabits a body, some of us do not stay grounded in that body, allowing, from time to time, other entities to enter into it and sometimes even to possess it, which can lead to actions, some of them quite violent, that we do not remember committing. Some bodies are particularly susceptible to this kind of possession, while others, under the influence of either drink or drug, periodically open themselves up to invasion, while others still are what are known as mediums, or conduits for other intelligences to come through them under controlled, and sometimes not so controlled, circumstances. Whatever the happenstance, each of us has a responsibility to remain within ourselves, for the consequences of not doing so can be ofttimes disastrous, with no one to take the blame for actions committed while we were temporarily "away" but the prime inhabitant of the offending body.

Thus, many innocents sit in both prisons and mental hospitals for deeds they did not themselves do but allowed others to do for them, and life takes on a far more complex depth than a surface reading of it by our previously accepted realities would indicate. As with everything else, all this falls within the realm of choice, and one of the primary lessons of this planet is learning how to take responsibility for all aspects of our lives: who we are, what we do, who we come from, who we produce, and how we play the hand we deal ourselves on each go-round.

RELATIONSHIPS

As our existences progress and we come into contact with more and more fellow denizens of this planet, some begin to take on a special flavor in our succeeding lives, and we have a tendency to incarnate again and again with them, both for better and, in many cases, for worse. These "soul connections," which manifest on the earthly plane in all sorts of varieties of relationships, are predicated many times on contracts and agreements made in the high spheres, which, though ill-remembered by the conscious mind, are as indelible as if dipped and sealed in blood. They can be responsible for many a bizarre action that otherwise would seem to have no rational substance to it at all.

Falling in love with someone you hate is an excellent example of this principle: a teaching of opposites that can manifest itself in all sorts of horrendous forms down through the centuries between two disparate beings testing the lengths to which their emotional essences may be stretched. In the same way, many an earthly marriage is a result of individuals eager to get even for past injustices imposed upon them by their equally hostile partners.

These contracts act as programs of the mind and heart, and they can be as murderous and destructive as they can be enlightening. Once set in motion they are exceedingly difficult to break upon the Earth plane, for they represent a will much higher than ordinary consciousness and oftentimes take many many lifetimes to be finally worked through. Thus, a husband and wife or parent and child can be thrown together again and again in all manner of connection until they finally find the right circumstance through which they can break their unhealthy ties and move on to better and more amenable relations with one another—or realize that there is no way their different selves can ever unite in harmony and move on to other beings with whom they can work out these same problems of the psyche.

Most of the unhappiness on this planet comes from situations just like this, in which we fail to see ourselves in the negative mirror of others and are forced to repeat the same mistakes of love and hatred over and over again, all to similar frustrating and unsatisfactory ends. The reverse, of course, also holds true in our repeatedly incarnating with those we genuinely love and who love us in return. Lucky indeed are the beings who can continually surround themselves with the deep and abiding affection of others, for they are well on the way toward the healing of themselves and adding to the light of the planet before their subsequent permanent transcendence from this plane into the higher (and hopefully far more loving) realms of the universe.

HIGHER & LOWER SELVES

Since all of us exist on some level as pure consciousness, our lives on Earth may be looked upon as singular hairs upon our greater head; and though each life is a definite reflection of that head, it is only a miniscule manifestation of it, a tiny detail of the much larger and more multidimensional entities that we are. In a sense, we are all puppet masters of the laughable beings who populate the planet, and though we may rail against the fates and curse our foul luck and blame everything but our own manifested inadequacies for what transpires all around us, on a higher level we are working on integrating our many aspects, and the choice of how we do this is largely up to us. We alone have the responsibility of writing our own dramas, and we alone have an equal responsibility to see that they turn out ultimately in our favor, no matter how many centuries and millennia and aeons we have to go through to finally get it right on this veil of illusions that constantly tricks us into thinking otherwise.

Since this realm is one of total choice, all of us choose unique paths to get to where we want to go, and there is no set rule as to how many times we have to incarnate or how often or even if we have to incarnate at all to enjoy the privileges of planetary citizenship. One being, then, can pop up every ten thousand years for a fast look-see, while another rarely lets more than a decade pass before submitting to the strictures and lessons of life, love, and death between each go-round.

Since this is also a circular world, if we don't get it right the first time, we probably wind up going through it again and again, for that is the rhythm of the teaching here. If this circle proves impossible to us, perhaps there are easier realities to which we can spiral off, before we once again tackle Earth. Perhaps our current incarnations are all involved in the ten-thousandth retelling of this planet's story, and all of us who are still here have not yet seen our way past its and our own trapped inevitability. Or perhaps this is the time all of us finally do get to spiral out of here together, having finally found the perfection that is at the end and the simultaneous beginning of this relentless circle.

SUICIDE

Each time we choose a suitable lifetime in which to incarnate, we probably sketch it out roughly as to duration, content, and substance, in accordance with the various agreements we have previously made with the people we plan to contact. Once having come down and lived out our lives, the normal avenues of death allow us to spiral back over to the world of the dead and there continue on with our existence until that time when we once more enter the waiting rooms of the ethers, make our agreements with our appropriate parents, and prepare for our next try at the world of the living. Most of those who commit suicide, however, do not seem to transcend this plane at all, for they abrogate the time span of their life contracts and must pay a heavy karmic penalty, which in most cases probably means sticking quite close to the Earth sphere in the etheric darkness. There they must await a chance to incarnate anew, for that is the only way they can leave where they are, usually to slightly worse circumstances than they thought they were escaping from when they fashioned their premature exits because of the added negative baggage they now carry. A person who commits suicide because he or she cannot emotionally cope with life probably has a far more difficult time in finding a parent, for that threat always hangs over any and all agreements made, and it must be considered a possibility in a mother's superconscious decision over whom she wants to bring into the world.

An extraordinarily selfish act, save in special cases such as life-threatening instances or symbolic political self-sacrifices, suicide is the ultimate statement of self-hatred. Those who get caught in its warp condemn themselves to succeedingly darker lives until they somehow can learn to love themselves, a task greatly compounded by the devastation they create round those who do love them and who are deeply pained by the emotional havoc their unexpected departures engender. Those who take their own lives in advanced age or to relieve themselves from some terminal illness operate outside of this law. However, those who cannot handle their own problems should think through the larger consequences and the effects on others in their draw toward self-destruction. A self-hating exit from this planet will do little to heal their wounded hearts, since the reason they incarnated into that form and life situation in the first place was to try to resolve it. Suicide also makes it a lot harder to get back on Earth the next time around, for it sets up a burden of deep loss and sorrow through which the suicided soul must struggle once again.

SPIRALING CIRCLES

For most beings on this planet, there is a continuity to life from one existence to the next, particularly when we choose to follow the flow of an entire cultural epoch. This means that there is a certain amount of repetition to our lives. We must go over past acts until either they work out to a more satisfactory conclusion or we understand the absolute impossibility of the particular task or tasks we have set for ourselves.

There doesn't seem to be any set rule as to puppet mastery on the physical plane, other than that each being does what serves her or his peculiar interests the best. Many beings choose to work out their private dramas on the public stage and appear again and again in positions of leadership and power. Thus, certain transcendental figures can be seen at the forefront of the entire story of civilization lifetime after lifetime. In addition, some run more than one body at once, a tricky bit of business when they are operating in the power arenas. Occasionally, several powerful beings can even get together to run a single body, sometimes with extraordinary results.

All the laws that apply to individuals, apply to countries, cultures, and civilizations as well. Upon incarnating into a specific race or society, we also buy into their legacies, for we are now part of a greater whole that is evolving along the same lines of healing or self-destruction as we are, which will dictate and shape our consciousness in the same manner as our private genetic, environmental, and hereditary factors.

Those of us who have been on the planet for a long time, then, have gotten to experience all races, both sexes, and all cultures. Thus, on some level we know we are a part of everyone, despite the forgetfulness of body we feel each time we incarnate anew, for that is the method of healing here, the nonremembrance of our deep pasts making us that much more cognizant of the present. In the forgetfulness of body, we always have the possibility of correcting past mistakes, no matter how many different times they have been repeated, for each time we begin afresh we always have fresh choice as to what to do.

As each of us once again asks those never-ending questions "Who am I ?" and "Why do I not love myself more?" we are given ample opportunity to find out through a multiplicity of guises, until our unmistakable essence finally emerges. In that moment, all that we have learned here finally comes together, and we can move onto different planes without the constraints of external realities for we no longer need physical definition to see which parts are still missing.

That is when we fully understand we all feed off the same "celestial egg" and act out each other's dreaded dreams. Who we love is who reflects our loving parts, and who we hate and fear is who we hate and fear in ourselves. And most important of all, at long long last we see that love is a state of being, a totality far beyond the excitation of emotion; it infuses our very fiber. But until we reach that golden moment, we will remain as children, bound to this planet of choice, until we finally choose not to be.

What follows is an almanach of magical stories woven round humanity's hidden and multileveled collective stay here. Through the alchemy of uniting the sublime with the mundane so that each reflects the other, a most unusual tapestry is created to retell the "her-story," "history," and mystery of our mortal world.

T H E
SACRED HEART
O F   T I M E

Part Three

Genesis

The *reader is now invited to recontemplate the heavens and then delve into the dualities of light and darkness before learning the sacred "rhythm of sevens" and seeing how they all helped create the mental, astral, and etheric worlds that give invisible resonance to our seemingly solitary physical presence here.*

If we could integrate all the different ways people on Earth view the heavens, the resulting panoramic empyrean, or heaven, would be a very large and multifaceted place, and perhaps it is. Perhaps we see the heavens so differently, or not at all, precisely because they accommodate the entire imaginative heart of humanity. Perhaps all the practitioners of all the world's religions ultimately do live in harmony and perfection there—god and goddess worshiper, atheist and agnostic alike—enhancing and complementing one another in the sweet understanding that all pathways that allow us to knock on heaven's door are ultimately one and the same. Perhaps, in the same way, all our religions have been divinely introduced to Earth to show us that this is not a planet of one truth or one way, but a planet of many ways, of choice, and that all the faiths that have appeared here through divine intervention are here to ultimately teach us to honor ourselves, without dishonoring anyone else.

THE ORGANIZED SACRED WORLD

Most of our earthly religions are based on sacred stories about the times divine beings have walked among us or acted through a selected channel to give intense grace to the planet for a fleeting, shining moment. Some of these sacred stories have come to accumulate ritual and ceremony around them and have gone on to become the cornerstones of the "organized sacred world," which has been with humanity in one form or another ever since some of our number first felt compelled to give the greater spirit of this planet an earthly orthodoxy and authority.

Our organized sacred world has told us all during its long existence that Earth is a place where humanity and divinity continually touch. There are enough varied testaments in our collected sacred texts to make a large percentage of the world believe this, for the greater imagination of humanity has always been highly receptive to our universe being populated by all sorts of different emanations of the divine.

The idea of one god, monotheism, has been the preoccupying religious sentiment of the West for a goodly stretch of time now, despite the irony that the organized sacred world built round that concept has come to house a number of different deep and highly defined beliefs based on one god. Because they all call their one god by different names, they have wound up creating a heaven, once again, of many gods, all very powerful, with the Earth as their competitive arena. In addition to a collective heaven populated by various "one gods," a second deity, this one lesser and darker, an adversary god, is also acknowledged in most of the canons of monotheism. This set of beliefs has given us a planetary one-god heaven that is actually filled with a whole host of deities, an odd contradiction that has caused much tension, separation, and isolation in the fragmented planet below, which seems to want to believe in a oneness of the heavens, but cannot get beyond the idea that there may be more than one oneness to its ultimate design.

Collectively, humanity has had a tendency to project out from its own insularity in creating its overview of things here. For a long time, Earth was considered flat and at the center of the universe, with the sun racing around it each day. This was an accepted reality up until the last several hundred years, and when it was finally questioned through scientific investigation, a great deal of resistance arose before the current model of our sun-centered, round-planet solar system came into popular acceptance.

Beliefs, even when they are wrong, are part of our collective and individual evolutionary processes. This is a planet of choice, and sometimes we have to make the wrong choice before we accidentally discover the right one. All of our lives here are riddled with choices, great and small, all the time. Since we always have the choice of leaving here anytime we desperately want to, more than likely we have had the choice of coming here as well. Constant choice is a wearing responsibility, and yet it is the mode of teaching all of us accepted in choosing this planet to be our temporary temporal home.

Because this is a planet of choice, there has never been a universal heaven that appeals to the greater heart of its planetary denizens. Even within the demarcations of the organized sacred world, schisms and factions and offshoots have always existed, so that the chaos of choice is always present even within our separate belief systems.

LIGHT & DARKNESS

When there is no illumining light on the Earth, this becomes a very dark world, for the matter of which the physical world is made is inherently dark and depends on outside illumination to make itself seen. Matter by itself is just palpable darkness, part of the intermittent physical workings of a great dark void we call space. The darkness here is deeply embedded in this planet's cyclic disposition, for each day the Earth has to dip into the dark before it can move back into the light. The dark is and always has been a major presence here.

In our human projection of the heavens, we have posited, through the bridges of our organized sacred world, great struggles between the forces of darkness and light, with Earth as one of the primary battlegrounds of that titanic conflict. In our eagerness to project our own imperfections on higher realms, we seem to have created a model once again of a greater world revolving around our lesser one, rather than Earth being a humble satellite of a much larger and more complex empyrean.

Perhaps the light of illumination and the darkness of matter have no quarrel with the existence of either realm in the ultimate design of things. Perhaps the conflict lies wholly with humanity and who and what it invites from both the light and the dark to represent its higher face. Perhaps our conflicted inability to honor one another's beliefs is not part of a celestial battle of supremacy and will, but a simple ongoing exercise in choice. Since light and dark form the opposite edges of choice, they have the ability to create all sorts of combinations between them. Perhaps it is these many combinations and the limitless choice they represent that has made Earth seem like an endless Armageddon between good and evil, when, in actuality, its inhabitants are following a chosen agenda of experiencing the joys and horrors and chaos and absolute madness of having endless choice.

In the beginning of all things there is the story, a never-ending tale that constantly changes each time it is told and each time it is listened to, for stories are products of both speaker and audience. They remain alive and vibrant only as long as they are allowed to transform, to alter, to spiral upward and downward in the collective imagination of all. Otherwise, they become the never-changing story, and they slowly deaden and their tellers become more and more strident and rigid. The stories consequently lose their meanings, and the civilizations built on them crumble and die, for such is the nature of myth that cannot accommodate change.

Following, then, is part of the tale that has no end. It can be accepted, disbelieved, disavowed, torn apart, and/or totally rewrit, for it is one of the many never-ending stories of this planet and wishes only to dance in the dreamscape of its listeners for whatever purpose it serves them.

There was once a runner who could move so fast he thought he could out-race that master athlete, Death. And so a race was run twixt the two, and when it was over, some said the runner had indeed beaten his adversary, while others claimed he had not. The controversy that rose from that contest is still with us, for this is not a planet that takes its reality laws lightly, particularly the one that slashes to the very soul of humanity: "Nobody gets out of here alive."

Now, this runner was so sure of his skills that he ran with his legs crossed, his arms spread wide, and all four limbs nailed into place, so that he stood frozen in a dancer's leap upon the starting line. Yet when the race was finally completed, three days later, his most loyal supporters all swore they saw him saunter across the finish line with a big, loving smile on his face, and they ran out jubilantly to the countryside to spread the good news "We're number one!"

Soon after that legendary race, the runner disappeared into the myth of the Christ, leaving the legacy of his accomplishment to a handful of publicists who rode it for all it was worth, claiming their champion had beaten the Old Master in a fair athletic contest and that the end of the world was now imminent, thanks to that superhuman feat. As a result, the fear that Death had so deeply instilled in the hearts and minds of the multitudes gradually fed into a popular acceptance of a new champion runner. Soon ordinary people were imitating the new master's cross-over pose, leaving life with the same open-armed leap and cavalier disregard for whatever adventures lay in the unknown beyond because prophecy had told them the end for everybody was only a couple of extended heartbeats away.

But somehow things didn't end, and a couple of centuries later the sign of the runner's victory, the cross-over cross, was emblazoned on the shields of the very symbolic empire he had run against, that of ancient Rome, which was looking for some symbol round which to rally its waning resolve and found it in the sawed-off sword of the crucifix. By then, the spirit of the race had long been lost, and the open-palmed, passive-fist stance of the runner had been altered radically to an image of a well-armed avenging warrior. This change left his former foe, the Old Master Athlete, to stand as mysterious and proud as before, an aged combatant whose skills remained as unmeasured, unknown, and as feared as ever. Now, some twenty centuries after that curious contest, Death, the ancient athlete, once more stands invincible, and the human race lies wrapped in abject ignorance of the power that the unknown and the immeasurable has over them.

Yet there was once a time when Death was known and people feared it not, for they knew it was but another doorway to life on this planet, where all who live in bodies experience the inevitable corrosion and decay of time. But in order to understand its true place here, it is necessary to go back to the invisible world of the past, way back to the very beginning of things on planet Earth.

Some five billion or so years ago, the Earth was a gaseous ball, vomiting smoke and flames as it uneasily digested itself into a breatheable, bouncible sphere. Despite the incendiary fury of the creation of this planet, a form of humanity was probably here from the very start, mind-surfing the flaming waves of the Earth as fire spirits, molten sheets of energy who wished to learn how to live in physical bodies in a four-dimensional world where space and time are the two limiting lords of reality and Death, that old master of the unknown, is their strange servant.

As this planet formed and reformed itself, so did humanity, passing down through the various planes that surround the physical earth until they were finally able to create hard, pliable, skeletal bodies to navigate the jungles, steppes, and valleys of their long-awaited new home. Since only the rude fossilized remains of this planet's primitive past have been revealed to the blinking eye of science thus far in the never-ending story of humankind, it has been assumed that no other civilization has ever trotted down the timepike of this blue-green paradise save our own two-legged, heavily armed variety.

Wrapped in the unseen layers of memory that envelop our outer world, however, is an extraordinary story from which most of our own myths, deities, and religions have come. This story covers the rise and fall of uncountable civilizations peopled by gods, goddesses, demons, and mortals alike. Though it would take a hundred million volumes to merely outline it, its basic flow can be summed up in four words: fire, water, air, and earth—the acknowledged elements. Before proceeding, however, let it be said that there are many ways to look upon the creation, continuation, and periodic destruction of this planet, and the following is only one of them. It is offered not as a contradiction to any existing system of belief, but as an imaginative alternative, another way of looking at things, based on the collective lore of humanity's hidden and revealed past.

RHYTHM OF SEVENS

Consider, then, the number seven. There is a cyclical rhythm to sevens that moves from a unity of beginning to a unity of end with a reevaluation of its various parts through the middle. In stage one, a unity (or a state of oneness) is introduced. Eventually, the unity begins to manifest different forces, and the two strongest ultimately divide the original state of oneness into a duality, or a state of twoness (stage two). This duality, which is a delicate balance of opposing forces, eventually manifests a third element from the struggle of the first two, thus dividing the duality into a trinity, or a state of threeness (stage three). This, then, does further struggle with itself and eventually breaks down to create a multiplicity of elements. This fourth stage of the cycle, that of manyness, at length, reverts back to the trinity (stage five), which eventually breaks down to the duality again (stage six). When the duality is resolved, then the original unity can be re-created, but this time it is quite intimate with all of its sundry parts. The cycle is completed with the unity at one with itself once again, through the experience of its own disintegration and reintegration (stage seven).

So, the rhythm of sevens runs as follows: unity, duality, trinity, multiplicity, trinity, duality, and unity once again. This cycle is a means for perfection to break down into its various components, resolve the many internal differences revealed in the process, and ultimately re-create its own completeness if it can make it all the way through the seven steps of the cycle. In addition, the first three stages reflect the last three, and the fourth—the middle—creates a bridge so that the second trinity may conclude the first trinity with what it has learned in between.

Much of what has transpired down both the recorded and the unrecorded roads of time can be laid against the seven-spoked cycle of "unity working its way back to unity," so that the circle rather than the straight line is the defining vehicle of time and space here.

In the very beginning of things only the Infinite existed, and it lived in its oneness beyond space and time. There it could have stayed into its own forever had it not made the choice one spontaneous moment to also become finite, so that it could mirror and experience its many dimensions and parts through the rhythm of beginnings and endings. This it did in an extraordinary explosion, the echoes of which still ring down through the many universes it created in that act of perfect magic. And long did it exist as the Two— Infinite/Finite—in perfect harmony with both its defined and undefined selves. Eventually, its finite side also chose to divide, this time into Light and Dark, so it, too, could experience its many dimensions and parts through not only beginnings and endings but illumination and shadow as well.

And long did the Infinite and Finite Dark and Finite Light coexist as the Three, until a further division appeared within both the Light and the Dark: the beginnings and endings and in-betweens of mortality and immortality. This time the three—the Infinite, Finite Light, and Finite Dark—and their mortal/immortal subdivisions could not find a balance among themselves because of the many in-betweens their endless combinations made, and so together they exploded into their countless parts. Thus, the galaxies and the stars and the planets were born, as part of a process of Oneness breaking down into its many parts in order to ultimately find its oneness once again, through the reexperience of itself.

THE MORTAL WORLD

Since that singular act of creation was one of choice by the power of the Infinite, choice most likely permeates all the levels of existence it created, for such is a natural legacy of a universe composed of both darkness and light. Within the many dimensions reflected by the choice-filled dynamic of those two lies our own, the mortal world of

Earth, a by-product of the explosions that formed the universe, the galaxies, the stars, and our own solar system, beginning with the sun and ending with the fiery emanations that came off it and hardened to ultimately form the planets.

Our solar system is an isolated place, sitting on the outer frontier of its master galaxy, the Milky Way. Its central sun is a finite mortal sphere, a self-consuming entity with a measurable life span, which nevertheless is capable of supporting biological life, but at a terrible price: its own ultimate existence. Those who dwell in physical form on the third planet out from the sun, our own Earth, are also heavily subjugated to the laws of the finite world, and like the sun, the very source of Earth life, they are prey to the same inevitabilities of decay and death.

The physical world of Earth, in fact, is largely a world of the dead, ruled by gravity and the laws of the grave, where everything is drawn down and back into the planet, while all life essence disappears into whatever lies beyond the living, breathing world. Despite the basically unappealing prospects its inevitabilities demand—aging, dying, and death—the Earth has attracted an overwhelming diversity of life to it. These life-forms have subsequently done endless battle with one another in trying to both survive and predominate here, all for the privilege of being asked to leave at any moment. On the surface, none of this makes much sense. Why would anyone want to live locked into a highly vulnerable mortal body on a planet constantly struggling with both the light and dark of its own ongoing existence? Unless, perhaps, they were an integral part of that planet and part of its story and subject to the same rhythms of beginnings, endings, and new beginnings, so that they, too, could see their many parts and understand their connections and their singularity in trying to find their way back up to the Oneness through the finite mirror of the Infinite.

THE BIRTH OF THE EARTH

In the beginning, all the Earth was afire. In its incandescence, it drew energy from all over the universe to it, some by choice and some by chance and all for the adventure of incarnating in multidimensional form around an isolated frontier world that would be rich in both resource and conflict, for it would be host to a multitude of beings who each would see their combined planet quite differently. Since many of these energy entities came from already formed worlds, they arrived in a variety of forms, some having already mastered whole universes, others in large-eyed and open-mouthed innocence, so that deity, space drifter, and undefiled alike were all witness to the birth of the Earth, and all could lay equal claim to it.

Those of us who had chosen to experience this planet in physical human form, and had in turn been chosen to do so out of the many who first applied here for admission, were given magic entry to Earth soon after its formation. We abandoned our previous shapes and existences to enter the dimensional atmosphere surrounding this planet in the absolute innocence and ignorance of rebirth, stepping through the first of four doors that would eventually lead to the actual surface of this sphere, once each of the other portals had been properly opened to us. The first door led to a vast plane that encircled the entire Earth, hovering within visual distance of the physical outline of this sphere, but sitting unseen, untouched, unsmelt, unheard, but definitely not unfelt, above it.

FIRST CIVILIZATION—THE MENTAL PLANE

The Archeozoic period, from 5,000,000,000 B.Z. (before the invisible year 0 of our current Common Era) to 520,000,000 B.Z., represents the Earth's first civilization and coincides with the formation of its mental plane. This period was symbolically dominated by the element of fire and reflected the first e-zone of survival on the collective body of humanity.

All who enter Earth's atmosphere must first pass through the ethers of thought that cover this world. There sits all the information a being could ever want to know about this planet in a limitless library of both fact and fancy, which has been continually created and re-created over a period of five billion years or so, an extended multilevel compendium of idea and fantasy, seaweed thick in its innumerable convolutions, involutions, and evolutions.

This is where we learned how our spirit essence would slowly be turned into matter and how we would gradually dip ever deeper into the darkness of the material world, with less and less illumination to guide us, save for whatever spirit we could keep alive within. We saw the degradations and abominations that would ensue from all this, as well as the ecstasies and passions, and we knew this would be no easy world to pass through.

Thus, humanity spent its first several billion years hovering over the planet, not quite on it, not quite directly learning from living on a world that is defined by time and space. All that time we watched as the fires receded into the Earth's center and the gases liquified and turned to water mist. Some solidified and the planet became alive with volcanoes under a thick canopy of clouds as simple carbon-based molecules gathered and linked to ultimately create the living creatures who would populate the planet's surface and sprout up through its unsettled ground.

Through observation, we learned the strictures of time and space by watching those even less evolved than we plunge into the physical and taste its initial fire and its slow-brained early evolutions. We also learned how all who journey here—animal, vegetable, and mineral alike—do so because they, too, desire to experience the phenomenon of choice, and within this sphere and its continual cycles of creation, continuance, destruction, and re-creation, all things are possible when there is constant choice. In addition, we saw that the question asked by almost every soul who walked our mind-world was, "Why do I not love myself more?" And we saw that the answer would be played out against the Earth's constantly changing scenarios of consciousness, until each of us could finally get to see our true selves, however long that would take.

In the same way, we saw that everything was continually in motion here, from the tiniest atom to the slowly moving mountains, and that everything was constantly changing so that to sit still and resist change was to die. For here all paid homage to time and decay, and everything was always birthing and blooming and dying and returning, again and again, so that Earth is forever young and forever old and forever in-between. Right from the beginning, this planet evinced itself as a cauldron of diverse wills struggling to express themselves at the expense of all in their paths.

We also saw that everything is precariously balanced on finite scales of plenty, so that those who hunt unsparingly soon find they have only hunted down themselves and disappear in starved shock to learn that lesson anew in different form. Thus, those who wished to be human learned all the laws of survival here and were introduced from afar to the Old Master Athlete, Death, who already had the reputation for great power even with the odd assortment of giant creatures who wore bodies at this particular juncture in the story of humanity. From our vantage point of being only bodiless spirits in the dimensional ethers that surround the Earth, we saw that although the Old Master holds complete sway over the physical world, the gray spectre of Death has no jurisdiction over the puppet-master souls who linger overhead on other planes to guide their physical manifestations through the forgetfulness of mortality and its limited consciousness.

This first plane, then, would be a repository for our relatively immortal essence, and each of us upon coming to this planet forms a body from its ethers, composed entirely of information garnered from this pure world of the mind. The mental body has no real defined shape; it is more of a storehouse of information appended to the personality of the being it represents. Because it exists on a plane that is almost pure information, it has access to the thought experience of all of humanity from the beginning of time until its end. Everything that has ever been or will ever be pondered, rationalized, discovered, discarded, created, and destroyed sits up in this fiery imaginative sphere to be rediscovered by beings upon Earth, when both the proper time and space open for it.

By the time the hovering fire spirits of humanity began to see that the planet was readying itself for more complicated forms of life, we came to the realization that our original thought-world, for all its brilliance, was actually a sand-castle civilization that would never progress beyond its own impermanence. We began, therefore, to look longingly at the second door that leads to the Earth and fantasizing about what lay beyond it.

The second door opened to all round about 520,000,000 B.Z., and everyone descended the step to pass through it, bringing the first phase of the First Civilization to a close and inaugurating its successor to all who had had the patience to make it through so far. Though no physical trace remains of this long introduction of human consciousness to the realities and illusions of Earth, it has all been duly documented and recorded in the Akashic Records and sits eternally above this planet, accessible through disciplined thought and undisciplined dreams in the first of our four human bodies, the mental.

SECOND CIVILIZATION—THE ASTRAL PLANE

The Paleozoic period, from 520,000,000 B.Z. to 195,000,000 B.Z., was symbolically dominated by the element of water and reflected the second e-zone of reproduction on the collective body of humanity. During humanity's Second Civilization, which came into being during this period, the physical planet began to become far more inhabitable, with a greater complexity to things, as the invisible dimensions of Earth suddenly expanded into two realms. At this time, the primordial ones, or creation deities, who had come from the distant galaxies and had supervised the formation of the planet, left for other worlds, for their work was now done. They were succeeded by their ancient children, the divine giants, who divided the spiritual domains of the world among themselves, as the second door of the four that lead to Earth opened for humanity.

This second plane also encircled the globe and was of equal size, shape, and strength to the first; the only difference between the two was that whereas our original plane was composed of fiery ethers, this place was woven out of watery essences. Though it seemed to occupy the exact same space as the other, somehow it seemed far closer to Earth, for its edges were less defined than the orderly fires of the mental. This was the astral plane, and it is where each of us who desires to be human creates our second body, the emotional, with all its irrational wisdom.

Like the thought plane, the astral is a world that is unencumbered by both time and space, and it serves as a theatre for feelings. It has come to extend from beneath the surface of the Earth to the very highest heavens, and it embraces all worlds in-between, for it is our collective and individual dream-scape and spirit-domain. It has also come to be an escape valve for the extraordinary pressures of trying to remain stable in a four-dimensional state, and it gives voice to a lot of the violence and rage and frustration that state entails. Unlike the material world, where the deed cleaves to the doer long after the deed has been done, in the astral world nothing lasts longer than a thought or a feeling, even if those thoughts and feelings are prolonged thousands of Earth years. When they vanish, so do their astral counterparts. This world is structured for fluidity, not permanence, and its laws revolve around that principle.

When the physical world disappears into sleep, the astral world comes alive. Much of the contained emotion of our material planet is let loose there, so that each and every night the astral suffers devastation and drama beyond belief. Yet it has the continued capacity to renew itself, for it knows how to transform its realities far more smoothly than its more rigid material counterpart.

Just as the First Civilization worked out the thought-story of humanity, the Second Civilization played out our feeling-story with the same creations, continuances, destructions, and/or re-creations, giving a depth to the fire of thought through the great waters of emotion, forging an ever more complicated reality in the process. Although humanity came to live fully in this astral world, slowly forming a body that would absorb all its information and yet remain flexible to its anarchic freedom of expression, we also continued to live fully in the thought plane. Now we were conscious of two worlds and active in both, so that each plane became a reflection of the other, and we often found ourselves dealing with similar dramas at once from the dual perspective of feeling and thought.

The Second Civilization saw a slight removal of the deities from our midst, adding a third pair, heaven/earth, to the light/dark and life/death dualities that were already in evidence below us. In the beginning, both were one, and we were as infants suckling at the empyrean breast of the greater universe. Now, on the astral, we became children, learning to walk and move around, each of us far more aware of our own specialness and yet still quite dependent on the greater whole. But we were somewhat separated from that whole, conscious of both a *greater world* and a *lesser world* and the idea that being human meant dwelling in the latter while searching for the former through the illusions of our limited senses. So our second body, the emotional, formed, and like the first one, it is relatively immortal, lasting for our entire stay on the planet, whether we spend a blinking millisecond here or several billion years.

Together, the mental and the astral comprise two dream spheres that are fully populated by all who dwell below them, as well as by some who choose to exist only on those two levels. Without the invisible presence of these two etheric spheres, the physical plane would never have been able to accommodate anything but its most primitive unthinking, unfeeling creatures. These two planes allow humanity considerable leeway before an action has to be committed to the four-dimensional world and its rigid laws of action and reaction, thus greatly enhancing the numerous possibilities to every situation by allowing them to be played out on two other levels before descending to the thick world of matter.

Everything that was conjured during the First Civilization was acted out during the Second, so its tale is every bit as detailed as its predecessor's, with the added intensity of the astral's emotional focus. This story has covered a period of more than a half billion years from its inception to this current era, and it, too, has left no tangible trace upon the Earth; it must be broached through the ethers in order to extract a full, recorded accounting of humanity's achingly slow development.

The astral allowed us to further learn and step ever deeper into the mists of this planet, peeking into every corner of the world below us, which would one day be ours. In addition to light/dark, life/death, and heaven/earth we saw yet another duality begin to form on the planet, one that caused a great rush for the gates to the outer universe by many of our number.

THE DUALITY OF THE SEXES

Since our astral and mental bodies exist for our entire duration here in quasi-immortal form, they have no need to reproduce themselves. They have the power of regeneration from within and are constantly shedding their outer skins so that they may remain eternally youthful. Because of this, there is no sexual differentiation between them, and they evince themselves as the trinity of he/she/it. This tri-sexed body is the standard corpus for most of this empyrean, with everyone allowed to give vent to their maleness, their femaleness, and their itness in equal measure. Those who have manifested as both gods and goddesses to the subsequent sexually divided planet have presented only part of themselves to the human consciousness of Earth, to add to the eternal illusions of this place.

In the beginning of the planet, the simple creatures who first appeared here had the ability to recreate themselves from within, splitting in twain or forming germ-buds of their essence, for they, too, lived in the oneness of the sexes. As life grew more complex, however, the complementary components of reproduction became divided between two slightly different bodies of all creatures, and the duality of sex was introduced to the Earth, over a long, long period. The prospect of manifesting only one-third of our sexual beings when at last we descended to the physical plane, in bodies that would be clearly labeled male, female, or, on rare occasion, a combination of the two, caused a great deal of angst on the astral. But we came to see that the basic healing method of this particular solar system would be in the separation of all our elements—our sexuality, our spirituality, our emotionality, and our cerebrality—so that they could be isolated and worked on apart from one another.

This process of rediscovering who we really are by allowing only limited manifestations of our true selves to appear on the physical is further compounded by then dealing with this phenomenon with an equally limited consciousness. The basic illusions of our existence, then, become thoroughly buried in all the misinformation that rises up out of them, and it is a sharp eye, indeed, that can pierce the veils this process creates.

And so the land and sea began to fill with creatures and the Earth began to grow thick with life. We then saw there was a definite pattern to all that transpired on this time-locked world, for everything seemed to move in chaotically ordered cycles, and each cycle either gave birth to another or abruptly ended itself. We also saw that the Old Master Athlete, Death, had absolute control over the world of the material and operated swiftly on all who did not adapt to the continually changing shifts of flora and fauna, making everyone extremely vulnerable to an immediate recall from the physical back up to the ethers until another opportunity would open to return to the world of matter.

As this first phase of our Second Civilization came to an end around 195 million years before the year 0, Earth began to become a paradise for tree-tromping reptilian giants. While most of us learning to be human shivered over this spectacle, the deities among us took to wearing both dragon dress and serpent garb in celebration of the monsters below us as mischievous reminder of the duality of all things here.

THIRD CIVILIZATION—THE ETHERIC PLANE

The Mesozoic period, from 195,000,000 B.Z. to 65,000,000 B.Z. was symbolically dominated by the element of air and reflected the third e-zone of power on the collective body of humanity.

In the beginning of this Third Civilization, a volcanic continent began to rise out of the sea, covering much of the Southern Hemisphere of the globe at its height. It incorporated a great deal of what is called in the Common Era the Pacific Ocean as well as the south Atlantic in its landmass, while embracing all of Australia, the tip of South America, the eastern and southern coasts of Africa, and patches of North America and Asia.

This continent, which came into being after an earlier Arctic and Antarctic world sank, was the original Eden of humanity, a tropical paradise that welcomed the last two bodies of the human form onto the actual surface of the Earth. This civilization became the first to both challenge the precepts of nature and destroy its world in the process, a sad tale that would be repeated over and over again through the many millennia to come. The land of the Third Civilization came to be called Mu, the Motherland, for all, in its beginning, was bounty and oneness and primeval perfection.

With the advent of the Third Civilization, each of us learning to be human opened our respective third doors leading to Earth and suddenly found ourselves down on the actual surface of the planet, but once more without an adequate body to deal with it, rendering us invisible to those already in residence here. We saw we would have to form yet another informational corpus for this world, the etheric, which sits right on the Earth's material contours and forms the energy plane here, being visible in the form of light auras around all living things for those who choose to see them. The etheric plane is as cojoined with the physical as the mental plane is with the astral, so that the first two reside upon the surface of the Earth while the second two sit above and inside it.

The etheric, as its name implies, also dwells in the ethers, but since these are fashioned of an airy substance rather than a fiery or watery one, the perspective on the actual planet is a lot clearer than on the higher planes. This is the level in which pure energy is created, and that energy has the ability to attach itself to any shape in the world of matter and give it both form and life. The etheric plane exists as a world of color and motion, constantly changing, constantly in flux, breathing the vitality of the ethers into the physical world and joining the upper worlds with the lower. This color con- duit of knowledge and life force sits between the two timeless, space- less levels of existence and the time-locked, space-locked planet itself. So although the Old Master Athlete has no real authority here, its presence can still be felt, for most of what happens on the etheric is tied into the actions and reactions of the physical sphere.

The three invisible planes—the mental, the astral, and the etheric (fire, water, and air)—hold the three invisible bodies of humanity. As the human presence has slowly evolved on Earth, so have these three bodies become interlocked, so that whatever happens on any of the four levels (including the physical) happens on all of them, and affects them all to varying degrees. Each has a reality to it all its own, with the story of humanity becoming ever more complex the higher we search through its physical, etheric, astral, and mental libraries. All that happens on planet Earth is recorded in the ethers, and that information is always open to all who learn how to seek it.

Humanity formed its third body on the etheric plane over the next 150 million years and began to experiment with the fourth and last plane, the physical. Much mischief and mind-bombing came of that experimentation, for the laws that govern the physical are more rigid and unbending than those of the three worlds that surround it. Thus was humanity finally introduced to the planet, after waiting nearly five billion years for the privilege. Our childhood was over, yet so was our childhood about to begin anew.

MU

The great motherland of Mu saw the birth of seven races on its etheric plane, each reflecting the color of Earth at its point of origin: black, brown, red, yellow, white, blue, and green. When it came time to add a physical body to that which already had been created on the etheric, the last two races politely demurred. They chose instead to remain solely as energy entities, becoming creatures of legend: fairies and nymphs and naiads and sprites, who would come to hide their electric presences from all save those special few to whom they chose to reveal themselves.

The other five races all subsequently came down to the physical plane in jellied form and slowly hardened over the geological ages in order to follow highly variant paths and become lost in the illusions of color. During the time of the Third Civilization, the physical world saw the advent of those who bore their young alive, the mammals, and a scant thirty-five million years later, the skies were aswarm with birds, great-winged reptiles who soared near the ethers. So it was that the land, sea, and air filled with life, and to those of us who hovered just above it in the ethers, it looked as if this place would be paradise after all.

LILITH & ADAM & EVE

When the door to the physical world first opened, a trinity of beings stepped through—a man, a woman, and a snake—each representing a member of the ruling triad of this planet: god/goddess/creature. It was the snake who led the man and woman into Paradise and then disappeared into the underbrush to leave them alone to marvel at the Eden that had been created for them. As they both stood naked and sexless in the absolute innocence of creation, the man called himself Adam and proclaimed himself lord over Eden, boasting of both his coming and his presence, for there were none to challenge him, and he saw that he could say what he wished. The woman called herself Lilith and proclaimed Eden a garden of wisdom, for she could see that this was a world of many worlds and that they all were interconnected.

When they had both finished making their entrances and had drunk deep of paradise's perfumed perfection, Adam turned to Lilith and told her he must have scraped his rib on arriving, and asked her to take a look at it. As soon as she healed it, Adam had another complaint, and then another and another and another, until all Lilith was doing was serving Adam. She finally berated him for it and cursed her servitude, and when he would not change, she stormed out of Eden, heading west to become a creature of the night, a figure of free will. Because she left Paradise on her own, she was the first being to exercise the power of choice so that she could experience the dark and the light on her own. Although she introduced the myth of freedom of choice to the planet, she would be condemned bitterly for it, and trace of her powerful spirit would be erased from the holy Adamic records as warning to others who wanted more than Paradise here. She would be replaced by another, named Eve, who would also suffer Adam's unending demands. Eve, too, would tire of them, for though she did not mind serving, she wished to be served herself as well, and this her earthly compatriot showed no interest in doing.

So she wandered into the jungle, her astral self feeling quite unraveled, for though this may have been a manly paradise, she saw it certainly was not a womanly one. As she lingered between a bush and a tree, the snake came crawling up and down out of both, for it was a creature of great magic and many manifestations. Running itself over her tired back, it massaged her gently with its movements, all the while quietly speaking, gently bestowing its mischievous wisdom on her gradually more receptive ear. Then it offered her a bite of the apple of knowledge. As she bit into it, the snake went on to tell her the story of men and women on this sphere and the vast differences and similarities between the two. It said that because females could conceive life internally and males could not, each would be sent down totally dissimilar paths of consciousness, and humanity would be given a dual perspective on itself from the viewpoint of its divided sexes.

Because women are the conduits of life, it continued, there would be a far greater need for them initially in any society that was interested in multiplying itself upward, with a lesser demand for men. While a fertile male can participate in endless couplings toward recreation, a fertile female can carry only a limited number of their results if she is bounteous. A handful of males and a tribeful of females could produce a thousandfold of themselves, while a handful of females and a tribeful of males would succeed only in recreating another handful of their number.

Because fewer males would be needed, they would become more expendable, for if their lives were lost, others could still take their place in the reproduction process. Because women would be looked on as the keys to the future, males would develop a greater need to prove their self-worth. They would begin either to aggressively assert it or create illusions around it if they wanted to insure their individual indispensability in the continuance of their kind.

Women, on the other hand, would not have the same need to declaim their self-worth, for it would be inherently understood that they carried the miracle of life within them, making their survival paramount to the survival of their clans or tribes. Consequently, men would begin to evolve around an egoistic path of consciousness, centering their concerns on their selves and how to make those selves individually needed, while women would operate out of a far more collective way of thinking, acting, and feeling. To them would fall the continuance of civilization, bringing in its new members, teaching them the wisdom of both past and present, drawing on the magic of the ethers to keep the planet forever stocked with fresh, new, angelic faces.

Men would, therefore, get lost in the illusions of their self-importance, while women would get lost in the illusions of serving that self-importance. This pattern would dominate many a civilization until these illusions could be transcended and men and women could both share in self-importance and the correct collective consciousness needed to maintain it as a constructive manifestation of self for everybody. All this the snake told Eve, who listened and understood, for she was now magically imbued with knowledge. However, when she went back to Adam, all he was interested in was what was for dinner. Instead of preparing it, Eve told Adam all the snake had told her and offered him a bite of the same "fruit of know-ingness" she had eaten.

To her surprise, Adam bellowed his outrage at what she had said and forbade Eve ever to taste of the trees of the Garden again. But Eve refused, and Adam wound up marching out of Eden to the north, to live in his thoughts. There, he found in his nakedness and vulnera-bility that he had taken the snake with him, to dangle between his legs, as reminder of his disconnection, of his creature-dom, of his need for union, of his incompleteness. Eve, in turn, went south of Eden, to live in her feelings, and in her nakedness she found the opened apple between her legs, as symbol of humanity's fear of the unknown, with its potential for mystery revealed or forever kept secret. And the two, man and woman, came to accept their separate-ness from one another and wound up dwelling in different worlds upon the same planet, driven from Eden by their own unresolved wills.

HEAVEN, EARTH & HELL

At the same time the first astral man and woman did their dream-dance of separation in the Garden of Eden, a selected group of beings who had been forming in the ethers and numbered exactly 144,000 alighted in physical form upon the planet, to begin its formal story. Each represented one of the 144,000 pathways to perfection here, and though all were completely different, all knew their deep connection to one another and to the world of spirit whence they had come. They were to be the storytellers of the planet, and though some had once been divine, while other had been mere sparks of energy, all had been selected to give future humanity its full legendary spec-trum, through both word and action. These beings lived in twelve valleys in the very heart of Mu and knew absolute planetary har-mony. Seeing themselves as a reflection of the very Name of Nature (a manifestation of the oneness of the heavens), they called themselves YSRL or Israel, after the four elements: fire, water, air, and earth.

And long did they live in peaceful plenitude, until one day a trickster came into their midst, a man who seemed woven from the very light of the sun. Word was quickly passed, and the beings from all twelve valleys came to see and hear this mysterious stranger. When everyone had gathered, he addressed them from a great rock and told them his name was Melchizedek, and praised them for their perfection. He said that now that everyone knew the possibilities of love and completeness here, they could begin their search for it on higher levels, for so they had come to this world, to learn about love through separation and reunion. For some, this would be a process of endless heartaches, while for others it would be swift and easy, for each represented a different pathway. Though some might regain their way into Paradise immediately, it would not appear again on this world until all 144,000 stories reached their full circle, no matter how long that took.

First, however, they would have to lose Paradise. Melchizedek bade them build him twelve towers to higher realities than their own peaceful perfection, one in each valley, which would stretch to the very heavens. The people who built the greatest tower would become his chosen people, and he would come to live in their valley; they would always know the highest of Edens, even while their brothers and sisters suffered greatly around them. With that, he left as mysteriously as he had come.

There was much talk over what he had said, and some said he was evil and that his words had no place here. Some said they did not want to disrupt the way things had always been, for that was part of the story they had to tell. Others did not know what to think, while the rest saw the adventure and challenge and brilliance of his coming, for that was part of their story. These were the ones who ultimately had their way, for they immediately began to build their valleys' towers. Gradually everyone was forced to deal with the competition of the separated towers, some to continually disclaim it as disruptive, some to try to ignore it as best they could, and the rest to become fanatically involved in the logistics and completion. Though there was great harmony in the building, since that was the way they had always done things, as each of the valleys got deeper and deeper into its own towers of separation, a keen sense of competitiveness began to assert itself, particularly after the towers started to grow appreciably in size.

It wasn't too much longer before each valley began to notice that persons unknown would sneak in during the night and do considerable damage on their structures, and guards had to be put around the towers. The twelve valleys became bitterly defined and defended territories, and their inhabitants began speaking among themselves in secret tongues, to keep their activities separate and private. Inside each of the twelve defined territories, different elements began struggling for control, so that each valley became separated even within itself. More secret tongues ensued, until the entire 144,000 were splintered and separated from one another, and all of inhabited Mu seemed ready to explode.

It was then that Melchizedek made his second appearance simultaneously in all twelve valleys. Opening the doors to each of the towers, he bid its builders to follow him inside into the very entrails of Earth, for in their struggles and disintegration, they had unknowingly given birth to yet another world where three more planes lay: one mental, one astral, and one etheric. All were constructed along similar lines to the three planes above the planet, save for the singular difference that they were fashioned from darkness instead of light. Melchizedek gave them this realm as yet another world upon which to tell and act out their stories, for now that they had lost Paradise they would need to see both the dark and the light to regain it, for such is the law of spiraling circles. Then he left them in their darkness to find their separated and collective ways to the light again. Some were able to rise immediately, while others are trapped there still, for such is the pattern of their stories and how they choose to tell them.

The legacy of the twelve towers of Mu is the foundation for all our legends and all our pathways and the eternal choice everyone who exists in a body on this plane has of whether to go ever deeper into the darkness or head unerringly for the light. With this new realm inside its surface, Earth now had seven levels of existence: the etheric, astral, and mental planes composed out of ethers of light; a physical plane composed out of matter and locked in time and space; and etheric, astral, and mental planes composed out of the ethers of darkness.

Melchizedek told them these seven levels of existence would be their mythic trinity of heaven, earth, and hell—the three ethers of light comprising heaven, the physical plane comprising Earth, and the three ethers of darkness acting as hell. Though none of these would be as they would come to be known in fable and story, all would represent very distinct choice, for each—even the darkness— would be a place of teaching and healing. Though the darkness is a much more torturous and painful path to climb up toward perfection, still it is very much a part of the process of this sphere, and some of those who wish to know light can know it only if first they taste its reverse side. Each body that transcended the physical plane would now be given the choice of dwelling in opposing ethers to learn what they had to learn in order to rise back up into the light, before being reborn back onto Earth, which would be the connecting link between the two.

An invisible civilization, then, came to live in the Earth's core, and rumors of its excesses soon shook the imagination of all who dwelt above it. It became a place of dread, and its darkness could be felt far beyond its boundaries. So was the underworld formed, and so did the light and dark of this planet become ever more separated.

HUMANITY DESCENDS

The first real humans to come here after all the stories of the 144,000 had been set in motion would look like total aliens to their latter-day counterparts. They were far more fluid and ephemeral than their hard-skeletoned successors. They also were egg-laying hermaphrodites, which means they were both sexes at once, who gave birth to full-formed replicas of themselves, while maintaining fluid, jellied bodies that were more gaseous than solid and more at home in the ethers than on the physical.

Slowly these bodies began to evolve and to divide into separate sexes and to reproduce in more and more helpless form so that near-ing the end of the long period of the Paleozoic—some seventy-five million years ago—there was a very real and palpable human pres-ence on the planet. These humans, however, would have appeared as quite shadowy to our modern eyes, like giant primitive dream figures, slow and dull in their movements and far more attuned to their unseen other-plane realities than to the physical Earth.

The three-eyed inhabitants of Mu soon found that being either man or woman was far different from being man/woman. Thus, the process of separation and incompletion was visited upon humanity, as our collective story began to take form: the descent of humanity from the oneness of the ethers into the fractured dimensions of time and space to see if it could rise out of the world of matter into spirit again—the one returning to the One. The eternal sadness of being mortal and being incomplete was introduced to the consciousness of Earth inhabitants at this time as deity-ruled civilizations came and went; however, not a trace of them remains, for they were carved far more out of the ethers than of the physical world, and they have dis-appeared into the mysteries of forgotten memory.

BACK TO THE DRAWING BOARD

The first three e-zones of humanity—survival, procreation, and power—had now been given their initial forms, and the outer frame of the human presence here had a structure on which to develop. All three would continue to evolve on humanity's collective body until power somehow took disproportionate place in that simple schema, and it was suddenly "back to the drawing board" time for most crea-tures here.

Around 65,000,000 B.Z., a major catastrophe occurred on Earth. Perhaps it was inspired by power struggles between the deities and their earthly charges, or perhaps it was totally natural in origin, as mysterious explosions set off volcanic chains that blanketed Mu and buried that continent in fire. Almost all large life perished, the huge saurians never to return, completing the Age of Giants, as new gods and goddesses appeared, children of the ancient children of the primordial ones. And the Earth cleansed itself and the seas swallowed Mu and all its human presence, and another continent, Lemuria, rose from some of its ashes in the area now called the Indian Ocean. Mountains appeared where there had been only water, great islands sank where they had once stood supreme, whole jungles froze underneath the arctic poles, and great ice stretches melted into lush tropic greenery. Thus did the Third Civilization come to an uncomfortable end, and it was once again the beginning of things.

○

C H A P T E R   S E V E N

Exodus

The reader is invited to continue to explore the evolution of civilization following the fall of the Age of Giants through the rise of the ancient continents of Lemuria and Atlantis, with their legacies of mystery and magic that ultimately brought about the Great Flood, which ended that ancient world in 11,000 B.Z. and brought us into our own epoch.

When the Age of Giants ended some sixty-five million years or so before the year 0, the Earth was inherited by the tiny shrew and all the creatures that would eventually evolve out of it. With the mass exodus of the giants, dinosaur and deity alike, Eden faded from the Earth, and the tropics that covered most of the planet's terra firma receded back toward this globe's center. This process allowed this world to gradually begin to form seven climates: an equatorial Eden girdling its center, two semitropics on either side of it, two temperate zones above and below them, and two polar caps at the top and bottom of the planet.

Thus, the unity of our tropical beginnings was divided into a septet of environments, the three upper reflecting the three lower, with the equatorial middle a bridge between the two. Some of the environments were blazingly hot, some were impossibly cold, and some were a combination and a moderation of the two, giving the denizens of this planet wide choice over where to live and what form to take in coping with the elements of survival on the physical plane.

With the Great Cataclysm that marked the end of the middle period of the planet's formation, or its Mesozoic Age, the ethers suddenly found themselves rife with a great many confused souls with etheric bodies that had been badly damaged by the fires that had destroyed their habitats. It was now obvious to beast, human, and divinity alike that this was a world of extreme volatility and that in order for all to descend into matter to learn the lessons of light through the inherent darkness here, everyone and everything would have to penetrate far deeper into the material world. Its mysteries could not be fully broached by the superficial etheric presence thus far visited upon it by its potential higher forms.

This process would also take more than the three energy centers that this long process of descent had opened up on the collective civilized body of humanity—survival, sexual reproduction, and power— for it to find its larger self here. The joyous and painful pathway toward its heart would have to be activated as well when at last the planet settled down from its raging fires to become once again the lush water-world it had previously been.

THIRD CIVILIZATION TO FOURTH CIVILIZATION

The Cenozoic period, from 65,000,000 B.Z. to 5,000,000 B.Z. was symbolically dominated by the element of earth and reflected the fourth e-zone of the heart on the collective body of humanity.

In the beginning of this planet's second manifestation of its Third Civilization, Earth was once again accepting more complex life-forms, and the word on survival that was heard throughout the land was a simple but direct "Adapt—or be zapped!" The naked-skinned reptiles that once freely roamed the Earth now found themselves quickly frozen out of all but the tropics and semitropics, while the little nervous insect- and grass-eaters that had previously shivered in their great shadows in hairy little coats fueled by warm blood suddenly discovered there was little to stop them from becoming large, imposing beasts. Cometh then the mammals in full force on many feet: some cloven, some clawed, and some padded; some herdful and some hunterly; and all producing themselves live, giving their young far closer physical contact with their mothers before their official entrance on the planet than anything that had preceded them.

With the mammals, the former shadow-humans of Mu returned under their gods and slowly settled over the continent of Lemuria, Mu the Motherland's vast successor. In their collective memory, however, was the dark nightmare of the Great Cataclysm, for Earth had shown its inhabitants it was not a planet to be trifled with and that its three sacred elements of fire, water, and air were as capable of consuming life as they were of maintaining it. That direct vision of the Apocalypse would never quite leave Lemuria's memory, so that it would forever be acting out of a pall cast by its deep past. Despite its many millions of years existence, its ultimate contribution to the ongoing story of the planet would lie not in the material realm, but in the deep spirituality that would evolve from its unconscious internalization of the time Earth caught fire and was consumed by it.

Around 35,000,000 B.Z., another anthropoidal, or humanlike, species, the ape, began to appear in goodly number as further reminder to humanity of its animal excesses, for many of these jungle primates were creatures that had participated in the mystery-shrouded Great Destruction that had ended the Age of the Giants, some thirty million years previously.

So after many many years of cleansing and regrowth, Earth was once again carpeted with both beast and shadow-human. The two roamed and ranged alongside one another, sharing similar space but living in completely different worlds, the former with both eyes focused on its immediate problems of survival and the latter, childlike, with its third eye still intact, sitting obliquely in the back of its head, so that it retained a dull awareness of greater realities than the temporal world had to offer.

MAGNUS MAGUS & LEMURIA

Along with the three-eyed primitive shadow-souls of Lemuria lived some of the godlike teachers, healers, and superiors who had guided humanity down through the mental, astral, and etheric planes to the physical Earth. These were called by the name of *Magnus Magus*, "great magician," and these Magi were revered as wondrous ones and great parents by a humanity that was incapable of anything above the animal level.

Some of the Magi took advantage of their station and got lost in the lusts of the planet and further degraded their charges, while others remained the incandescent fires they had always been, giving humanity kingship for the first time. They began incarnating among the humans as incorruptible priest-rulers, who lifted their children to far greater heights than any they could have achieved on their own. Many of these beings became both the prototypes and the legend-basis for the later gods and goddesses who came here, and their stories became woven in with the sacred myths of many of the succeeding religions that arose here.

Darkness and light came to live side by side in Lemuria. Because of that duality, many of the masters and "mystresses" of the ethers who had stood as high and pure souls in the dream-spheres of the planet became lost in the illusions of matter. Descending to the level of their inferiors, they became locked into interrupted mortality with those they were supposed to uplift and edify, as Earth became home for fallen god and rising human alike. Civilizations came and went, and the Lemurians gradually lost their third eyes, and became like those around them, as both they and their fellow primates slowly evolved their way on up to their current form, Homo sapiens, the apelike being who "thinks that it thinks and therefore thinks that it is."

While some of Lemuria participated directly in the ongoing evolutionary process of adapting to and spreading out over the planet, that continent's more spiritually advanced members began to recede from the surface of Earth and live underground in caves, growing ever more afraid of the light, for they could no longer see the connection between spirit and matter. As the higher presence of

Lemuria became more and more ghostly, it faded back into the ethers while it watched the world of matter take stronger and stronger shape all around it. This process allowed the more primitive and solely physical beings of Lemuria the full space of the continent to develop their physical selves, while the more advanced among them remained in subterranean solitude, buried in darkness, creating further worlds and underworlds and stories that would feed into the imagination of humanity, as Earth reverberated on all levels with the hidden and overt heart of its combined denizens.

The introduction of heart would signal the introduction of an interior to the collective body of humanity. If the first three e-zones are the outer structure of humanity, then the last four are its inner, and Lemuria was the bridge between the two, raising the human presence above its animal instincts for the first time.

Around 5,000,000 B.Z., Lemuria began to stir from its incredibly long sleep of sheer survival, as the higher presence of that continent at last came to understand that only by thoroughly embracing matter could they ever touch on spirit again, for the darkness here is the path that must be crossed, not avoided, in order to reach the light. Thus, they slowly began to rise and reintegrate themselves with their lesser brothers and sisters, and as they grew in number they would appear as speakers and sacred storytellers to tell the tales of creation, continuance, and destruction over and over. These stories drew Lemuria out of its underground hiding and long sleep into the light of day once again, as those who wished to be human continued their physical evolutions into a form that conformed to the laws of the world of matter, allowing them to give birth to the Fourth Civilization and the final emergence of humanity onto the physical plane, as a naked, mortal presence.

ATLANTIS

As the last segment of the long race that had spanned the Third Civilization made its presence known once again on the planet, from its seed sprang a new species of humanity who would go on to claim the Fourth Civilization for its own. As they did so, a second continent, named Atlantis, which at the time occupied most of what is now known as the Atlantic Ocean, arose to house them. The Atlanteans, who, like the Lemurians, wound up evolving in seven different segments, were the aggressive complement to the spiritual passivity of Lemuria. They were ruled by war gods who were interested in nothing less than absolute dominance over the rest of the planet, a limited focus of vision that hastened their complete and final departure from this sphere around 11,000 B.Z.

Beginning as soft-boned and soft-shelled creatures living in a heavily misted, vaporous environment, they eventually evolved into the hard-boned, hard-shelled variety that we who are human today recognize as our own. Their landmass also solidified and became four-dimensional over many millions of years.

Just as Mu and Lemuria were begat in the full force of the sun and came to flower as the combined motherland to complement the blazing directness of the day, so Atlantis began under the aegis of the moon, for only that lunar ball's diffused light could penetrate the mysterious shroud of clouds that continually covered that lost continent's hidden countenance. So it was that the moon begat Atlantis and showed that long civilization the secrets of the nighttime and the arts of darkness and the other side of Illumination. This allowed Atlantis to ultimately become the fatherland and eventually to emerge from its own shadows to try to command the planet again and again in a series of highly aggressive cultures that lost their initial highly spiritual sight and came to see this planet solely in terms of the myopic self-interest of conquest and domination.

CAIN & ABEL

The differences twixt the two cultures can be seen in a pair of brothers of different mothers. One was an Atlantean tiller of the soil and the other a Lemurian herdsman. The tiller, whose name was Cain, was as violent and earthy as the planet, a man of chaos and ill humor, who chose to be unconnected from all save himself. His brother, Abel, was a shepherd and charged with the responsibility of his flock, and he deeply understood how both shepherd and herd all dwelt together in a sacred oneness. Abel lived his life in the circular rhythms of nature, celebrating the connection that all creatures have with one another here, while Cain lived only in the straight line of his plow, looking solely at what was in front of him, feeling peace only in his own strength, his personal power, and his muscular dominance over the earth.

One day, Cain came upon Abel playing his flute in a hilly field, while his sheep peacefully grazed around him. Abel smiled in greeting, but the larger Cain only scowled in return, complaining he hadn't eaten in several days, for his crops had mysteriously withered and a disease had taken his animals, and so he demanded some mutton to soothe his growling stomach. But Abel gently protested that this would upset the flock, for there was a time for slaughtering and a time for sharing their fleshly bounty, but this was not it, and to destroy the flow of the natural order of things would be a grave dishonor to his herd.

Overwhelmed with both hunger and rage, Cain slew his brother and tossed his body over a precipice before killing one of his sheep. But as he began skinning it, a great remorse came over him. He lost his appetite, and felt the shame and weakness of what he had done, for he saw his earthly strength was but an illusion against the true power of the beloved shepherd. He buried Abel and, weeping bitter tears, put a mark upon his own forehead and dressed in penitent cloth, so that he would be set apart from other beings and they would be able to see his difference at a mere glance.

Then he went somewhere east of Eden, to learn the passivity and spirituality of the East, and he came to dwell in the land of Nud, or Nod, the land of sleep and dreams, to learn how to become a shepherd, a priest, an inner man, and his brother's keeper. He became father and brother to all priests here, for he had experienced Death intimately and learned to be troubled by it, and he could no longer be comfortable with the limits of his mortality. By symbolizing spirit as an expression of loss, remorse, and disconnection to the planet, his would be a deep and long-felt legacy to the many generations of priests who would follow him. Cain's enforced exile also represented the beginning of humanity's fractured stay here. No longer an extended family, the human presence became torn asunder by the rift between its outer actions and inner feelings. Such is the price of heart, and so began the straight line of human history, where life and death are no longer a part of the same great circle.

FRATRICIDAL LOVE

From 5,000,000 B.Z. to 1,500,000 B.Z., the Lemurians bore the endlessly obsessive aggression of the Atlanteans as well as the periodic glacial sheets that covered most of their land for long stretches. Their existence came to be defined by defeat, slavery, and continual retreat, while the peoples of both continents intermingled and intermarried and infused each with the wisdom and ignorance of the other.

The constant battering that Lemuria took from both the elements and its fellow inheritors of the Fourth Civilization gave that continent a deeply contemplative overview, for its denizens were forever rationalizing one adversity or another. Yet an extraordinary will to survive also pervaded Lemuria, and its tenacity to continue to exist under the most oppressive of circumstances helped forge a rich, deep mode of thought that has been passed down unbroken into our own Fifth Civilization, where it reemerged on the subcontinent of India in slightly altered form as Hinduism. Thus, the Lemurians became a race of both philosophers and slaves, creating a culture of acceptance of greater wills than its own, which was able to survive beyond the self-destruction of the continent that gave birth to it.

Atlantis, in the meantime, became a repository of mystresses and masters, women and men of the red race who knew well the magic of the ethers and could perform great feats of sorcery. Darkness came to battle light for dominance over these highly assertive peoples, who slowly evolved from fish-framed shadows that glided effortlessly through the perpetual fog that enshrouded their domain to brittle-bodied warriors whose footsteps could be heavily heard all over the planet.

By 1,000,000 B.Z., Atlantis had risen to dominate the civilized Earth through the auspices of one of its peoples, the Toltecs, who created many nations run by hereditary and harmonious patriarchal monarchies that relied on the magic of their sorcerers to keep to the high pathways here. Their center of power was the legendary City of the Golden Gates, which lay in the mid-Atlantic, fifteen degrees north of the equator. With their magical powers over the forces of nature, they truly commanded this planet from every level, operating as they did from its very middle. It was here that the secrets of our larger universe first began to be taught in "sacred library schools," so that the magic of the ethers and the gift of co-creation of the gods could be codified and brought down to the physical planet.

The Golden Age of the Toltec Empire lasted 100,000 years, then went into a demonic decline, as their unbroken link with their mortal divinity began to be fragmented by the forces of self and self-interest. The dark and the light came to do apocalyptic battle with one another, until the City of the Golden Gates was destroyed around 850,000 B.Z. Darkness and light would continue to be a duality that would dominate the Atlanteans' fascination with power, but they would never rise again to the unearthly heights that this segment of the Fourth Civilization manifested.

In 800,000 B.Z., Atlantis ultimately fell to a self-inspired cataclysm as did Lemuria, and both suffered a great loss of land to the sea. This was repeated in 200,000 B.Z., reducing that huge continent, which once stretched from the British Isles all the way across to the eastern Americas, to two islands in the middle of the Atlantic Ocean.

SEMITES & ARYANS

Following that second debacle, a new people came to power on Atlantis. They called themselves Semites, a white-skinned race from the north that appeared where Ireland and Scotland now sit. They were the children of Melchizedek, the master storyteller, and their story would be the bridge that would link the Fourth Civilization with the Fifth.

As clever marauders who became masters of the seas, the Semites had a deep sense of story about themselves, feeling they were the thread through which the true tale of humanity ran. After holding sway over the rebuilt City of the Golden Gates, they were driven from power around 95,000 B.Z. to become wanderers. Their various nations separated, some to be swallowed by succeeding cultures, others to pursue their original outlawry and get lost in their own underworld of self-interest, while a small segment continued on as storytellers, keeping the sacred story of their long existence alive so that they could once again grow in power and might.

The Semites' loss of station was a great puzzlement to those who maintained their sacred traditions. They had always felt they were a people of destiny, ruled by gods of destiny, and the ancient magic they had learned in mutated form from the preserved inner mysteries of the City of the Golden Gates seemed to indicate their story was far from over, even if they were no longer capable of dominating the overt world. Still soft-skeletoned themselves like their other Atlantean counterparts, the Semites were not capable of individual thought, save for their god-priests, and relied instead on the huge memory banks that all Atlanteans carried with them in their etheric bodies. If something happened that never had been dealt with before, ordinary people were unequipped to handle it, for they did not have the faculty of problem solving.

Around 80,000 B.Z., just before the third of Atlantis's four cataclysms, a great leader arose among a small select tribe of wandering Semites, and he led them into the Arabian peninsula to create a new race, a "chosen people," who would fulfill the destiny of the Semites as the uniters of all humanity. This Magnus Magus saw that his people were living in a doomed culture that had sentenced itself to endless and mindless self-destruction, so he knew they would have to create a body-form that could dwell in the outlying physical world, where the Fifth Civilization was now rapidly forming. These hard-boned bodies would have to have the ability both to digest information and to synthesize it in order to deal with the physical world as its masters, rather than as ephemeral spirits. Unlike everyone before them, the "chosen people" would be thinkers. They would lose their psychic nonrationality to the far more earthbound rationality of cognitive thought.

So began a long, slow process of god-magic and biological experimentation and separation that eventually produced an entirely new strain, which called itself Aryan. These were the chosen of the "chosen," and a tiny band of them was picked by their god-priests from the resettled Semites and were led off once again from Arabia to central Asia to develop in even further isolation. There they lived for tens of thousands of years untouched by other civilizations in order to maintain their deep and all-abiding sense of self. They were taught self-consciousness by their gods to become a thinking, acting people far removed from the debasement of power now engulfing the last ebb of Atlantean might. However, some of the resettled Semites, out of whose initial number the future Aryans had been further chosen, also shared the same claim of being special even though they had not been picked to complete this process, and a deep antagonism would continue twixt the two down through the hidden memories of the ages into our present civilization.

With the creation of the Aryan race, humanity's etheric body became a much closer and more integrated part of the physical body. This, in turn, gave birth on a mass level to the seeds of self-awareness, a province heretofore restricted to only the most advanced of souls who walked among lesser humanity: the deities, sorcerers, and Magnus Magus–incarnates who already knew how to claim their individual uniqueness on Earth. As this happened, Atlantis began to retreat from its strong psychic connection to the ethers and to dwell more on the mundane four-dimensional fields of Earth. The perceptual immortality that the other planes represented now began to give way to far more mortal concerns, as matter began to really matter in the lexicon of planetary existence.

All these transmutations were part of the process of completely opening the final door to Earth and making the physical plane a reality unto itself. The two doomed continents that had comprised the Fourth Civilization, Atlantis and Lemuria, had succeeded in bringing the human race down to the material surface of the planet, while opening the warrior and spiritual hearts on the collective body of humanity so that it could learn to see its connection to its divine origins in civilizations to come.

In 80,000 B.Z., the Earth shook and the sea swallowed ever more of Lemuria and Atlantis, reducing the latter to one island, called Poseidonis. The physical map of the Fifth Civilization with its five mainlands—Africa, Asia, Europe, and North and South America— and its two island-continents—Greenland and Australia—began to take the shape it would ultimately bear when the last traces of those now lost continents finally disappeared: Lemuria in 26,000 B.Z. and Atlantis around 11,000 B.Z.

NOAH

In the last days of Atlantis, there lived an old Semite sacred librarian named Noah, who dwelt by himself off the eastern coast of Poseidonis on an island wildlife preserve, which he diligently tended, knowing virtually every creature and plant that chose to exist under his protective wing. Because he was a man of deep magic, he was conversant with many of these life-forms as well, for he knew the secret language of nature and served its tenets justly.

Although he needed no human companionship, he allowed his four sons and their wives to dwell on the other side of the island, though he rarely spent time with any of them. They accepted his isolation as his way and held him in awe for it, for his visits were always a special treat. Noah's wife had been a magical conjuration—a spirit-wife—and had long since disappeared onto other planes, allowing him the solitude of his own realities, which he treasured greatly. He spent his days in the care and protection of his vast charge, while his nights were passed in a small hut in the pursuit of his ancient craft of sorcery and dream saying.

Now, Noah was extremely partial to the fermented fruit of the vine, and each eve he would imbibe a large glassful of magic and settle back to watch the fantasies of his interior eye unfold. One eve, after nestling down on his pillows and sipping a healthy snortful of nectar, the four-lettered name of his sorcery master manifested to him in astral form. The apparition told Noah to build an ark, gather a pair of each the creatures of the field and sky, and take three of his sons and their wives and prepare for a long, watery voyage, for the land was about to be washed clean of all its unhappy past.

When Noah protested that he had four sons, the invoked deity repeated its previous message, emphasizing the urgency of the request by thundering that there would be need for only seven people to survive the devastation—himself, three sons, and their wives—and he had exactly one week to get it all together. With that, the apparition disappeared, leaving a suddenly sobered Noah to do just what it had said.

All that night, the sacred librarian worked on plans for his boat. When morning came, he set out for the other side of the island, still unsure of which son he should exclude, since he barely knew any of them. When he arrived, he found them all out in the fields, tilling and planting, and when they saw him, they all hailed him and tensed, for they had always perceived him as a person of great power and feared him greatly, as his love was never directly expressed.

Now each of the sons was markedly different from the others, for they came not from a woman of this sphere but from a spirit-mother who had held many races within her womb. Ham was the earthiest, a dark-skinned giant of a man who was well-skilled in the practical arts. Shem, the next, was the airiest, somewhat lighter and smaller, who was always talking, arguing, verbally defining his realities and contradicting everybody else's. Japheth, the next, was the fieriest and lighter still, somewhere in between the sizes of his two older siblings, always aggressively asserting his presence wherever he stood, in continual fraternal battle with his brother Shem. Dov, the last, was the most watery, a lithe and pale-skinned dreamer, who, like his father, was interested in matters that went beyond the ken of nature.

After Noah had called them all to him, he unfurled his plans for the ship and showed it to them, explaining exactly what he wanted before announcing that he would be back in a week with creatures aplenty and the full expectation that the boat would be ready. And with that he left.

While Shem and Japheth immediately fell to arguing about who would build what and Dov stared after their father, Ham looked closely at the plans and noticed there was only cabin space for three of the brothers. He shouted out the oversight to his father, but Noah called back over his shoulder that that was the way it was supposed to be, before disappearing into the safety of the island's other side.

The four brothers looked at one another and all began talking at once. Ham, Shem, and Japheth fell to loudly disputing the relative merits of each, never listening to their youngest brother, Dov, who, growing tired of their repetitious bickering, finally wandered off by himself. When Noah returned, seven days later, with a column of birds and beasts neatly trailing behind him in twos, he was shocked to find the three brothers still arguing, all of them bleary and bloated with their continual declamations of self-importance and their equally dark pronouncements on the claims of their brethren.

Totally astonished that his word had not been obeyed, Noah balefully addressed his sons with his eyes, as the first droplets of rain began to trickle down slowly from the heavens. Reaching into his supply sack and pulling out a goatskin of fermented fruit, he took a very generous swig, as the suddenly thickening rain began to pelt them all with hard, heavy droplets. The boys, who could not meet his gaze, all stood drenched in silence, each morosely contemplating their combined failure.

Suddenly, from around the corner of the inlet, a large boat hove into view, and it was sized exactly to the specifications of the old man's plans. As the four stared in wonder, they could see Dov and his wife at the helm, guiding and steering it into shore, where they dropped anchor, lowered the gangplank, and disembarked to approach the others.

Dov said he and his wife had built the boat together out of "mind-wood," using tricks that Dov had picked up by watching his father. Then they told the others not to worry about who wasn't going, for it would be the two of them. If the other seven were going to be as unloving toward one another in the brand new world, there wouldn't be any place for the likes of the two of them anyhow. With that, they hugged each of the now silent and crying seven, and then they were off and running toward Noah's side of the island, as the remaining crew watched them dodging raindrops till they passed from view. As their departing words sank deep into the heart-mind of each, each saw for the first time how unloving they had been to one another—fathers and sons, brothers and brothers, wives and husbands—and Noah embraced his remaining progeny and they him. Everyone held closely to each other, and all wept into the rain before they slowly boarded their boat, two by two with Noah the last, silently thanking his lost son for the one gift that would make the coming world truly different from the one they were departing: the gift of love.

And so came the Flood, and the few who were lucky to escape its devastation passed its legend down to all who followed in all cultures of the world, so that they would know their planet was once cleansed of its unlovingness and would be again if future generations did not learn from the hatred and anger of the past. Noah lived to yet an even greater age after the waters had receded and never forgot the words of his wisest son, wishing that he had known him and loved him better when he had had the chance instead of spending so much time by himself.

Ham went on to father all of Africa, and Shem gave seed to the Semites and their Islamic and Judaic divisions, while Japheth sired the Gentiles. Although the descendants of all three prayed to different deities and continued the perennial arguments of their fathers, they, too, held in their blood-minds the memory of the fourth son who chose to bear not a race but rather an idea that would help all races one day to transcend themselves.

Thus, the vast aquarium of Atlantis finally disappeared into oblivion around the year 11,000 B.Z., and the Fourth Civilization passed to give birth to the Fifth Civilization. The ice came and went, and glaciers reshaped the land. The motherland and the fatherland gave way to the coming new world, and it was once again, as it always is, the very beginning of things.

○

Numbers

The reader is invited to enter the Fifth Civilization, our own, and to see how men and women became thoroughly divided, and how the idea of self arose to redefine modern humanity through the re-creation of Israel by the Semite storytellers and their all-abiding belief in the One God in a world of many gods and very few well-defined selves.

The first four civilizations of humanity gradually brought our human presence down to the physical planet. In the rhythm of sevens, the fourth stage is the bridge between the first three and last three stages.

Stage one saw the mental plane of humanity opened, as Earth worked out the laws of survival that would govern its multidimensionality. Stage two saw the astral plane of humanity opened, as Earth worked out the laws of reproduction for those who would exist within its mortal boundaries. Stage three saw the etheric plane of humanity opened, as Earth worked out the laws of power between its various time- and space-locked species. This process reached its explosive climax in an incendiary cataclysm sixty-five million years ago that left both the powerful and powerless alike in stunned awe of the devastating powers of the planet, as it wiped itself clean of its Edenic beginnings to become "Paradise Lost" for its succeeding inhabitants. Stage four saw the physical plane finally opened to humanity, as Earth began to toy with its collective heart and allow its mortal human inhabitants to delve into their interiors for the first time. Once that bridge was crossed by the warriordom of Atlantis and the spirituality of Lemuria, humanity was ready to begin its ascent back upward through the etheric plane to continue its cycle of moving from the oneness of innocence to the oneness of experience. Its first four collective e-zones had been opened, and it was now ready to manifest in higher, more complex forms.

First, though, humanity's Fourth Civilization had to be destroyed so as to disconnect stage five from its civilized roots and allow it to begin anew, unprejudiced by anything save its most unsophisticated past. Atlantis and Lemuria were only too happy to comply, disappearing in a deluge of water, to elementally complement the earlier fires that had consumed Mu. Once more the planet purged itself to allow its denizens fresh perspective. Not only had Paradise been lost, but Paradise Lost had been lost as well.

Fifth Civilization humanity also had to divorce itself from the magic of the ethers, so as to proceed upward from its own spiritual innocence and ignorance. This it gradually accomplished over the many millennia of its existence, culminating with the advent of our modern age, and its accepted dominance of science over mystery. While the fifth stage of this process has slowly opened up the powers of communication on the collective body of humanity, or its fifth e-zone, it has also gradually mired us ever deeper in the world of matter and progressively ever further away from the heightened mortality that awaits us, once we learn to collectively claim our true place here.

FIFTH CIVILIZATION

The Anthropozoic period, from 5,000,000 B.Z. to 2000 A.Z., has been symbolically dominated by the element of air and reflects communication, the fifth e-zone on the collective body of humanity.

This Fifth Civilization of humanity is conveniently divided into two parts, the Age of Stone and the Age of Metal. The Age of Stone, which goes back several million years, contented itself with living inside its own dream-tales to explain away the unexplainable. It was tuned into celebratory mystery, and saw this world as one of sacred lore, which gave magic life to all the natural elements here. The Age of Metal, which has encompassed the last few thousand years, has been far more interested in scientific mystery, and sees this world as one of physical law, while treating all the natural elements here as if they are unnatural impediments to humanity's divine right to predominate upon this planet.

When the primates who were priming themselves for future humanity first descended from the trees, they did so in amazon clusters, groups of females with one large, strong male in their number. The male would serve as seeder and protector against others of his brutish ilk, while the females would have the freedom of their own extended company to create the social texture of their society. Because of this, the two would come to vary greatly in size, since only the largest and strongest of the males would get a chance to spray his sperm, while females would give themselves the opportunity to reproduce in all shapes and sizes.

This largely female world, which kept its male presence highly occupied with the presence of other males, eventually worked its way down through the many millions of years of evolution into small clans that were bound by lunar blood and long generations of connected mothers, with their female element dominant to give order and structure to the group's survival. The focus of concern of everyone was always on the welfare of the women. They were both the creators and continuers, while the men, who assumed roles of sons and brothers, were basically spear fodder for intruding presences, as well as hunters, destroyers, and protectors, channeling their aggression outward so as not to disrupt the internal balance of shared power this system created, based on a hierarchy of motherhood. These small groups were able to survive at peace with themselves because of a sharp division of the sexes and an all-abiding credo that "Great Mother knows best," making them into extended families of mothers and brothers, where the power of women was deeply respected by all. This pattern was all to gradually alter when a universal change in climate, brought about by the waning of the last ice age, spread humanity around the globe, concentrating itself in the Eastern Hemisphere around four river-worlds: the Yellow in China, the Indus in India, the Nile in Egypt, and the Tigris-Euphrates in Mesopotamia.

Once the planet had been resettled, the Fifth Civilization was then allowed to break down into its various components, which subsequently divided even further according to the two hemispheres and the five visible races, or color-worlds. It is one of these subdivisions, the White West, and its oft-chronicled story of fathers and sons that will be further followed here, for the mortal and material concerns of this group would have a profound effect on the spiritual and social evolution of the Fifth Civilization, particularly as it came to enter its modern age.

This white-skinned world arose on the outer edges of the planet, where resource was scarce and where resourcefulness was the only alternative. Tempered full blast by the various ice ages, this human color-world came to see Earth as a largely inhospitable place and shaped its consciousness accordingly. Mortal space would become the overweening concern of those who wore this sun-shy skin, for they had to struggle so hard to maintain it, and this situation would trigger, particularly in their more driven members, a continual need to dominate and disseminate their presence wherever the Earth offered any semblance of acceptance to them. These were not a people who saw themselves in terms of natural harmony, and their restless presence and resourceful will would give rise to an ethic of "self interest above all else," which would be a predominating theme of the future rise 'n' fall rhythm of the civilizations they would ultimately create.

THE RISE OF EGO

During the Third Civilization on the continent of Mu, men and women had first separated into opposing, complementary sexual bodies to learn the art of cooperation, which is the cornerstone of creating civilization. The two, however, lived at opposite time ends of one of their greatest mutual responsibilities: reproduction. The female was a seed-carrier to full fruition, while the male was merely a quick-release sperm-sprayer. Seed-carriers would then be further weighted down by the time-consuming task of giving their helpless seed enough strength to deal with this world on their own. Sperm-sprayers were exempted from much of that responsibility, which, in turn, gave them a lot more free time and space.

This separation of duties eventually set up a time dynamic between the sexes that would have each looking at the world through far different temporal eyes. The female eye-set would become predominantly collective, plugged into the larger cycles of creation here. They would be both intimately linked and hemmed in by time via the awesome responsibility of maintaining their bodily creations' continuance. The male set would view life from a far more separated perspective, being a much smaller part of the creation process. Because they would be given much more freedom from domestic time constraints, they could begin to pursue pathways of separation, of selfhood, of self-importance, so that this unity of mothers and brothers, as they saw themselves, could break down and see its separated parts.

This process was long and slow, for humanity's sense of its individual self was not part of its early essence but something that had to be developed over a long period of time. As soon as a sense of self began to rise in primitive consciousness, it was largely the male of the species who grabbed onto it. He was less connected to the larger cycles of collectivity and so was far more open to the possibilities of separation and private experience.

While collective consciousness stems from a sense of being a small part of a greater whole, egoistic consciousness does quite the opposite, re-creating reality in terms of individual truths and perceptions, and fragmenting and redefining all phenomena through the prism of self-interest. All those who come to live on the physical planet as human beings operate out of both of these modes of thought. We are all the product of a dual sense of collectivity and individuality, but during the rise of the Fifth Civilization in the White West, it was men who gradually claimed the sphere of ego for themselves, supporting one another in their mutual exploration of the excesses of self. Women, on the other hand, tended to their collectivity and underwent the same process of development of the "I," but

under increasingly subterranean circumstances. They slowly relin-
quished center stage to their male counterparts, and the old order
of mother and brother began to give way to the new order of father
and son.

As the egoistic character of the male continued to evolve, it began
to center around two attributes, might and reason, the former coming
from having to deal with the more dangerous aspects of survival and
the latter from being divorced from the higher awareness of collective, nonrational consciousness. Though women had the same
potential for developing these egoistic traits, they didn't have the
same initial need. So, after many tens of thousands of years of chest
thumping, skull smashing, and hair splitting, men finally convinced
the majority that not only were they the sexual presence who
counted the most, but that might and reason were their sole
provinces and were to be prized over all other human attributes.

In addition, since males were only brief contributors to the time-
consuming process of insuring their immortality through reproduction, it became increasingly important to the more powerful of their
number to insure just which little creation was truly theirs. This
meant their seed-carriers had to be controlled and separated, and so
the unity of tribe began to break down into the separated unity of
family, with father as its nominal head.

As father began to define things more and more, his word gradually became the unwritten law of might and right and wrong and reason. Father became patriarch, and he came to represent the wish and
will of the whole of the human race while, in actuality, he was only
a part of it. So it came to pass that all of humanity was placed under
the common name of "man," and the long story of our evolution
came to be called *his* story—"history"—with its emphasis placed on
the individual and collective deeds of men.

THE GREAT MOTHER
& THE HORNED GOD MEET THE SKY GODS

When Fifth Civilization humanity first touched on its invisible
spirit, the Great Mother sat alone in the skies over them. She ruled
equally over the spheres of life and death and represented the great

circle of existence here. As the male sense of self slowly began to rise, her position was augmented in gradual degrees by the appearance of a consort, a horned male god. The two came to symbolize the maternal-fraternal linkage of clan and tribal life, and the "as above, so below" connection of men and women with the greater rhythms of the overt world they saw around them.

As Earth became resettled, its fields and forests and river-worlds rang out with lusty moans in the endless celebratory dance of procreation, with both Great Mother and horned consort nodding their full approval. The planet was crying out for more humans to share its fertility and abundance and to read its circular hidden secrets before they all disappeared into straight-line science. All this was to change as the migratory patterns of those on the outer edges of the world began to widen. These rampaging nomads, mostly from the ghost-skin territories of the north, had little use for anyone save themselves. They drove through the circular agricultural world of their southern neighbors and imposed their company on whomever they wished, for they believed in power as sheer will, and no one had the opposing will to stop them.

With their coming, their aggressive sky-gods steadily began to replace the Great Mother in the consciousness of humanity, and our universal sense of unity with the natural forces around us began to be superseded by our ability to transform that very same world through the sheer will of conquest, dominance, and invention. Power was now a force of earthly self-interest. Might was in and everything else was out. Good-bye immortal circle of nature, and hello straight line of mortal deed.

DEATH

When humanity lived simultaneously in the ethers and upon the Earth during its earlier civilizations, it had a much wider view of life and could see that the loss of the physical body meant that only one plane was denied the soul who had inhabited that corpus. It was a mere shell that housed a far more complex being, who continued on in the other planes that surround this planet, despite its loss of earthly life. Death was, therefore, very much viewed as a part of the life process and signaled neither an end nor a beginning, since everyone had access to everybody else no matter on what plane of existence they chose to dwell, or whether they elected to even appear in bodily form here in this circular world, where beginnings and endings are often the same.

However, as a result of access to the ethers being closed down during the Fourth Civilization, and shut off entirely during the more recent rise of our Fifth Civilization, human perception has become more and more limited to the physical plane. All else has become sheer imaginative speculation, since nothing but the four dimensions can be perceived and verified directly save by the few among us who have kept their clairvoyant and clairsentient centers alive.

So by the time the conquering northern hordes had established themselves over most of the western portion of the Fifth Civilization, Death had become one of their primary political weapons, for whosoever could control the evolving weaponry produced by their endless conflicts with one another could also insure the continuance of their rule. Their ruling patriarchs now had a deitylike power over existence and nonexistence. Their subsequent conjuration of Death, then, became one where their most egoistic fears were realized: disappearance, disconnection, and absolute nothingness.

The ideas of ego and separation and self-interest that these patriarchs represented swiftly divorced humanity from the invisible planes that surround Earth, and placed the concern of all on the immediacy of mortal existence. By transforming Earth into a thoroughly mortal sphere, the fathers of Western civilization created a state of ignorance round the death of the physical self, which has been well-exploited by those masters of violent departure from this plane: the generals, the kings, the emperors, and even the high priesthood, who have continually invoked the Old Master to thwart any threat to their continuance in power.

Thus, as fathers have passed down their legacy of ignorance of the ethers to their sons, Death has disappeared into the realms of the rationally unexplorable in white Western culture. It is used as a means of fear and punishment for all who disavow whoever is in command and rationalized as a state of being totally divorced from life, creating a proscribed reality that looks at existence through but one visual portal—a masculine, earthbound one that trusts only its five senses and its heart hardly at all.

THE RETURN OF THE SEMITE STORYTELLERS

The Minoan civilization of Crete represented the last gasp of the Great Mother. When it was finally conquered and hybridized, it concluded a history-eating sweep that began around 4500 B.Z. and ended in 1200 B.Z., allowing the warrior forces of will and self-interest to lay total claim to the ongoing overt saga of Western civilization.

It is around the year 2100 B.Z. that the story of the White West once again moves back into its cycle of beginnings, as two ancient antagonists from Atlantean days, the storytelling Semites and their "chosen" offshoots, the genetically engineered Aryans, start to make their presences felt. The Aryans who entered the Fifth Civilization en masse came from three separate areas: the mountains of central and southeastern Europe and the central Asian plateau. These tall, fair-skinned, inventive people held the six elements—sky, earth, sun, water, fire, and wind—as the sacred magic behind all life and personified each as god or goddess. Existing in the eternal present, they burned their dead and left their deeds unrecorded. They were conquerors and scourges and history-eaters, imbued with all the predatory force that once was Atlantis, waiting for the rest of the world to eventually open its gates to them, so that they could descend and place their presence everywhere. Their patriarchal forebears, the storytelling Semites, were destined once again to come into deep conflict with them, and it is the struggle of these two ancient Atlantean forces, each still feeling itself to be "chosen," that has given the Occident much of its philosophic and aggressive overview.

Around 2100 B.Z., a man by the name of Terah, a high priest of royal descent who lived in the Sumerian city of Ur, took his son, Abram, his son's wife and half-sister, Sarai, and one of his other son's sons, Lot, and crossed over the Euphrates River to begin life again elsewhere. This group of four—a grandfather, a father, and a grandson, or the immortal patriarchal triune of past, present, and future, and a related female to serve them—came to be known as the

Hebrews, from a priestly ancestor, Eber, whose name stems from the Sumerian root word "to cross."

After that conscious act of crossing over and separating themselves from their pasts, the group resettled, and when Abram was seventy-five years old, his father, Terah, died. With that death, for reasons still shrouded in mystery, a Father Aeternal descended full force from the ethers and into the modern sacred storytelling realm of the planet. Unlike the other active deities of Sumer and the rest of Mesopotamia, this Immortal Father stood totally alone and was unconnected to a deific family. He was a thoroughly unique emanation of the Divine—the One God—and his choice of Abram as his earthly channel would begin a whole new spiritual connection between the heavens and Earth.

Abram followed a series of instructions, predictions, and peregrinations that bound him ever closer to his deity, and when he was fourscore and nineteen, and had done all that was asked of him, he made a covenant or agreement that would unite both heaven and an earthly people through a spiritual/physical rite of removal and exposure. This covenant stated simply that if Abram would uncover the hood of his own organ of reproduction in a rite of circumcision and then circumcise every male born to his house at the age of eight days, as well as every other male who converted to his faith, then he would be mortal father to the divine nation of an Immortal Father, and that nation would receive a Promised Land in which it could celebrate the glory of the heavens on Earth.

This he did, and though his wife, renamed Sarah, had been barren for all of her ninety years, still she bore him a son, Isaac, and this son proved to be the seed of that new nation. Abram's own name was widened to Abraham, changing him from Sumerian to Semite, so that the blood of a mighty civilization that was now dying might be reborn in yet another people.

The "Foreskin Covenant" not only removed the hood from the old externalized serpent from Eden, it also gave its bearer graphic reminder that even in his nakedness that bearer's bodily connection to eternity was still clearly manifest. The agreement was also an added insurance of cleanliness in the reproductive process, allowing the subsequent Covenanted Brotherhood of the Foreskin that adopted this practice a better chance at regeneration without the transference of disease and thus a better chance at continuance and survival—their collective pathway to immortality in a mortal realm.

The One God of Abraham was a highly judgmental father figure who was surprisingly human in his temperament, a force of nature who was divorced from nature and yet who dwelt in the spiritual heart of anyone who chose to see him. By making his presence known in direct human terms, he made himself remarkably accessible, a Father Aeternal who could be talked to and prayed to anywhere and at any time. That accessibility would be the cornerstone of the highly personal and highly patriarchal religion that would emerge from this union of the divine with the mundane, through a talking, listening, watching, emotional, highly active God—a Father Who Is Everywhere to his covenanted people. Thunderous and old, this Immortal Father was a constant judge of the moral rectitude of his mortal charges, responding benignly to obedience but extracting terrible revenge for disloyalty. And since he existed unmated, alone and untouched by his female side, he was as distant as he was approachable; he made his minions earn his love, rather than giving it away freely, a picture of a heavenly and an earthly father for a long, long time to come.

Although the private face of the God of Abraham would come to be seen as compassionate and loving by future generations of his worshipers, the face he presented to everyone else was harsh, vengeful, and totally intolerant of any expressions of the divine that did not begin and end with him. In the One God and the one self as reflection of that One God he created with each of his worshipers, nothing else really counted. God and self were a completion—a singular ticket to immortality.

This spiritual union, however, precluded all other relationships—with the physical planet, with the sacred stories of other cultures, and with the larger and less self-involved family of humanity. It was a covenanted marriage of separation and isolation, whose role was to teach the rest of the world the many hard lessons it had to learn about the dangers and disconnections of the separated self through the pupil nation of Israel, the nation of Abraham's seed, which had, by embracing the One God, also chosen itself to be an earthly teacher of both unity and disunity.

The One God of Abraham also stated he was above all other gods. This declaration of competitive supremacy would further alienate his followers from all the other cultures around them and set up a dynamic of endless confrontation between the future adherents of all the patriarchal one-god religions that would spring from this ancient root.

CHILDREN OF ABRAHAM

When Abraham's son, Isaac, was a young boy, Abraham was told to take his beloved seed into the mountains and sacrifice him. Though this cut to his very heart, he did as he was asked, binding his half-grown child to an altar of wood and raising his knife to prove his absolute trust in his Father Aeternal, who now asked him to destroy virtually everything his loyalty and righteousness had created. When Abraham showed that he readily consented to this, his hand was stayed at the last moment by angelic force, and a far more significant and subtle covenant was made between the Hebraic heaven and Hebraic earth. The "Covenant of the Stayed Sacrifice" was an unspoken submission on the part of Abraham to his God's unfathomable will and wisdom, as well as to his hoped-for mercy. This would be the covenant that would create the overt spiritual personality of the One God of monotheism in all his subsequent manifestations: the All-Powerful, All-Merciful Unfathomable Father whose acts are beyond the comprehension of all who wish to live in the fearful and loving grace of his light.

After being given life anew, Isaac grew to manhood, took a barren wife, and, like his father before him, saw his seed come to fruition through divine dialogue. He was granted twin sons, one a skilled hunter, the other a clever but seemingly ordinary soul.

When Isaac, the second patriarch, reached great age, he lost his sight, and when it came time for him to give his blessing to the future generations of the children of Abraham, he unwittingly chose the clever son, Jacob, over the strong son, Esau, despite his preference for the latter, thanks to the manipulations of his wife, Rebekah, and her preferred progeny, Jacob.

Though Esau swore he would hate his brother forevermore for stealing both the birthright and the blessing of their future nation from the traditional hairy, strong-armed force that he represented, he eventually came to see that Jacob was a mighty warrior, too, one with the ability to wrestle with the heavens and the larger heart of humanity. Jacob's persona was built on the all-abiding love of his mother, as well as a deep faith in his own abilities and an even deeper one in the One God of Abraham, and this would be the legacy that he would hand down to the nation of Israel as its third patriarch. After wrestling one night with an angel till dawn, he was given the name Isra-el, meaning "Wrestler with God," and his would be the subtle warrior spirit that would sit over the future nation whose appellation he now bore. Twelve sons sprang from Israel's loins, and twelve tribes sprang from theirs. Thus did the children of Melchizedek, the master storyteller, once more enter history, to carry their ancient unremembered threads into the Fifth Civilization of humanity's many separations and reunions with its divine aspect.

YAHWEH

Israel's singular god was named YaHWeH, after the four letters of nature: Yod (fire), Heh (water), Vav (air), and Heh (earth). His solitary standing in the heavens set several practices in motion that would further separate the Hebrews as a "chosen people" from the pagan belief systems of their neighbors.

Since the children of Abraham had but one god, once YaHWeH had fashioned the firmaments Israel's story could begin with the first humans, Adam and Eve, unlike other creation myths that started with forces far beyond the scope of mortal life. This allowed the Hebrews to center their belief structure totally round life on the earthly plane, making them far more rooted in the realities of day-to-day existence than their fellow planetary beings. This also helped them to enhance their own egocentric view of existence, for their males were a direct manifestation of the image of YaHWeH, and each became a patriarchal king and priest within his own household—a god unto himself—which greatly augmented the male sense of self-importance.

Although males and females had long since diverged along the separate paths of separated and collective consciousness, up until that time a strict sense of self had still been limited to those men who had achieved considerable power within their tribes, acting as the egos for the rest of the benighted populace who were still very much connected to their collectivity. Here, then, was the very first nation whose entire patriarchal population had achieved an individual sense of self-worth, and it was this state of affairs more than anything else that earned them the undying enmity of their fellow planetary denizens.

The strong evocation of individual superiority by the adult males of this tribe was enough to thoroughly outrage their neighbors for the many millennia to come that it took for the rest of the White West to achieve an equal consciousness of self. This, along with the conceit of being the "chosen" on a planet of choice, has been enough to ensure the Hebrews more than their share of planetary wrath, despite the extraordinary teacher role they have played in the unfolding story of Western humanity.

From their beginnings, the Israelites were geared toward a culture that would be continual while all else around them declined and fell into oblivion. Their four-dimensional immortality would come through collective continuance. This is how they would defeat Death. This would be the key to their long story, for the Hebrews have managed to bridge the entire span of the White West, despite continuous efforts to the contrary on the parts of their many conquerors, enemies, and, quite often, themselves. They have been teachers of continuity on a discontinuous sphere, and thanks to their equal gift for written exposition, their lessons and errors have not gone unnoticed by the larger hostile world around them, which has never quite known what to make of these separated but unified-in-their-separation peoples.

Some of the descendants of Abraham ultimately wound up as slaves in Egypt for several centuries, until the emergence of a child who, legend has it, was set adrift by his mother and found by a servant of a princess of the royal court of the pharaoh. This child would be raised as an Egyptian prince, a secret Hebrew who knew not his earthly father but rather his heavenly progenitor, and who would learn firsthand the mysteries and the wisdom of one of the Fifth Civilization Western cultures that had secretly and directly maintained some of its Atlantean roots.

MOSES

The name given this child was Moses (ca. 1510 B.Z.–ca. 1430 B.Z.), which meant "son" in Egyptian, and he became as his adopted people, living a life of privilege. As an initiate in the sacred library schools of Egypt, he was made aware of his deeper past and his own divine destiny, and one day, when he was about thirty, he took the life of an Egyptian taskmaster who was whipping a Hebrew slave. Fearing reprisal, he fled into the desert, where he created himself anew through a new identity. After becoming a pastoral nomad for many decades and taking a wife and family, Moses buried himself in the harsh routines of his primitive desert existence until the God of Abraham suddenly appeared to him in a bush aflame and announced, "I AM THAT I AM," before informing the startled and fearful patriarch that he would be an earthly deliverer.

Moses returned to Egypt, where he proved himself an adept manipulator of the forces of nature and led his blood tribes out of their bondage and into the Sinai Desert. There, on a mountain of the same name, he received a decalogue of commandments, outlining the moral strictures that would unite the heavens and earth of Israel. It was a unity, however, that precluded all who did not adhere to its ten basic beliefs, and so it was a unity of exclusion—isolated, alone, and un-united with the other unity of existence, the family of humanity. This created an even greater separation between the people who called themselves chosen and everyone else.

Moses was a Builder in the deepest sense of that ancient initiatory title. While he served as the master mason who laid the foundation of stone tablets upon which the ethical civilization of the Hebrews could be built, he also served as a channel for the Egyptian mysteries, bringing their subtle undercurrents into the esoteric hidden traditions of Israel, so that they could survive and be passed down intact into the Fifth Civilization.

Two worlds, then, flowed through Moses: an exoteric one, which held a divine plan for a nation that would be unified in its diligent separation from everyone around it, and an esoteric one, which linked the lost world of the past with those who wished to be the builders of the future. While the former would be well-chronicled and looked upon as the very Word of God, the latter would persist in far less accessible form, keeping its mysterious face hidden from succeeding cultures that are still still working their way through all the implications of a one-god heaven.

This would be monotheism's legacy, then, through all its subsequent manifestations: an outward orthodoxy, with a rigid, carved-in-stone story at its base, and an inner tradition, rich with mystery and far more fluid in its vision of the divine and the mundane. Being a Builder who knew through the personal experience of being reborn in the bulrushes, and then re-created in the desert, that what is once built sometimes has to be destroyed, Moses served as the channel for both the visible and invisible foundations for monotheism, which he knew would soon diverge.

After having been given the Law, Israel's lawgiver died, and a warrior, Joshua, rose to replace him. In most cultures, the warrior comes first and the law follows after. But here, most uniquely, the law came first, and with it came a far greater sense of purpose, as a law-imbued warrior nation trumpeted its way into its Promised Land, destroying sacred knowledge when it did not fit its own and incorporating it when it did. Israel's religion, Judaism, which was still forming, would become both a repository for and a denial of many ancient beliefs, all centered round the concept of a singular god, sitting high and mighty over all and reflecting the singularity of presence that each of the Hebrew males felt about himself.

Having attained the promise of a Promised Land, the fantasy of a deliverer or a messiah began to seep into Hebraic consciousness. The sense of unity the Israelites felt in their heavens was not reflected at all upon Earth, for Israel was a nation of a dozen strong tribal divisions.

Eventually, the city of Jerusalem became the symbol of the Hebrews' earthly existence. A magnificent temple was built there according to the architectural precepts of the sacred library mysteries, to serve as substantive reminder of how worldliness and otherworldliness had been united through the One God.

PROPHETS

As Israel embarked on the pathway of earthly Empire, it began to lose sight of itself and its outer traditions, becoming more deeply buried in material affairs. Prophets rose to remind the Hebrews of their higher role here, and some were listened to and some were ignored. Through them, YaHWeH rose to the level of world ruler, for so did Israel begin to secretly think of itself in those terms with their One God as part of everyone and everything.

Israel's early prophets were part of the Egyptian sacred library school traditions that had passed into esoteric Judaic teachings. They were the public voice of these schools, and their combined vision saw that the unity of Israel was divinely conceived to be a beacon and a blessing to all nations, so that all who lived upon the planet would one day be able to ultimately touch on their oneness with the heavens, through the shining example of the nation that had first embraced the One true God.

They also saw that visionary Israel and everyday Israel were two entirely different places, and this they could not countenance. With their abilities to penetrate the astral and prefigure the future through the sheer ecstasy of faith, the prophets were out-of-time figures, four-dimensional voyagers trying to rouse a people who did not have the capacity to fully hear them. Though they opened Judaism to some of its larger possibilities, they also condemned the children of Israel to dissolution and disintegration by collectively conjuring an inescapable future of exile and defeat as punishment for not adhering to the higher pathway created and forged for them through the ministrations of Abraham, Isaac, Jacob, and Moses.

Collectively, the prophets represented the vast separation that existed within the uneasy unity of Israel and the impatience between its higher and lower aspects for not having the ability to integrate vision with practice. From the prophets came three basic doctrines: that YaHWeH and no one else was the ruler of the universe; that YaH-WeH was exclusively righteous, but was not omnipotent enough to curtail the evil impulse of humanity; and that it was up to the earthly religion of Judaism to create an ethical base to help humanity transcend its own innate evil.

This ideology, in turn, set the Hebrews on a most unique path, for their priests and proselytizers were no longer merely custodians of rituals and rites—they were interpreters of the ethical conduct of their people, teachers and analyzers and judges of human behavior. They were spirit as a thinking, evolving phenomenon instead of the blind ceremony it was elsewhere. Where other belief systems preyed on humanity's fear of Death and the unknown, seeking to assuage the frightened hearts of their followers through sacrifices and incantations, Judaism and its subsequent monotheistic outgrowths geared themselves toward humanity's fear of life. Their method was to control behavior through strong ethical codes, seeking to explain away the unexplainable by focusing attention on the four-dimensional sphere of human interaction, where the wayward forces of nature and the wanton appetites of the secular world could be dealt with by rules and laws and punishments.

By removing the material paraphernalia of rites and rituals, and by abandoning graven images and idols, the religion of the Hebrews became a moveable feast of the mind, to be transported in non-material manner wherever Israel stood, be it on its home base or on alien shores. Thus, the concept of being a Jew was totally internalized, for this belief system was soon to find it had no four-dimensional home to give it continual life.

True to prediction, Israel, which had divided earlier into northern and southern kingdoms, lost its upper half after a couple of hundred years and, with it, ten of its twelve tribes. The southern half fell in 586 B.Z. when the walls of Jerusalem were finally breached, the temple was destroyed, and the Hebrews were dispersed. Thus began a period called the "Babylonian Captivity," where their task as custodians of the mythos of the One true God would be further defined and would give them far more focus than when they were empire dreaming. Just as the lawgiver gave way to the warrior, now would the warrior give way to the sacred librarian.

This process brought the disunity of Israel in contact with the duality of the Aryan Persians, beginning the second epoch in the serial struggle of fathers and sons for consciousness supreme over the rapidly forming White West, making it once more, as it always is in this circular world, the very beginning of things.

○

Chronicles

The reader is invited to follow the flow of the Aryans, those direct descendants of ancient Atlantis, through the duality of the Persians, the trinity of the Egyptians, and the multiplicity of the Greeks and Romans, as wandering Israel lives with and learns from them all before producing the major prophet of modern Western mystery from its own unsettled midsts.

Around the time the unformed nation of Israel heard the clarion call to make its presence known in the civilized world, the Aryan nation, in its three separate hiding places, also revealed itself. Streaming out of the mountain passes that had isolated it for so many years, it poured into India, Persia, Mesopotamia, Egypt, Greece, Italy, and points westward, covering all of Western culture in one rapacious sweep, the chosen of the chosen on the loose at last.

All this happened between 1900 and 1600 B.Z., and despite their relative barbarity to the civilizations they invaded, their vigor, weaponry, disregard for the past, and mastery over the horse gave the Aryans easy conquest over wherever they chose to go. One of the places was Persia, and they gave that ancient arena its basic population as well as one of its names: Aryana, or Iran, "the country of the Aryans."

This strongly patriarchal society took a long time to enter the recorded story of humanity, for it did not bury its dead and did not record its deeds on clay. By not acknowledging any sense of the past, it remained forever in the present, achieving its own sense of immortality in this unusual way.

The Persians were an extremely aggressive people, and part of the continual practice of overstepping one's boundaries is the desire for acquisition of knowledge. And so among the warriors and berserkers of every army are always the information-gatherers, as eager for battle as anyone else of their ilk but with the added curiosity of the untrained scientist, collecting facts and relics and experience to add to the mass weave of human existence.

War has been a continual mine of mutual physical investigation and exchange of cultural consciousness through abrasive means from the beginning of civilization on this planet, and it has been the one consistent element that ties together most of the civilizations that have existed here. The threat of imminent removal from the earthly plane always lays its participants open to intense learning as well as allowing them to directly confront the mysteries of the Old Master and that gray spectre's strange dominance over the unknown here.

ZOROASTER & MITHRAS

Around 600 B.Z., a Persian by the name of Zoroaster (ca. 628–ca. 551 B.Z.) felt that he received a divine revelation that the true nature of nature was a constant battle between dark and light. He was subsequently forced to flee to the backwaters because of his teachings, where he ultimately disappeared into the mad duality of his mind, making him a most fitting postulant of the two-sidedness of the universe. His teachings on the twin face of moral reality here would become the spiritual mainstay of Persia and allow that aggressive empire-to-be, which lasted from the middle of the sixth century to the last third of the fourth century B.Z., to become a symbol of the West's second stage of religious evolution, the acknowledgment of good and evil, with the warrior imperative to do battle over those precepts. Since Zoroaster saw everything as a struggle between light and darkness, the Aryan Persians, too, looked upon themselves as a mass wave of redeemers of the planet, warriors working under the auspices of the heavens. In this way, they established the physical plane as an important manifestation of much higher struggles, and this would be their main legacy to the western part of the Fifth Civilization: aggressive moral purpose.

After a series of conquerors had established Persia as a planetary power, an offshoot of Zoroaster's double-sided vision rose to challenge Zoroastrianism for supreme belief among the Persians. It was named after a demi-deity called Mithras, who would later vie with other deified "heart-masters" of the area for the soul of the Mediterranean peoples for the first three centuries of the Common Era.

Mithras was originally a minor figure in the heavens who, legend had it, descended to the planet, lived an earthly existence of suffering, sacrifice, and magic, and then ascended to the ethers. He was a pagan runner who inspired much of the ritual of Zoroastrianism as well as the temporal observances that were later incorporated into a future resurrection cult, such as employing Sunday as a sacred day of worship, marking the 25th of December as a lordly birthday, and celebrating Easter as a festival of nature's capacity for renewal.

In addition, many of the stories of the Hebrews dovetail with the Mithraic accounts of early creation, as do the priestly interpreters of this religion, called Magi, who also wound up playing a role in the legend of Mithras's magically reborn Christed successor. Mithraism flourished for almost seven centuries, incorporating into its belief system the many cultures it touched as it expanded and contracted with the times.

ISRAEL'S DUALITY

During its Babylonian Captivity, which lasted from 586 B.Z. to 536 B.Z., the displaced nation of Israel was introduced to all this stellar speculation, while still being allowed to maintain its own oral tradition. This freedom of belief allowed Israel to augment its monotheistic view of the heavens with a second deity, one to balance the righteousness of YaHWeH and give rational foundation to the presence of evil in a world that is ruled by a god who is seemingly the personification of good. Thus Satan, the Adversary, was born, and he gave a ready rationalization for a heaven that seemed to look on its earthly minions with less than all-abiding love.

Although Babylon would become an important host to a large, exiled Hebraic community for the next fifteen hundred years, its "king of kings," Cyrus the Great (d. 529 B.Z.), wanted Israel as a protective buffer state. He encouraged a return to Palestine, which was accomplished in several waves over the next century, and a second temple, this one far simpler than its ornate predecessor, was completed there in 516 B.Z.

Cyrus, who was a Zoroastrian, would become a heroic figure in Jewish mythology. He was a great believer in the unity of the heavens over a diversity of peoples under one unifying leader; that belief, coupled with a distinct gift for conquest, made him a secular archetype for God on Earth. A little over a half millennium later, a Christed figure would rise, whose title would be a variation on Cyrus's name (pronounced Ky´-rus). This second king of kings would give Israel a counterbalancing spiritual archetype for God on Earth, one they would have a great more difficulty in accepting, for his rule would be far more challenging than that of their original larger-than-life host.

As some of the exiled Israelites slowly began to return to Jerusalem, the ideas of a last judgment, a resurrection of the dead, and the coming of a spiritual savior were all introduced into the minds of the Hebrews, to later take hold and be woven into their belief structure. From this time onward, there would be exiled communities of ex-Israelites all over the Middle East, some to be assimilated and disappear, with others to serve as long-time homes for a people who had now incorporated the duality of a hostile outer world into their unity of belief in the One God.

So the Persians, with their empire and their many conquests and their many dualities, came and went as many before them had done and many after them would do, and the nation of Israel—defeated, risen, defeated, scattered, and risen again—continued on as always, for so it had chosen and so it believed it was chosen to do. Its version of the sacred library, the Hebrew Bible, a detailed chronicle of the many stories of the One Father and the fathers and sons that comprised the story of Israel, would now be its main source of renewal, a bridge between the dimensions of time and spirit upon which Israel's immortality would now be thoroughly based.

EGYPTIAN TRINITY

Several hundred thousand years ago, the gods who ruled Atlantis first put their imprimatur on the ancient lands of Egypt and established a series of empires there that were based on divine teaching. They enter the records of the Fifth Civilization with the reign of the god Ptah, some twenty-three thousand years ago. It was this hidden civilization that first brought the Egyptian mysteries to light, and these mysteries, in turn, became closely linked with architecture as symbol of the outer manifestation of the intricately structured inner workings of humanity. Following the final cataclysm of Atlantis in 11,000 B.Z., the god-presence of Mesopotamia and Egypt began to lay the foundation that would allow humanity to claim this planet for its own. There, both the gods and the priestly adepts who served them would gradually bestow the gifts of civilization—agriculture, architecture, writing—that would connect humanity with its higher sources and put it on the collective pathway of mortal godhood.

Understanding that the marvels of the human universe could be gained only after a thorough knowledge of the physical had been secured, the Egyptian god-priests trained their future initiates accordingly, gradually deemphasizing the psychic to let them master the material. Part of their rites in this process was an initiation ritual where candidates for the higher priesthood would lie in a state of near death in a sarcophagus, or coffin, and their souls would leave their bodies through the inducement of drugs or trances. These souls would then experience the worlds beyond this one, before returning to the physical sphere far the wiser for their experience.

It was in this way that the hidden past was passed down from adept to adept and kept alive despite its invisibility to the normal state of physical consciousness. Though this privilege was reserved for the very few who had shown the purity and willingness to undergo it, it would become a graphic manifestation of the Egyptians' ability to ground all wisdom through the practices of the physical plane and to preserve everything that came within their grasp-

ing touch. Consequently, the river-world of the Nile came to be a
repository for the Fifth Civilization's lost-continent past, as that past
eventually blended in seamlessly with the subsequent rise of the
Land of the Pharaohs as spiritual arbiter of the concept of the trinity,
to complement the later unity and duality that postdated them.

From the point that the hieroglyphic inscriptions of the Egyptians
first began to limn their country's long tale until Egypt was conquered
in 525 B.Z. by the Persians, this monumental civilization falls into
three distinct periods of unity: the Old Kingdom, the Middle Kingdom, and the New Kingdom. During the Old Kingdom (3100-2200
B.Z.), the practice of mummification, or preserving the bodies of the
dead, came into being, first for the reigning monarch, the pharaoh,
who was considered a son of the sun god, and then for the wealthy.
This was done at the behest of the priest adepts to alter the course of
soul evolution on this plane.

In the ordinary course of physical death, a being transcends its
body and returns to the ethers whence it came, there to await a
proper time to reincarnate, or return to the Earth in a new body,
while it mulls over the lessons of its previous lives, divorced as it is
from the physical sphere. When that body is preserved, however, the
soul within remains far closer to Earth than it normally would, dwelling in the etheric rather than the higher spheres, for its bodily form
is still manifest upon the physical plane, not having been totally
released and allowed to undergo natural deterioration. Although a
relatively small number of souls ultimately underwent this preserva-
tion process, a great many more in the state beyond death observed
their entrapment in the lower ethers, and with that came a far greater
awareness of the physical plane and its central position in the seven
levels of consciousness connected with this world.

If Egypt had one singular contribution to the flow of the West's
planetary awareness, then, it was to give humanity far more cog-
nizance of the material world and its special importance in the healing processes of this planet. Prior to the Egyptian culture, the focus
of life for most of humanity had been on the etheric levels of this
sphere. The first four civilizations had all dwelt mightily within that
invisible realm and had deemed the ethers as their true home, since

the punctuated mortality of the physical sphere seemed but a brief nightmare-dream in comparison with the endless life span of the upper and lower regions of Earth.

With the Egyptians and their preservatory practices, their monumental buildings, and their attempts at immortalizing their earthly existences, the course of Western humanity's story was to change for everyone, whether they had been part of this longtime culture or not. Here was where the Fifth Civilization became thoroughly grounded and wedded to the planet, for better and for worse. All that has transpired since that time has been a further investigation into the possibilities of being truly on this globe without recourse to the greater magic of the greater universe that surrounds us.

Following the fall of the Middle Kingdom (2000-1786 B.Z.), a mixture of Semites and Aryans called Hyksos invaded and conquered Egypt. Within two centuries, however, the Land of the Pharaohs rose up, reconquered itself, and reclaimed its rightful place in the spiritual evolution of the West.

AMENHOTEP, PART IV

During Egypt's last gasp at greatness, the New Kingdom (ca. 1567-1069 B.Z.), there lived a pharaoh, a son of the sun, named Amenhotep, part IV (1397-1357 B.Z.), and he was the West's first true "separated self." His earthly father, Amenhotep, part III (d. 1372 B.Z.), had broken precedent by taking a commoner for a bride, thus making the kingship of Egypt a position of temporal sovereignty rather than the divine office it had been. When his son assumed the throne, he was determined to reverse this pattern, assuming himself to be not only a servant of the absolute truth, but its very earthly manifestation. To do this, he felt he had to unify the disorganized heavens of the Egyptians under a single deity and then make himself the planetary representative of that high spirit. Declaring himself the son of the sun and renaming himself Akhenaton, he announced that Aton, or the sun, was the universal force controlling this planet. He then banished all the other deities and their worship while attempting to restore order to Egypt's embattled etheric realms by streamlining the divine down to its essence, One God.

In doing so, he severed the divine channel of the office of the pharaoh, and began the process of divorcing humanity directly from the divine. He was a reverse Moses, in essence, for in his consuming mania on monotheism, he entwined his own persona with that concept, demanding godly obeisance, breaking with his more traditional nobility, ignoring external matters of state, building a new city to house both himself and his religion, and, like father, like son, incestuously marrying one of his daughters when his wife failed to produce a male heir. These various gestures not only hastened the ultimate fall of the New Kingdom, but they also foreshortened his own life, when this sonless son of the sun was assassinated by his successor.

The successor was a product of Akhenaton's father and sister's royal union, one Smenkhkere, who ultimately married one of Akhenaton's daughters, making him brother, nephew, and son-in-law all in one to the immortal he summarily brought back to earth by killing him. The implications of Akhenaton are many, for after his death, his memory, his city, and his singular deity were obliterated with such all-consuming passion that he was thoroughly forgotten by his people in a very short time span. This was strange, indeed, for even the most heinous of rulers used to inspire secret cults after their death. But Akhenaton's conceit of declaring himself god/man/king, that ultimate trinity of egoistic male power fantasies, was enough to expunge all trace of him after his divinity was exposed by Death in the guise of a rapacious incestuous relative.

In addition, Akhenaton established a mortal precedent that would add a considerable amount of confusion to earthly psychology and spirituality. As father to the West's ongoing obsession with its own individual self, he was profoundly instrumental in beginning the process of dividing humanity from both its heavens and itself, for the oneness that he seemingly stood for did not have the ability to integrate itself with anything that fell outside its self-glorifying boundaries. It was a oneness of separation—and ultimately of disintegration—and its dynamic would gradually filter down to embrace and deeply affect the entire individual consciousness of the West in the centuries and millennia to come.

OSIRIS, ISIS & HORUS

The collective consciousness of the Egyptians was ill-prepared for a pharaoh who worshiped his singular self, for they were a people who had long been directly ruled by their gods and did not know the meaning of self, save where it applied to the high and the mighty among them. This final state of transition into the Fifth Civilization, where the gods would allow humans their own wills, now began to speed up, as their presences diminished even further save to the priests and adepts who kept them alive on Earth.

In Egypt's ordering of the empyrean, there had been various traditions of a triad, or a uniting of three heavenly figures. It wasn't until the final millennium that one trio became universally recognized over the Land of the Three Kingdoms, and that was Osiris, Isis, and Horus—king, queen, and prince of the heavens. Though many stories are connected with them, they all revolve around a similar theme.

This story was set in motion by a fourth being, Set, the covetous brother of Osiris and Isis, who first radiated with light and then came to dwell in his own darkness. In that darkness, he coveted Isis as well as his brother's kingdom, so he killed Osiris and tossed his body into the Nile. Isis discovered his fratricidal deceit through magic means and reclaimed Osiris's corpus and buried it in the mud, before seeking out her son, Horus, to avenge this disgrace. In the meantime, Set dug up his sibling, hacked him into fourteen pieces, and scattered him to the winds, before claiming the immortal river-world for his own. By experiencing death and mortality, the divine Osiris was rendered human, thus linking the two, divine and human, and giving humanity the possibility of higher origins.

The loss of Osiris's immortality at the hands of his shadow brother was the fragmentation of consciousness that all who forgo their divinity to live on this planet must undergo in their subsequent self-destructive and self-healing stay here, so that in death, Osiris was able to give humanity life. Isis managed to find all but her husband's severed genitals, and she gave him a proper burial, minus his missing parts. She then used her considerable powers to revive Osiris's etheric being, thus enabling him to claim the Kingdom of the

Dead for his own, where he could watch over the less dramatic resurrections of his lessers, imbuing them with the same transcendent immortality that he had experienced at the hands of his extraordinary sister/wife.

Horus, who had been privy to all this, went on to slay his double-uncle in a titanic struggle that cost the former his fabled eye and the latter his dangling manhood. When the battle was over, Set went to live in the underworld while the trinity of light—the emasculated father, the magical mother, and the avenging son—rose to claim the heavens for their own.

Osiris's dismemberment into fourteen parts, and his subsequent magical piecing together by Isis, the lunar goddess, represents the two fourteen-day spans of the moon, from new to full and from full to new again, reaffirming woman's position as re-creator. Having been unmanned by Set, Osiris lost his powers of re-creation and became dependent on Isis to become whole again, showing woman to be the pivotal bridge in the cycle of destruction and re-creation, making her the continuer of all life-forms.

Isis and her avenging son, Horus, also symbolize the maternal/fraternal origins of humanity's Fifth Civilization, with the two acting in concert so that destruction, Set, may be destroyed, as mother, father, and son replace the duality of good and evil of Osiris and Set. With Osiris's resurrection, humanity becomes conscious of both its self and its mortality and is now ready to begin its story. The darkness of Set is the dark that sets the light free, so he, too, is part of a much larger process.

In addition, here is the father, Osiris, butchered and buried because of his own vulnerable mortality and then inadvertantly castrated while given life anew, so that his impotence among the immortals is doubled. Not only can he be easily separated from his body by the mere will of another, but also he no longer has the physical weaponry to reproduce himself and so must rely on a woman and a man-child, his own holy son, to make amends for his failings.

He thus becomes Lord of the Dead, for that is where his true power lies, beyond the world of flesh and feces, where his vulnerabilities are far too apparent, which allows him to move into the twilight world of life beyond the body. There he acts as moral magician, passing judgment on all who shed their skins in order to live forever among the shades, sending them off to their proper place. His is the imagination of Death, and all his works and art and philosophy reflect his fascination with that curious spectre, a spectre he may never hope to transcend with his limited powers of judgment, rationalization, and organization. He is the unknown made accessible through the planetary face of our spiritual patriarchs, and he bears all the power that has been given them as accepted arbiters of humanity's potential for immortality.

Magical mother Isis, on the other hand, has the gift of life, Amazon warrior and "holy cow" that she is. She does not view the Master Athlete as unconquerable for she knows the secret of turning spirit to blood and bone inside her own body and thus knows that nothing is eternal, not even the void beyond conscious consciousness. Together with Horus, the two are a match for the very forces of darkness itself, for they have the power of both the sword of destruction and the wand of creation to play with and therefore are unlimited by the conventions of ordinary reality and the mundane concerns of mere life and death.

This trio—the father as invisible lord of death, the mother as the magical vehicle of life, and the son as the force of resurrection/revenge/renewal—would be reenacted anew in the collective consciousness of a later epoch with global consequences through the Christian trinity of the Lord, Mary, and Jesus, for it is a story filled with deep and profound implications and with the flexibility to appeal to a multitude of cultures.

In the epochal evolution of the White West's consciousness, Egypt stands as stage number three, having added its trinity of father, mother, and son to the unity of the Hebrews' One God and the duality of the Persians' light and darkness, while placing a whole new perspective on mortality. By giving the planet both a material and an earthly focus, Egypt also readied the West for its next stage of evolving consciousness, that of the multiplicity of deities of the Greco-Romans, who would bring the separated self of the Hebrews to full secular flower.

GREEK MULTIPLICITY

The fourth epoch in the White West's formation of consciousness occurred in the Mediterranean's twin bastions of "me" and "me-first," Greece and Rome, as Egypt's trinity gave way to the multiple pantheons of the Hellenes and Latins.

The Aryan invasions of the second millennium B.Z. fused those remnants of ancient Atlantis with the long-standing Aegean and Minoan civilizations already established there, creating a hybrid culture called Minoan-Mycenaean, which flourished for several centuries before falling to natural disaster and further invasions. Wedding their patriarchal sky god, Zeus, with the region's goddess of fertility, Hera, these earlier Greeks created a family of gods and goddesses that were more of an astral extension of earthly life than a religion. These were father and mother figures who lent a certain air of security to an otherwise highly insecure plane, and they interacted with most Greeks on a rather prosaic level, as familiars rather than fearsome powers. These planetary immortals, like their human counterparts, were as easily susceptible to evil as they were to good, so the afterlife that awaited all who acknowledged them was not divided by earthly deed.

Since outer worship consisted mainly of individually inspired sacrifices, there was no need for priests or rites or intermediaries interfering with each citizen's private relationship with the ethers. In the same way, temples were considered guest-houses for the deities rather than houses of ceremony, serving as way stations for the unpredictable peregrinations of the divine host of Greece. In time, heaven was brought down to the planet and given an earthly site, Mount Olympus, a nearly ten-thousand-foot peak in northeast Greece, which allowed the people the illusion they were created from a cloth similar to that of their empyrean superiors.

These early manifestations of Grecian civilization paid homage to the finite and the natural. They believed in the divinity of humanity and perceived the Earth to be just another trapdoor in heaven, while basing their solipsistic culture on the view that all things emanated from them rather than on the prevalent planetary belief that humans were but a mote in the eye of the eyeless empyrean. Because of this perspective, the ideals of beauty and truth, particularly the former, would become of paramount importance to Grecian sensibilities, and this culture would give a further grounding to the Hebrew concept of the separated self, divorcing it from its One God/one self origins, so that earthly ego could at last stand alone upon the surface of the planet and pursue its material destiny.

Following an age of darkness and a century of light, the story of Greece is officially divided into two distinct eras, an "Archaic Age" (700-500 B.Z.), when its institutions and culture came into sharper focus, and a "Classical Age" (500-338 B.Z.), when they came to full flower. The latter ended when a neighboring father-and-son team—Philip, part II (382-336 B.Z.), and Alexander the Great (356-323 B.Z.) of Macedonia—effectively ended the Hellenic influence of Greece proper and spread a bastardization of it called Hellenistic culture throughout the rest of their known world. During the first age, the city-state became the powerful center of commerce, and two in particular, Sparta and Athens, came to symbolize the duality of Greek culture, the former representing the masculine principles of might and reason, while the latter came to stand for the feminine ideals of wisdom and expression.

This duality of metropolitan body and mind would also find its expression in two deities whose subtle unity of purpose went unacknowledged, Apollo and Dionysus. These two would further exemplify the tensions of a civilization that had the ability to isolate its component parts but did not have the subsequent genius to unite them into a larger whole.

APOLLO & DIONYSUS

Apollo was one of the Grecian gods of light, the deity of unity, perception, and revelation, representing the mind in all its glory. He was clarity and all that could be perceived in the sunshine of rational thought, a figure who illumined the surface of all things and made them accessible to the perceptual apparatus of humanity. There was a cold brilliance about him, despite his identification with the sun, and in the legends of the Greeks, his singular failures were always in the realm of love, for his hard, brittle vision could not penetrate the murky hearts of others. Because of this vision, he came to be associated with prophecy, and had many oracles, or earthly mediums, the primary ones being at Delphi. There, a group of women called the Pythia acted as his prophetic voice to bring his crystalline wisdom to any who asked for it. Apollo, then, was the master of the knowable, the revealer of mysteries perceived, and the patron of the higher expressions of humanity, in poetry, music, and the arts—the spiritual consciousness of the ethers divorced from the emotional excesses of Earth.

In contrast with Apollo's lofty and serene sensibilities was the ecstatic figure of Dionysus, also a son of light, but a light of a very different sort. He was the light of passion, of the invisible forces of feeling, of all that could not be revealed by the surface illumination of things. Dionysus was the unknown question answered, the murk of the moon revealed, the descent of the divine into the world of matter, the death of immortality and its ultimate resurrection, the fusion of the deific and the material, the very story of humanity itself.

Dionysus was the son of the chief deity of the Greeks, Zeus, who was also Apollo's father, but his mother, Semele, was a mortal, who upon seeing her cohabitor was consumed by his lightning, so that this future god of the grape was sewn into his father's thigh in order that he could be properly born. When Dionysus grew to young manhood, he was driven mad by Zeus's jealous wife, Hera. He then traveled to the ends of the civilized world, where he taught humanity the miracles of the vine and accumulated an entourage of celebratory spirits, while passing his madness onto all who denied him his divinity. Through his many adventures, including a descent into the underworld to rescue his mother, he came to know the joys and sufferings of those who called themselves human, forced as he was to endure the full range of human emotion in his long and arduous journey both upon the surface of this planet and beneath it.

The two Gods came to represent the totality of humanity's presence upon this sphere. Apollo was the divine soul of all who initially come here in their perceptual but unloving wisdom, while Dionysus was the subsequent immersion of that soul down through the ethers and onto the ecstatic madness of the physical plane, to learn of death and mortality and to taste the sweet and sour wine of life before transcending back to the greater universe as a healed and whole being once again.

THE GRECIAN MYSTERIES

At the end of the Archaic Age, another religious phenomenon began to rise in popularity to complement the loftiness of Olympus. This was the mystery cults, of which two came to ultimately dominate the nether-consciousness of the Hellenes: the Orphic, based on Dionysus's death, descent, and resurrection, and the Eleusinian, rooted in a similarly structured tale with female participants, Demeter and her daughter Persephone, symbols of the great motherhood of Earth and the dying and rebirth represented by winter and spring.

The Grecian mysteries touched the heart of Greece far deeper than its mythology, for there was little to truly celebrate in the weave and warp of the gods and goddesses. Their original male creation deity, Uranus, had shown no love for his children, many of whom were monsters, and he was ultimately unmanned by one of them, Cronus, the father of chronological time. Cronus in turn swallowed all his progeny to save himself from a similar fate, but through a ruse, one of them, Zeus, escaped. He grew to full godhood and ultimately upended his sire, before dividing the world by lot with his two brothers, Neptune and Pluto, whom he had rescued from his father's stomach. This less-than-inspiring story of paranoid fathers and patricidal sons resembled the patriarchal story of humanity far more than it did the divine spheres that ruled the Earth; and in essence, it freed the Greeks to pursue a much more secular pathway than they would have if they had had a heaven that demanded far more of them.

Although the Grecian mysteries were tempered by the same secretiveness and exclusiveness as those of other cultures, their outer trappings were better known to the general public. They, too, would combine with elements of the Hebrew, Persian, and Egyptian religions in creating the mystic dynamic of the earth-shaking spiritual epoch to come.

The rational and irrational mind of Greece was eventually superseded by the muscular body of Rome. By the time the Common

Era rolled around, the Grecian deities had been reduced to cult status, while a variety of highly delimiting philosophies were defining human roles on Earth. The separated self had become secularized through the Greeks and brought down to the planet minus its spiritual imperatives, so as to see its many isolated earthly parts and to briefly glory in them before larger forces moved the focus of Western spiritual evolution elsewhere.

ROMAN MULTIPLICITY

In the four epochs so far described, the type of terrain strongly dictated the male consciousness of each and how that consciousness would develop. The desert with its harsh forces gave the Hebrews the desire to continue above all else and to reflect that singular obsession with a singular deity and a singular purpose: to survive and to persist no matter what.

The irregular valleys of the Persians with their equal physical pathways to both east and west gave that empire its continual concern with dualities, for it was connected by land to two different worlds and was strongly drawn to each. The river-world of the Nile gave the Egyptians a predictable regularity in dealing with the rhythms of nature, allowing them to see in their monumental scheme of things the fruits of continuity and the importance of trinities: past, present, and future; birth, life, and death; and over-world, river-world, and underworld. The broken terrain of the Greeks, with its islets, waterways, mountains, and separated pastures, allowed that culture the separation of self-inspection, and its subsequent worship of all things divinely human.

The homeland of the Romans, in turn, was a long, narrow Mediterranean peninsula whose mountains created several fertile valleys but offered little resistance to invasion, which brought out the territoriality and martiality in whomever could hold the land. As with Persia, Egypt, and Greece, an Aryan presence had earlier intermixed with the tribes who already occupied the area.

The eventual seat of this empire-to-be was the city of Rome, which was founded, according to legend, in 753 B.Z. when a wolf-suckled brother slew his twin to claim the city as his own. This fratricidal myth of Romulus, where his father was a deity and his mother was an animal, speaks volumes on the subsequent consciousness of Rome. There, patriarchal fantasies would be acted out to excess, allowing the propertied males to identify totally with the power that their citizenship in this colossus engendered, making the title of "Roman" redolent with superiority over everyone else who dared dwell on the same planet.

ROMAN COLLEGIA

Following Romulus, the second legendary king of Rome was Numa Pompilius (seventh century B.Z.). It was his long and wise rule that gave the Romans the basis for both their outer and inner traditions. Well-versed in the mysteries of the various cultures that preceded Rome, he created the Roman Collegia, guilds of builders and architects who would accompany the future legions on their conquests, building fortifications and temples and houses and roads, while giving spiritual substance to their works through the rites and ceremonies that lay at the heart of the mysteries. The Collegia would rise to significant political power and at times be seen as a threat to the emperors-to-come, for they were the connectors of both the physical world with itself, through their skills at material manifestation, and the higher world with the lower one, through their practice of divine principles in creating earthly structures. It was this ability to both overwhelm and to connect that would give Rome its greatness and allow it to lay the basis for the West's predominant emphasis on the material sphere in its succeeding story.

OUTER RELIGION

Over Rome lay a pantheon of gods and goddesses who were worshiped in most orderly style, as befitting a heaven that sat over such an earthly power. This pantheon had grown out of the beliefs of the Latins, a rustic tribe of central Italy who saw spirits in everything, making both home and field rife with higher life. When the "Eternal City" of Rome rose, those same spirits grew in importance to the Romans and were magnified into deities. Eventually, an organized sacred college of pontifices gave both ceremony and order to this controlled brand of paganism, as they regulated sacrifices and consecrated temples and immersed their beliefs in the large earthly power that supported them. Electing their own spiritual emperor, a "pontifex maximus," they gave direct root to the structure of the next epoch's central church, once the White West had turned in its gods and goddesses for the simplicity of a rude cross.

This process produced a priestly class with considerably more power than their Grecian brethren and therefore with considerably more interest in maintaining things just as they were, for so their power would continue as such. This clergy would manifest again in the next epoch as part of the legacy of a culture that saw everyone as ultimately subservient to the will of the state, but because that state was so all-powerful, all its recognized individual members could also claim a high self-worth in its reflection.

Within this state, a huge rift existed between those who *had* and those who *had not*. This split was compounded by the *lex*, or law, which was continually being rewritten to incorporate inevitable change to the benefit of the most powerful. This was a culture that greatly respected material power and did its best to maintain those who had attained it. Even the afterlife came to be covered by this *lex*, for Rome was the first of the Fifth Civilization cultures to bestow upon its citizenry the legal right of last wills and testaments, thus giving them control of sorts over the earthly plane even after they had exited it.

In Rome's outer traditions, then, self became grounded and materially defined. It was now a legal entity with certain rights and privileges depending on rank and station, and it was protected by a much larger concern—the state—that had effectively replaced the heavens as absolute master of the planet. In the process, its official citizens now had the sense that they were mortalized divinities, complete unto themselves.

Never a particularly reflective people, the Romans believed in the power of their immediate presence and attacked life in the very same way, expecting to overwhelm it with the sheer force of their patriarchal might. They viewed themselves as political animals, sons of a son of a she-wolf, whose territorial mandate was to bend all the other beasts of the world jungle to their subjugation, so that all property would one day be theirs. In the same way, the Roman religion was far more political than spiritual, demanding of the deities that they protect the state and augment its prosperity, making the denizens of the ethers citizens of Rome as well, only of a slightly higher order. The deities, then, assumed a divorced posture from humanity below, acting as abstract personifications of virtues, ideals, and flaws, thereby draining themselves of most of their emotional appeal, cold and distant as they were.

Those without property and citizenship could find little sustenance in the worship of such gods. Thus, like their Grecian cohorts, the lesser Romans reveled in the uninitiated mystery cults, with Dionysus, also known as Bacchus, once again inspiring such orgiastic enthusiasm that his celebrations had to be quashed by the authorities for fear of giving voice to more ecstasy than they felt life on Earth warranted.

A second figure, Cybele, a former Great Mother, also inspired cult worship after she had transformed herself into the wife of Saturn, the Romanized Cronus. The two were the inspiration for a yearly festival in mid-December called Saturnalia, which was a grand letting loose of the various restraints imposed by living in such orderly disorder.

When Egypt finally knelt to the "Eternal State," Isis and Osiris were quickly pulled into the Latin pantheon, as were numerous Asiatic deities. This synthesis resulted in more than a hundred different religions, with thousands upon thousands of spirits, all of them quite acceptable to the state as long as they didn't interfere with business as usual. With this many deities, an extremely chaotic heaven stood over this controlled citizens' paradise on Earth, as everyone under Rome's banner began to feel a need to express their self-importance, particularly those who had little to call their own save their anger over having nothing. Thus was the slow process of bringing humanity down to the physical plane finally completed, as all its remembrances of its etheric past disappeared, save in the secretive practices of its mysteries.

In 27 B.Z., Rome officially became an empire, with an emperor, titled "first citizen," at its head and seemingly no power on Earth with the ability to stop its complete and utter drive for absolute dominance over the physical sphere. As the marching footsteps of "ego rampant" reverberated throughout the world of the Mediterranean, the people who had originally coined that concept, the Hebrews, suddenly found themselves beset by a civilization that shared the same concerns of self-importance, albeit through a totally different perspective. This threat would ultimately undo Israel from its homeland, for the "I" of Rome would have no other "I" before it. The two cultures were destined to do battle from the moment the Eternal City cast its first covetous glance at the rest of the known world.

ESSENES, SADDUCEES & PHARISEES

Well before the inevitable confrontation between the Hebrews and the Romans, the political/social voice of Israel had split in trine to give three distinct voices to the problem of proper planetary consciousness and behavior for the Hebrews. This trinity would manifest as the Essenes, the Sadducees, and the Pharisees, and each would come to represent a displaced face of Israel and its splintered unity of the heavens.

The Essenes were a group of teachers, healers, and sacred librarians who garbed themselves in the pure cloth of spirituality, eschewing the complex world of the senses for a simple life of well-ordered homage to the ethers. Living by the toil of their hands, while sharing their slim bounty with one another, the Essenes could be seen all over Judea, the Grecian name of the land of the Hebrews—in its cities, on its hillsides, and most notably near the Dead Sea, where a set of scrolls that they left revealed them to be a religious sect of a most unusual temper.

They were firm adherents of the pagan idea of resurrection, for that fantasy seemed to hold within it every mortal's wish of uniting with the divine. They saw their own continuance eternal in the idea that the flesh could rise again and be as one with their immortal souls at such time when a messiah—a savior—chose to descend from the heavens and give them the enlightenment to do so. This craving, to unite with the divine, became more and more prevalent as the great time clock of recorded events ticked its way down to the year 0, for the further humanity moved away from its collective sense of the ethers and the more it sank into its own egoistic self, the greater became the desire to reunite with what it had lost as a civilization.

Thus, the Essenes, in their purity and piety, gradually withdrew from the material world, to live in a state of timelessness and await their deliverer. They baptized one another against the uncleanliness of the world of matter, while living in close communal bond, an extended band of God-fearing communards who knew in their heart-minds that both an ending and a beginning were near at hand.

The second group of the three was far more material in its overview, consisting of assorted aristocrats, priests, and wealthy merchants, who called themselves Sadducees, after an ancient high priest. Looking for compromise rather than confrontation with their neighbors, they drew their moral inspiration from the written Law, as propounded in the Torah. The Torah consisted of the first five books of the Bible, called the Pentateuch, which the nation of Israel had held very close to its own bosom, editing and reediting it before finally letting the alien eye of the rest of the world see its genius for story, symbol, and language. The Pentateuch detailed the Law as interpreted by both Moses and the subsequent scribes of Israel. This was augmented by another work called the Talmud, which supplemented the Mosaic codes with added civil and canonical edicts.

The Sadducees did not believe in a messiah or afterlife, for they were grounded firmly on the planet. As a result, none of their writings outlived them, since they were forever looking to the material world for their spiritual sustenance.

The third member of this triumvirate, the Pharisees, or separatists, eventually separated from the Sadducees, much discontented with their lack of adventure of the spirit, body, and mind. Drawing their support from equally discontented countrysiders, they became the teachers of a far more fiery brand of Judaism. They believed in the oral Law of Moses, while replacing temple, priest, and sacrifice with synagogue, rabbi, and prayer so as to remove the static pall they felt the Sadducees had cast over their religion and make it alive to belief, analysis, and feeling.

With the emergence of the Pharisees came the idea of the Rabbi, the Teacher, the Master of Law, the Spreader of Wisdom, the Walking Word. This concept gave Judaism a host of interpreters to allow it continuance in the face of the rigid orthodoxies of its more conservative establishment.

The Pharisees also augmented their beliefs with some of the ideas of the Mithraic Persians, adding a resurrection of the dead, an angelic host above them and another world beyond them, while sharing with the Essenes the fantasy of a savior and the ideal of touching on the divine through human righteousness. This triad of views of one god—one passively spiritual, one material, and one aggressively spiritual—ultimately saw the latter, that of the Pharisees, come to full power. By that time, Judea was an argumentative kingship with various forces vying for that title, while a council of elders, called the Sanhedrin, tried to temper the intrigues, power struggles, and mayhem of their ruling court.

THE DELIVERER

There arose at this time, during the last century before the Common Era, a Deliverer, who appeared among the Essenes, and they called him the Teacher of Righteousness. He walked among them and healed the halt, levitated the lame, and gave succor to the sick, all the while preaching the single word of Love. Though his message was but a simple one, he was thought to be the long-awaited divine who would teach humanity to touch upon its immortal soul, for so he had both the presence and the light to look like Love itself.

Though he was received with a mixture of adoration, belief, curiosity, ignorance, skepticism, disbelief, and intolerance, it was the very last of these that ultimately prevailed. The Sadducees, fearing his power, condemned him to death by stoning, and he died a martyr for his various conceits, proving himself quite mortal in the process.

Although his name was soon forgotten by the larger public, his memory was revered by his followers, many of them Essenes, for he had said before his inglorious exit that he would come back with his divinity unaltered, and so they believed he would. Though his tale lacked divine drama, it did serve as a base for a future prophet the following century, who would repeat the exact same message before effecting a most memorable departure from the material world to insure that his word would be heard forevermore.

With the coming of the Common Era, Judaea, its name now Romanized, found itself a culturally Hellenistic nation under the political aegis of Rome. This was a galling state of affairs to a patriarchal people who had introduced the idea of individual self-importance to the Fifth Civilization and then saw that concept carried to its least spiritual extreme by an empire that had re-created itself into a material theocracy centered round the worship of the state as the eternal "I" of humanity.

And so the chosen of Israel, whose genius for continuance would even allow them to outlive this material monster, prepared themselves for the coming of the White West's fifth epoch, as the pagan fantasy of resurrection and immortality began to make inroads into the one people who had heretofore collectively resisted these concepts, since they had already learned how to transcend Death through their continuing ability to continue. As the year 0 approached, a mass belief in that continuity was being sorely tested, for Israel was a much-divided nation despite its unity of One God. Many elements were vying for its damaged heart, including the desire for a Deliverer who could teach humanity about the higher continuity of its immortality.

Thus, as Western civilization's sense of self and self-importance grew ever thicker and its hunger for its lost divinity grew ever greater, the first four epochs of consciousness of the White West came to a close. The deathless continuity of the Hebrews and their oneness of "immortality through continuous survival" was about to be challenged by the resurrection mythos of the larger world around them. One of their very own number would eventually violate the basic tenet of their patriarchal rule that "Nobody gets out of here alive," and usher in a new era by upending that conceit in extraordinarily spectacular fashion, making it, as always, once more the very beginning of things.

○

The Gospel According to Melchizedek

*The reader is invited to listen
to a retelling of the basic story of modern Western mystery,
in which a magical being appears and challenges the very
tenets of mortality.*

There was once a Man of Light who fell to Earth and proclaimed himself a prince of the Invisible Realm of Peace. This being, who took male form and walked without casting a shadow and talked in a tongue that was lit by the sunshine of infinite wisdom, had a magician's touch to his hands and could raise the dead and give sight to the blind all in the flick of his long, thin fingers and the flow of his thunderous heart. This Son of the Sun knew Love both inside and out, and he preached and taught it in a ministry that was as loose as his high-glowing logos and as tight as his glacier-cool eyes. Yet in his lovingness and gentleness there also dwelt within him another soul, this one provocative and challenging, claiming authority over all the earthly authority around him, unwilling to peacefully assert his message of pax, daring his adversaries to act out their weakness of vision upon him. This soul within went on to assume the sufferings and sins of all humanity in the brashest act of humility ever recorded in the mythos of the peoples of this world. Though his story has been writ and told many times, still it bears yet another retelling, for its message has been much misunderstood and misinterpreted in the two thousand years following his momentous coming.

In the beginning was the Word, and the Word was Love, and it begat a son to teach humanity its essence, and that son was born of a mortal mother and an immortal father, to show the denizens of this planet that they also are a product of the human and the divine.

On the winter solstice of the year 4 B.Z., there came into this world two beings of extraordinary luster, born simultaneously into the Roman province of Judaea to two women named Mary, who could not have been more opposite, the one having never known a man physically and the other having known far too many. Though of different wombs, these two infants were identical twins, sculpted as they were from the mist and ephemera of the deities and the ashes, bones, and breath of humans. They came to Earth simultaneously, heralded by prophecies and a whole celestial circus of empyrean fireworks, Joshua ben (son of) Joseph and Jesse ben Mary: the Son of Man and the Son of Woman, identical down to the signet crosses on their brows. The sole physical difference between the two was a pair of magical goat feet that Jesse bore, which could transform themselves into human appendages at a mere wish so as to hide his unearthly origins from any prying mortal eye.

Joshua was born in a manger in Bethlehem, a pallid child almost translucent in his delicate, finely formed features. He was a baby who never nursed or cried or wet his swaddling, as he stared out of the oceans that were his eyes and swept everyone he saw with love, a beatific smile continually gracing his infant lips. Jesse, in contrast, was born in a cave outside Jerusalem, a dark and robust child with a rich earthy color, who nursed and cried and wet lustily.

Both boys were immediately befriended by shepherds following their emergence, but Joshua soon had to be spirited from his birthplace, following his initiation of circumcision according to Mosaic Law, his little life in deep peril; it was only the message of three Magian magicians that saved his young heart from the sword. Taken into Egypt, he spent his first three years in the isolated company of his virgin mother, his carpenter father, and a priestly couple who acted as teachers for him.

Though he was extremely fair skinned, Joshua was a true child of the sun, filled with the perceptions of Light. He possessed an extraordinary mind that could see through all the illusions of this plane and knew that love sat atop all living things, for he had been blessed with a full vision of the ethers, Son of the Sun that he was.

If Joshua was the Son of the Sun, then Jesse was the Child of the Moon, for he had the vision of all things concealed and could see to the heart of all matter. Nothing was hidden from his deep, penetrating eyes and he understood the emotional essence of all things, the absolute madness of this sphere and its crazed passions and ecstasies.

At the age of three, Jesse, along with his mother, the shadow Madonna, went to live among the Essenes to share and learn their ways, while Joshua returned to the home of his parents in Nazareth, there to prepare himself for his most unusual calling. Thus did the boys spend their early childhood, Joshua buried in books and learning, Jesse running free in the streets and along the hillsides. The one filled his mind with the high and ancient laws of love, while the other filled his heart with the unwritten edicts of the same, the two accruing a complementary knowledge that would one day unite in one being who could truly say he knew all there was to know about this planet's illusory and depth-filled character from a male point of view.

When both boys were twelve, their mothers took them to Jerusalem to celebrate the citywide feast of Passover. By this time, Joshua had been working for a full year under the stewardship of his father as an apprentice carpenter, while Jesse had become an accomplished and entertaining beggar, always sharing his bounty with those less forceful and fortunate than he.

By chance, the two boys passed on the street, and through telepathy they arranged a secret meeting by the Court of the Gentiles near the temple, for each knew the other was a secret part of himself. Clasping each other as brothers, they marveled in the superficial similarity of their appearances, and then talked on and on almost till the dawn, Joshua in well-wrought phrases, Jesse dancing out his thoughts on spry goat feet. The two made plans for a mutual journey to the East, for both felt they had learned as much as they could from Judaea and now had to stretch their minds and hearts elsewhere.

Joshua visited the temple the next day and elicited the curiosity of an Indian prince named Melchizedek, who was very much interested in Western ways. He followed the boy to his home in Nazareth and offered him a position at his court as a carpenter in exchange for food, shelter, and lessons in the mysteries of the East. Gaining his parent's reluctant permission, he was off the following week, joining the prince's large retinue, while Jesse attached himself to a merchant's caravan, meeting his secret brother sometime later in Babylon, where he was introduced to Joshua's benefactor, who was much taken with both the goat-foot boy and the carpenter's son. That night, by the flickering light of many candles in his tent and in the presence of a holy slew of ghosts, the prince told the magical boys a tale that they devoured with rapt attention, for it was a tale of the Christ—his coming, his wandering, his temptation, his teaching, his torture, his death and resurrection, and his life forevermore.

All this happened long, long ago said the prince, and it would happen again. The coming Son of the Word was a wandering teacher of the cosmos who had performed his tricks on many other planets as well as this one, all with highly divergent results, for he had the capacity to prick the peculiar consciousness of whatever world he dwelt on and create for it a myth that struck at the very heart of its imagination. When the Prince had finished his story, the three looked deep into each other's eyes, each knowing he was in the presence of beings who were more than human.

"Who are you?" echoed both boys, and the prince answered, "I am from the Kingdom of the Other Side of Light, come to show you what life and love and death are all about." This the boys accepted, for they knew they would have to be masters of both light and darkness if ever they wanted to reach the higher souls of those who dwelt on this planet, for Earth is a combination of the two, and all who come here to master this plane must learn each. So it was that both boys readily accepted the prince as their teacher, and he took them across Asia Minor through many of the ancient empires and kingdoms of old. Many were the marvels they experienced and saw, until at last they crossed the Khyber Pass into India and continued on until they reached the veiled and walled city of Piscespuhr, sitting high in a mystic valley of the Himalayas. There they saw a vast metropolis with broad streets and many terraced houses and public gardens, whose very center housed a magnificent palace of such airy grace and majesty that it seemed to be fashioned from the very clouds themselves.

Joshua was immediately made a carpenter of the court, while Jesse was made an elephant handler, for his way with animals had become quite apparent during the journey. The two boys entertained their work with great enthusiasm, learning through their environment rather than by direct contact with the prince, who remained invisible their first year in his city.

Finally, one day both brothers were summoned by their host for their first private audience with him since the three had initially met. They were formally escorted up the palace steps and into its mysterious portals by an honor guard. Entering the prince's candle-lit chamber, they found him, much to their innocent surprise, lying wounded atop an array of cushions. His groin was heavily bandaged, and his face was contorted in abject anguish, reflecting in the flickering light a greater suffering than any either of the boys had ever witnessed. Numerous women silently tended him, wiping his brow, bringing water to his dried lips, rearranging his pillows, and comforting him each time his contorted body moved in a spasm of agony.

Next to the prince sat a crowned cup, uncommonly aglow. Out of its mouth hung a dead fish, its face equally etched in pain, its life having long left it, its gray scaly skin reflecting the darkness all around it.

Although Joshua was filled with a thousand questions, out of the politeness of the moment he asked not a one, though he was deeply aware of his host's wound and could feel it inside himself. Looking through the prince's bandages, he could see that somehow he had been emasculated, castrated, unmanned—but what kind of force could have accomplished this? Still, Joshua could not ask the nature of his ailment. It was as if his tongue was totally stilled by an even greater presence than the two magic boys and the dying prince, and it was all he could do to consume the unwanted dinner offered him.

Jesse, too, was rendered totally reticent by this tableau, for the prince's wound seemed to be his as well, and he could feel his own adolescent masculinity torn asunder from him. The boys pondered all this as they sat silently and ate with no relish whatsoever, for their meal tasted dead, causing them even more discomfort, as their host, in the utmost of agony, watched their every gesture and move.

When they had finished eating, the two women who had served them silently returned and took their plates. As soon as they did so, all the candles flickered out, and the boys found themselves in the total dark. The entire scene around them faded to the echo of hideous laughter, and to their astonishment, they were suddenly outside the gates of the walled city of Piscespuhr with no recollection of how they had gotten there.

As the two stared at one another in astonishment, both women who had served them appeared as apparitions, and they spoke in a rasping unison that shivered the boys' spines. "Away with you," the two harpies shrilled, "for you are now lost in the hell of your own darkness. May your souls rot forever in the Other Side of Light. You have lost your powers. Now shall you know the torture of being merely mortal on this planet." With that, the women disappeared in a shriek of raucous delight, leaving the boys wrapped in the darkest of night, the manifest world totally invisible to them as they stood shrouded in their own torment.

Suddenly, Jesse clutched himself and folded to the ground, a silent scream upon his lips, as he lost all control of himself, shuddering in abject misery while his light-brother bent to heal him. But Joshua soon discovered his powers of healing had totally deserted him in this dark place. It was all he could do to hold his suffering other self and rock him back and forth, begging him with his inner heart not to leave his body, for he knew that in order to escape this nightmare realm, both would have to go together—if he lost his goat-foot half, he would lose himself as well.

But Jesse continued to sink within, until at last, when Joshua could barely feel the beat of his life, he asked, in anguish and despair, "What ails you?" As soon as the question was posited, a sliver of dawn appeared on the horizon, and he knew their crisis had passed.

As the sun slowly rose to define the sky and earth, Jesse's breathing became more regular; he could open his eyes, and they were filled once again with the vital fluids of life. Looking about them, the two saw no sign of the walled city in which they had spent a happy year, although the landscape that flooded their vision was exactly as they used to view it from their windows and their arenas of work.

Though lightly clad, neither of the two seemed to feel the cold, so they decided to hie up the road northward, into the awesome rise of the Himalayas and the distant spectacle of white-hatted peaks that touched the very skin of the sky. After several days, they came upon an old hermit, who greeted them in their native tongue and told them he had been expecting them. Surprised and yet not surprised at this, both boys eagerly followed him when he beckoned to a nearby cave that seemed to be his abode.

At the mouth of the cave, lying coiled asleep, was a large serpent, which awoke at the sight of the three and slithered back inside, causing the brothers some slight pause. Nevertheless, when the hermit entered after it, so did they, understanding that this creature was an adjunct to his solitude, for they had heard that in this part of the world the snake was both revered and dreaded and that some had powers that stretched back to ancient days when dragons and other scaled creatures ruled the mountains and mists that were the Earth.

Once inside, neither could see in the darkness, but both felt comfortable within, for this was obviously a darkness woven from light. When their host lit a fire in its center, they were astonished to see his dwelling was shaped exactly like the inside of a human skull. After the hermit had fed the flames so that they were properly dancing, he offered the boys two seats round the fire and proffered them each a golden fruit, of which they partook—Joshua out of courtesy, Jesse out of ravenous hunger.

The hermit, in softly speaking to them, seemed to know all about their adventures, as well as a great deal about themselves, although when they asked him questions about himself, he revealed nothing.

When he had finished speaking, he directed their attention to the fire, from whose center a great flame-spirit suddenly rose and threw the cave into brilliance, chasing out its shadows so that all were now bathed in their purest essence.

As the flames grew higher, there appeared in them a four-armed being, a dancer, a spectre of light with one goat foot and one human foot. Both boys watched in awed fascination as it began to move to the music the fire created. As it danced, it called the snake into the fire, and the creature came forth and slid into the brilliant inferno although it remained unscathed. It then wrapped itself round the body of the furiously spinning being within, entwining itself around the flame-spirit until the two became one. As it did so, both boys felt themselves mysteriously moved by no known force, till they were each occupying the same space. And so the two, of exact same physical proportions, became one, a single entity, Joshua/Jesse, now forever bound in one body, with human feet but with the invisible intimations of a cloven heel and toe around them.

When this had been done, both dancer and serpent were consumed by the flames, which immediately ebbed to their previous modest glow. It was then that Joshua/Jesse, now a single being, looked at himself in astonishment through his one mind and one heart. Then he stared long and hard at the hermit but questioned him not, for he knew there were no answers to what had just happened.

When the last tiny spark had flickered out, the hermit rose and beckoned the boy with invisible gestures to follow him out of the cave, which he did, only to find himself stunned by the light outside. Breathing deeply of the air and stretching his sore muscles, he listened carefully as the hermit told him his composite form would now be called by its Grecian name, Jesus, and that in order to leave this magical valley he would have to find the Prince of Fishes again, through internal means, and once he did, he would have to ask him the nature of his ailment. If he did that, he would be free to pursue the extraordinary path that awaited him.

The grateful Jesus thanked him, and the two embraced, incipient and aged masters that they were. Each bid the other a heartfelt farewell, for the magic in which they had participated was engineered by forces far greater than they, and each had felt it a deep privilege to be part of it.

Jesus stayed in that magical valley for four years, this time a singular entity, a combination of the two people he had been: one studious and quiet and ethereal, not quite of this plane; the other vibrant and earthy, a trickster of the highest order. The serene Joshua and the laughing Jesse were now forever melded into a singular being who was destined to alter forever the story of humanity. Not once during those four years did he see another human soul—not even the hermit—only the natural wonders around him, with which he communed deeply. As he meditated and drank of the air, the wind came and brought him messages, telling him of his carpenter father's death and of his two mothers, the Madonna and her shadow, longing for him.

One day, the wind told him it was time to leave this valley, for he had garnered all the strength and wisdom from it he needed to face his strange nemesis, the Prince of Fishes, who was all things that the young, pure, and loving Jesus was not. So he bid the little creatures of the valley good-bye. They were greatly saddened, for they did not wish to see him leave, but knew he had to, as he was meant for a much larger world than theirs; they felt blessed that he had chosen to share a small portion of his life with them.

Traveling through the mountainous deserts of Central Asia, Jesus moved on bare feet, barely feeling the cold dark of the winter on his lightly clad frame and unbothered by any of the fierce tribespeople there, who allowed him uncontested trespass. Maintaining his polite aloofness, he said naught to any of them, moving in his own light, slowly and steadily, until at last, somewhere in the Caucausus mountains he stopped by a well, suddenly incurring a rare thirst for something more than air, the substance that had totally sustained him thus far on his journey.

As he approached the well from a distance, he saw a beautiful young woman drawing water there, and he was powerfully drawn by her absolute perfection. She, too, was magnetized by his ethereal handsomeness, and when he drew near, the two stared at one another transfixed, for neither had ever beheld a creature who so closely reflected the inner soul of the other.

As they stood together in their own timelessness, he asked her what her name was, and though she responded in a tongue that was totally foreign to him, he could easily understand her. She said that she had the same name as the spring that fed this well, Mary, which meant "the darkness of light" in her language. But when he asked if he might have a sip of her water, she warned him that whosoever drank of that liquid would have a thirst that only the darkness of death would quench, for this was a spring that rose from the wounded bosom of the gods in their eternal struggle for supremacy over one another and all who drank there took on that struggle within themselves.

As they were speaking, there suddenly appeared on the horizon seven horsemen, clad in such fierce colors that even the sun paled in comparison. These were the daemonguard of Ahriman, Lord of Darkness of this region of Persia, and they shone with all his malevolent brilliance, riding on chargers who bore the mark of the underworld on their flanks. When Mary saw them, she stiffened in fear, watching in statued terror as they thundered to the well, encircling the two with their steeds.

One of their number loosened his Hades-hair rope from his rude saddle and threw it around Mary, yanking her tied figure to him and flinging her cross the rump of his mount, all in two expert motions. As Jesus stepped forward to protest, he was immediately imprisoned between the other six, who laughed at his outrage and his puny form against a crew as armed and evil as they. "If you ever wanna see her again," hissed the fiend who had her, "you're gonna have to waste yourself on this water."

Then drawing a knife to her throat, he bellowed in triumph as Mary stared at the young Prince of Peace with eyes that were already flecked with death and whispered, "Do what thou will." Without hesitating, Jesus quaffed several mouthfuls of the bitter liquid before falling to his knees, overwhelmed by a great dizziness; the entire scenario before him melted into geometric patterns, and he sank to the ground unconscious.

When he awoke several days later, the breath of life barely in him, he was amazed to find the same hermit he had met in India, kneeling over him with a flask of water, dripping it onto his lips and wiping his brow of all its fever. As the future Savior slowly crawled back into his body, he looked about to see all trace of the horsemen and the woman gone, and he felt a deep ache in his heart, for she had touched him as no other being ever had—not even his combined mothers, to whom she bore an extraordinary likeness.

After several hours, he could sit up without any of the fogginess that had so besmeared his brain earlier. But it was not until Jesus had regained his strength that the hermit addressed himself to his queries, revealing himself as a wandering Semite who had been on the physical plane continuously since the time of Atlantis. Because he had scorned an earlier figure who had been Christed, or made into a vehicular channel for the larger Love of the universe, he had been condemned to roam the planet till the next Christed figure appeared—and now that possibility existed in Jesus. So he was pledged to follow his wanderings to insure that his Christ-cycle would be completed; that was why he had followed this young Son of the Sun and used his modest magic to restore life to him. When Jesus asked this mage his name, the hermit said it was Judas.

Then Judas told him all he knew of the well. He said these were the waters of the two Persian gods, Ormuzd and Ahriman—Lightness and Darkness, Heaven and Earth—and now that he had drunk of their dualities, now that he had touched upon the invisible woman inside himself, he would never be free of his incompleteness without her unless he once again went off by himself to bring his separate parts together.

This Jesus agreed to do, for now that he had seen his complementary opposite, all he could think of was to release her from her captors, which he knew to be the other side of himself: his darkness, his desire for power, and his desire for death. Judas told him what he must do and that this would be a far more treacherous test than his first go-round with the Prince of Fishes. There he had only to transcend his own innocence through meditative experience in order to unite with his lower half, but here he would have to deal with a far more basic duality, his male and female sides, this Son of the Sun and Child of the Moon.

With that counsel, Judas and Jesus once more parted company, and the wounded Savior came one more time to live in a nearby cave. But this valley that had chosen him for its mysteries was far more forbidding than the paradise he had experienced in India; few creatures dared live here, and the vegetation was as sparse and unfriendly as the terrain, with all life looking out solely for its own survival.

By day, Jesus could lightly feel the presence of the God of Light, the Solar Word, Ormuzd, who shone down on him and allowed him to slowly heal his wounds. However, by night, Ahriman, God of Darkness, the Lunar Moan, opened those wounds anew, showing him the blackness of his soul, torturing him about his human imperfections, his vainglory in feeling he was the savior of a planet that could not be saved. This made him struggle mightily within himself, for little by little he felt the darkness within winning, and each day it became harder to recover from the night.

After nearly four years of this, Jesus found he was wishing only for his own death. He felt that he had drowned in his own waters and that he was no longer worthy of the task for which he had been chosen, for if he could not save himself, how could he hope to save humanity? As he lay close to dying once more, the sun sent him a wounded dove, a creature of the air far off her course, the first being with which he had had contact in the entire time of his solitude. He saw it immediately as a symbol of himself, and he tended to it and put all his healing power into its feeble wings.

All that night, as Ahriman taunted him with evil magic, he hovered over the dove and breathed life into it, and in the morning, as the solar word rose in the sky, the bird was still alive. As she gained strength, so did he, until several weeks later, the bird was able to fly away and Jesus knew he would prevail. And so he did, for one glorious night, soon thereafter, Ormuzd appeared in the shadows of his cave, and the demon-magic of Ahriman was gone, and Jesus stood before this spectral radiance, dazzled as he had never been before.

Ormuzd sat on a golden throne that was supported by four

figures, three of them—a winged bull, a winged lion, and an angel—standing in full force, while the fourth, the vague outline of an eagle, lay in shadow. All bade the Prince of Peace to step forward as the God of Light gave Jesus a robe of air and told him he could now return to the well and drink of its waters freely, for he was whole again. The Savior donned the garment that he was given, and as he did so, the god disappeared into a cheshire smile, leaving behind him the permanent light of his Word, as a continual mantle for this young man, now twenty-two years of age, to wear through his further trials.

As dawn spread its roseate kiss across the sky, Jesus returned to the barren oasis that had almost undone him, dipped into the well, and drank deeply of its waters with no ill effect. As he did so, the seven horsemen appeared once more on the horizon and rode toward him. Their presence was even more frightening than before, for they were greatly angered that they had been undone by a being still in mortal state, even one as godlike as this. The fiend who had roped Mary cursed him with the vilest of blasphemies, but Jesus was intimidated not, for his darkness had left him; there was no part of his heart that they could enter, so pure and high did he stand after successfully withstanding his trial.

When the daemonguard of Ahriman saw this, they contemptuously threw a dark blanket at him, which had been furled atop one of their horses, and it landed at his bared feet as they galloped back off to the horizon. Jesus unfurled the blanket to find the body of Mary, its soul long departed, its previous perfection marred by the stone-cold sadness of death. He drew her up into his arms and wept anew at her demise, for she had been that part of him that had had to die for his drinking of her water. And he buried her there, scratching out the earth with his hands, burying his ambition and his desire for glory and the uncleanliness of his human desires with her.

For four days, he stood over Mary's grave, releasing all of his grief within, until, at last, an eagle appeared overhead, and he could see that it was she. He released her from his heart, as she had released him from hers, and he watched as she flew into the moon to rejoin it. Then he beheld that heavenly sphere face-to-face, and it shined down on him in total love, for he was now truly its child. So Jesus again took to the road, to continue his journey westward and pursue the destiny that he had both chosen for himself and for which he had been aptly chosen.

After several uneventful months crossing the face of western Asia, Jesus arrived back at the second starting point of his journey, Babylon, and decided to encamp there. He was well aware of the long story of this land, for it fell right along the trail of the Aryans and their sweeping conquest of consciousness of the White West. He knew that the legend of the Messiah, the Savior, had been born here, with the rubbing together of the forces of ancient Atlantis. And standing here in this sleeping city, which, like its neighboring river-world, Egypt, used to worship its divinities in triads, or threes, he pondered why he had incarnated into immortal Israel, with its Apollonian respect for law and literature, its Dionysian draw toward self-destruction, its ego supreme in its One God deity, and its arrogant conceit of superiority through "chosenness," as well as its belief that it could continually rise from the dead no matter how many times its beaten bones lay lifeless in the sun.

As he thought about all this, walking the predawn streets wrapped in his magic robe of air, he came upon a ghostly woman holding the dead body of a young man in her lap, while weeping streamlets of tears over him. To his astonishment, the woman looked just like a combination of his mothers to him, while the deceased body was his, pallid and death hued, with bloodied holes through both palms and feet, one of which was cloven and one humanly five toed.

Unsettled to the extreme, he stared at their tableau for a long time, but the woman gave no sign of being aware of his presence, as she showered her emotional attention completely on the pietà pose she had assumed over the spent life upon her lap. At last, he asked in a low sweet voice, "What ails you?"

This startled her out of her shadow, and she stared in displaced shock at this figure of the living who could see and address her ghostly etheric form. As she revealed herself to the equally struck Jesus, he could see that she was, indeed, the mothers Mary garbed in the cloak of love lost, her great heart exposed, dripping the gray blood of sorrow from out its many wounds.

For a long time the two drew each other in with their eyes, and then at last Jesus began to speak, telling her of himself—who he was, what he had done, and who he had chosen to be. When he had finished speaking, dawn began to throw its first breath of light over the horizon, and the woman bid him deeper into the shadows so that they could continue talking, uninterrupted by the curiosity of the slowly awakening city.

Without hesitating, Jesus followed her as she led him into the Realm of the Dead, abandoning his physical body to the magic of invisibility, where it lay in shadow upon the street. He stepped through a hole between the barriers of time and space to enter the etheric plane that surrounds Earth, called Purgatory by some, a place where life does not exist in material form save for the pure energy of consciousness.

Once through to the other side, the Son of the Sky realized he had abandoned his earthly body far too easily. He had seduced himself into thinking his powers would serve him there when he could see, as soon as he stepped through, that they would not, as the ghostly pietà before him disappeared into the thick murk of his surroundings, and he was suddenly all alone in the darkness. All around him he could feel the chillness of unspeakable creatures and smell their befouled breath and hear their grunts and groans in a nightmare world of no-light, where his vision was totally denied him.

Yet in his blindness, he could also see that here was the trinity of life, love, and death. He knew that if he could only find them again in the person of the weeping Madonna and her dead son, he could complete himself and perhaps resurrect back up into the world of the living, where he would then be fully prepared for the task he had chosen for himself.

Thus he understood what the path out was, but he did not know where to begin his search because of his diminished sight and the monstrous presences all around him—great fear-filled ghouls, who seemed equally afraid of him in their excited chatter, squeals, and moans. Recognizing their fear of him, Jesus sent out his own light to reassure them, and gradually they disappeared back into their own dungeon darkness, satisfied with the intentions of this intruder on their eternal night, and he was able to proceed without their further interference.

So the Prince of Pax once more found himself alone. His only recourse seemed to be to surrender to the awesome mystery of this place and follow it wherever it would lead him while he gained the proper wisdom to resurrect with his humanity and life intact. He began to walk, but all he ever saw and all he ever felt was the same blank space in which he was now entrapped.

At first he deemed this situation a hearty challenge, a true test of his spirituality, and feeling absolutely no strictures by either time or space, he walked as far from his starting point as a month's time by his reckoning took him, yet still the landscape remained exactly the same. He then walked two, three, four, ten times that length of time, but all he ever experienced was the eternal sameness of this place. Finally, the repetition began to make his purpose waver, and he began walking slower and slower and slower, till that inevitable moment when he stopped and sat down to ponder his plight.

As he let his mind overtake his heart and feet, he suddenly felt flooded with the futility of what he was doing, and he was ashamed at the arrogance that had propelled him into this journey through the underworld. He had been ill prepared for it and could feel the sickening embrace of failure descend over him as the shadow of all his sorrows engulfed him. He felt the pathos of his own mortality, the helplessness of being alive when everything else was dead, the whole horror of his humanity.

So he began to tear at his many wounds of ego: his martyr's call, his delusions of Christhood, his obsessive belief in his chosen role, his monumental pride in claiming the heavens for his paternity. He ripped them all open and let them bleed into the darkness, as he washed the unlovingness out of himself and lay helpless and spent in the murk, sliding off into total unconsciousness, letting his diamond mind lose itself in sleep, for it served him not at all here.

When at last he awoke, he found himself lying in the lap of the ghostly Madonna he had first seen, for somehow he had managed to replace the dead replica of himself she had been holding earlier with his own highly weakened, but still alive, corpus. As he stirred in her lap to signal this transformation, she disappeared, and he was left in the thick darkness once again. However, her evanescent form had been enough to give Jesus his purpose back again, for she had been the first sign that he was no longer alone in his eternal sorrow at being lost.

Further, he also saw that he had somehow united his living and dead selves and now had only to find love to make his trinity complete. He understood that having once found love in the person of his elusive ghostly mother, he then had the possibility of returning live to the physical sphere. Springing to his suddenly eager feet, he resolved to wander, no matter how long it took him, until he found lost love. He began to walk and walk and walk for what seemed like years, decades, centuries, yet all he saw was the sameness of sameness and nothing else.

Finally, he stopped and sat down again, spent from his labor and its awful, aimless repetition, as his purpose drained and his self-loathing rose to replace it. But this time, instead of agonizing over his difficulties, he surrendered to them and was rewarded, shortly thereafter, with a sliver of light upon the horizon. He immediately leaned toward it and bathed his body and mind and heart and feet in it, and he felt their strength return in this sudden manifestation of hope. As he rose to pursue the light with his spirits greatly resurrected, he suddenly understood that he had found this path not with his feet nor with his head, but with his unconscious heart, and he knew now that it was through that confused and confusing organ he must travel if ever he wanted to rise from this Land of the Dead.

Eager to be free of his own darkness at last, he set out for the horizon, running at full speed. The light grew larger and larger and then totally enveloped him. He danced in its all-consuming glow, seeing no less than seven suns above him, blazing away in such unbearable intensity that it ultimately made the darkness seem inviting by comparison, and soon the withered figure of the Prince of Pax began to search for some shade.

But in this place, he soon found out, there was no darkness whatsoever, for the seven suns were positioned to shine everywhere. Even the long, dark landscape from which he had just emerged had already disappeared behind him so that he was consumed by light, and in its shimmering heat he could see a vague outline of a city begin to form. As his eyes grew accustomed to its wavering lines, so did his ears begin to pick up its discordant sound, a continually raucous cacophony that grew louder and louder until it matched the pitch of the heat, the two combining to overwhelm the senses, which were equally assaulted by a rancid rotting smell that pervaded everything.

As his vision sharpened ever more, he could see that this City of the Seven Suns was filled to overflowing with naked-fleshed people, millions upon millions of them all searching for some respite from the heat. The streets were scorched to such degree that no one could stand in one place, so that they all had to keep eternally moving, lifting their blistered feet high in the air with each tortured step, while coughing and spitting with that mad exertion in twisted, misshapen bodies aching to rest.

Though this great horde was obviously human, there was nothing but cruel suffering and self-hatred upon their pain-wrenched faces, as all of them continually bellowed their outrage and shame as well as their complete self-absorption and their total lack of love for any and all things, including themselves. Yet, despite all this, the newly awakened heart of Jesus opened to them with love, for if ever a place needed a manifestation of the Word, this was it. Uncomfortable as he was in these stultifying environs, he nevertheless raised his loving arms and exposed his great heart to all who wished to embrace them in this City of Neverending Light.

So great was the hunger here, however, that he barely escaped being swallowed alive, as everyone grabbed for his love and gave absolutely nothing in return, draining him quickly and completely of all except his naked essence, which now lay prey to this infernal eternal city. Save for his robe of air, Jesus soon found himself just like everyone else here, as the streets began to seep into his feet and the blaring monotony of this city's existence began to invade his mind, so that all he could feel was his own extreme discomfort.

This descent was duly acknowledged by the citizens all around him and brought with it a derisive chorus of insults and jeers, for his brief beneficence of love had been deeply resented: this was deemed a fine comeuppance in this peculiar place where the excesses of ego seemed to be carried to their ultimate extreme. Eventually, he was ignored in favor of everyone concentrating on his or her own misfortunes, and he fell ever deeper into himself. His magic was now totally gone, his heart emptied, and his mind consumed by pain as he sweltered in his robe and lifted high his burnt soles to cool them from the flaming street in this City of the Seven Suns, which, curiously, seemed to resemble Rome.

Drifting off into unconsciousness and dropping to the pavement, he awakened to the sizzling realization he had burnt his right ribcage beyond recognition. Leaping to his feet to perform the slow, high-foot fire dance of this place once again, he was indistinguishable from everyone else now in his self-absorption and resignation to a fate beyond his control.

A despair fell over him that was far deeper than any he had ever experienced before, for his labors seemed to lead him into ever more complex circumstances. He felt himself to be totally fragmented by all his failures, unable to save himself any longer, for his mind, heart, and feet had all been enflamed by his conceit of believing he could rise from the dead. So he hardened his soul and accepted his high-stepping lot, using all his resolve to stay himself from his own darkness to compensate for the all-consuming light here. Slowly he found an uncomfortable equilibrium through which he could survive, a thread of self-love that somehow made this place bearable. As he slowly moved over and over the same streets through the same bellowing herd and maddening crowd, he never ceased his search for love, for that gave him meaning; even if he never found it, it mattered not for he had purpose, and that was enough to keep him going until eternity.

But gradually his sense of purpose began to fade into the ceaseless monotony of his existence. As he felt himself fade into the shadeless obscurity of this place, he placed all his power in his waning heart, asking it for one droplet of love with which he could replenish himself in a last-gasp dance of light from within.

Though he invoked but a tiny flicker, it was enough to annoy numerous people around him, and they turned from their bellowed mutterings to vent their displeasure on him. This was all he needed to regain his strength, for he could, at last, see love in their hatred. So he loved them even more, and they responded with even greater revilement, threatening him physically if he should continue, and he turned that into love as well and grew even greater, for at last he had seen that the Word is truly everywhere.

He danced in rapturous joy at his discovery, for he had finally found love and knew it would never desert him again. He was now complete unto himself, a true Son of the Sun and Child of the Moon, very much male in his substance and yet open to his female within. As he danced, a single sun appeared in the sky as sign of this understanding, and the city cooled and the people complained about the relief and worried about what they would do with their time now, feeling that what they had been through hadn't been so bad after all. Though his dance could bring no smiles to the faces of these people of the seven suns, still it had brought great laughter to his own emotion-seared cheeks, and that was more than enough to heal him and make him whole.

Now he at last knew who he was, what he was about to do, and how he would do it, once he had risen from this Land of the Dead. In the light of the one sun that shone above him, he could see he was standing just above the surface of the planet, not quite on it but once again connected to it, and the City of the Seven Suns was not Rome but Jerusalem, now sitting quietly in the predawn. As he stared at its familiar contours, it changed once again, becoming long-lost Piscespuhr, misted in veils in the moonlight, and Jesus let out a great cry of delight, as his mind, heart, and feet knew their journey had come to an end.

Striding through the familiar wide streets and past the neatly terraced houses, the Prince of Pax headed straight for the palace of the Prince of Fishes, mounting its steps four at a time and marching down its mirrored hall until at last he came to the private chamber of the Monarch of the Dark. Only then did a touch of fear and doubt enter Jesus, but he knew exactly what he had to do. He opened the door to find the prince exactly as he had left him, lying deep in the throes of dying, his groin heavily bandaged, while numerous women silently and diligently attended to his wasted figure. Next to him was that same crowned cup out of whose mouth hung the same dead fish, its gilled face a picture of torment and desolation.

Although he stood for several minutes of uneasy transport in the doorway, no one acknowledged the presence of Jesus, ignoring both his discomfort and ill ease in the face of their own tasks and suffering. Though it was all he could do not to turn and run, he stood his ground firmly on very human feet as his mind churned and his great heart opened up to search for love in the pathos and misery here, for this small group seemed to replicate the entire human race with all its depredation, degradation, self-loathing, and pain. Jesus wished to cry out, to embrace them all, to take them deep within, for he understood their anguish to the very depths of his being. His healing instinct pleaded with him to throw himself on them to absorb their agony and to accept his own death through them—to be swallowed alive by the darkness so that the aged Prince of Fishes might live.

And that surely would have happened had he not known that love was somewhere here. He found it in his own draw toward destruction and his laughable desire for martyrdom, and he became full of himself once again as he stared straight into the eye of the dying prince and leveled all his power within against the anguish of the human universe that lay there. He asked him a question in a voice that revealed not a whit of the horror and terror he felt within but instead all of the love and laughter he felt without. "What ails you?" said he.

As soon as those words were spoken, the thousands of candles there flickered out and a total darkness descended upon the room. The young Prince of Peace wavered for a moment on his mission, feeling the cold clam-hand of failure upon him, but this feeling quickly passed as he felt the strength of his own love and the knowledge that it would transcend all situations. Moments later, a great light permeated the room, revealing no one else save the two princes, each suddenly healed of their doubts and pain, both as radiant and aglow as when they had first met so very long ago.

The Monarch of the Dark unwrapped his bandages and flexed his arms and legs before doing a spry little jig to test his rejuvenated body, after which he graced his healer with a broad grin and clapped him handsomely on the shoulders. Jesus, feeling his heart deeply touched by the warmth of this strange and curious being, smiled in return, for even though this prince was his opposite in every way, he was also an extraordinary teacher, and it was through his fearful lessons that the Son of the Sun had, at last, learned love.

All this was spoken silently between the two regal beings, as they embraced and thanked each other for the wisdom bestowed, even though both knew that they would do battle again, for they were masters of opposing worlds. As dawn suddenly showed its glorious face through the windows of the palace, Jesus bid his benefactor/malefactor a twinkling good-bye and left to see if he could stand once more in the light of day.

As soon as he left the confines of the house of the Prince of Fishes, he found himself standing in the main marketplace of Jerusalem. People were staring at him, wondering at this wondrous creature, who was touching himself to see if he was actually alive again. And he was.

Breathing deeply of the air and drawing it into his lungs, he raised his arms in praise of the holy trinity of life, love, and death. The most joyous laughter was upon his lips, for somehow he had survived all his lessons and had resurrected his damaged heart. Now, at the age of thirty years by earthly reckoning, he was at last able to begin his fabled ministry, and once more, it was the very beginning of things.

Revelation

The reader is invited to contemplate the inner and outer temples of Christianity and to search for the Grail that lies within all who search for illumination here with their hearts.

Christianity's great genius has been its ability to synthesize, since it is based on the teachings of a master who taught that love draws everything together here. The highly organized religion that it was to become was ultimately able to unite the One God/one self of the Hebrews, the moral imperative and mystery of the Persians, the grounded monumentality of the Egyptians, the resurrection mystery of the Greeks, and the order and organization of the Romans into one all-encompassing explanation of the unexplainable. This synthesis would allow the postulants of Christianity many powerful avenues to give spiritual expression to their own longing to embrace the divine, insuring its continuance by constantly making it deal with its diversity. The many faces of Christianity have thus changed mightily down through the near two millennia of its existence, and because of that, it has followed many contradictory pathways in its attempt to unify the isolated spiritual God-Self of the Hebrews with the larger world around it through a singular, highly identifiable deity-inspired figure who had also tried to do the same.

In the beginning there was the Word, and in the end there was the Word and the "ShadoWord," and both shone like fire to all who heard them. Though the Master spoke the Word, most of his adherents heard it in reverse, and so the ShadoWord came to stand in its stead, for such was the legacy of that Logos that before it could be ultimately understood, first its other side would have to be made manifest, so that from out of its own darkness, its pure light could eventually be spun.

If the Word was love, then the ShadoWord was "love conquers." Twixt these two sentiments lies an ocean, for love alone is an all-encompassing state that needs nothing round it to make it lesser or greater than it is, while love conquers is an aggressive assertion of that statehood, more intent on devouring obstacles to its continuing manifestation than living peacefully in its own light.

For three years, the rabbi Jesus preached his ministry throughout Judaea, gathering both friends and enemies in most provocative fashion. A confrontation with those in power was inevitable, as he gave himself up to the people's call for self-destruction through martyrdom and that ultimate test of personal magic: transcendence over the finality of Death and a linkage between the human and the divine.

But Jesus was a master trickster, an illusionist of the highest order. There were a thousand meanings behind each of his well-chosen words, for in his secrecy he had fashioned two coteries of followers: one masculine, filled with the delusions of the patriarchy and its call for spirituality through might and reason, and one feminine/masculine, with its greater attunement to the mysteries of the larger universe and its fuller understanding of the ideals of love. Consequently, his teachings came to be divided into their exoteric, or outer, elements and their esoteric, or inner, components. The former followed a path of One God/one self and the earthly appearance of one God-Self to unify the two, while the latter pursued a path of collective or higher-consciousness awareness. Portions of the two would intersect and portions of the two would be forever disparate, giving continual confusion to the subsequent adaptation and reinterpretation of his earthly message in the millennia to follow.

The Word and the ShadoWord, then, demark those two lines, for inherent in the former is a total spiritual state that needs naught but a human heart to house it, while inherent in the latter is an entire warrior ethic that looks at life in terms of submission and conquest and at death as the ultimate failure, save for a heroic or martyred end. Therein lies much of the metaphysical confusion that the White West has experienced in its incorporation of the ideas and ideals of a master who had transcended mortality, for a warrior credo dictates strict codes of behavior and belief so that its various postulants do not do excessive injury to one another in their aggressive expression.

Thus was the spirituality of love incarnate swiftly institutionalized by the shadow of the Word, so that it could properly house a warrior elite of fathers who, not being able to create sons from their own seed, had to concern themselves with the orderly passage of their memories through a rigid edifice that would continue to honor its dead via its unchanging rituals and rites. The "church of the material" that they subsequently created to celebrate the conquering power of love had little to do with the teachings of the master mage in whose memory it was erected. In order to maintain itself, it soon found it had to delve deeper and deeper into the gross physical domain so that it could protect its lands and wealth, and it became as the world it was trying to transcend: lost in the illusion of the shadow of its logos.

JUDAS

In exoteric tradition, twelve disciples were chosen to gather round the Prince of Light. Of them, the least understood is Judas Iscariot, who played a pivotal role in the Race of Resurrection, which, like all true mysteries, remains veiled in the sensationalism of its outer wrap.

Judas was the only one of the twelve who was larger than human, for he had been on the planet for thousands and thousands of years without the relief of death, an immortal mortal, cursed by circumstance to wander from one age to the next because of a dark pact he had made with a previous Christed spirit. Once a mighty sorcerer/priest among the Atlantean Semites, he had exercised his considerable powers with an unloving heart. When a Christed spirit appeared among his people, he challenged it to grant him immortality, to allow him to touch upon the divine on Earth, and this odd gift was given him, much to his everlasting regret. He became the original "wandering Jew," passing down from century to century through the long story of civilization with the curse of endless life upon him, his body forever metamorphosizing from old age to young manhood and back again to decrepitude. He was eternally denied the magic of childhood and youth and the forgetfulness of reincarnation, in an endless chain of experience without the innocence of new beginnings.

This being who had mocked a divinity was made to suffer mightily for that act. Yet in the process, he was placed upon a most unusual path of illumination, for he was made to breathe the mortal air of Earth as an immortal in order to see that the divine and the human are one.

By the time he received dream-word that the universal Christ-force was once more preparing to enter the body of a planetary soul, Judas was more than ready for his coming, for his heart had been opened to his immortal humanity and his sense of self had been set free from its earlier narrow strictures. Using his powers, he found a cave in the remote southern Himalayas in India where he would meet the two conduits for that force, Jesse, the Child of the Moon, and Joshua, the Son of the Sun. So he was able to help and heal and to make into one the two that came to him and to aid their combined figure on his journey back homeward through a world choked on its unlovingness and drenched in the sorrow of its humanity.

Once this was accomplished, the wandering Jew transformed himself for the last time, slipping into the body of someone who drunkenly slept and had left his corpus unguarded, allowing Judas to send that soul back up into the ethers so that he could claim one last human body to finish out his endless curse. The body he chose was one that was riddled with conflicts, one Judas Iscariot, the son of a sicarius, a member of a knife-wielding sect of Judaean Jews who saw themselves as the avengers of the Lord, sworn as they were to expel the presence of Rome from their midst through violent personal confrontation. This assassin priesthood was so dedicated to purity through the letting of blood that it eventually showed little discrimination in its fervor, dispatching both chosen and unchosen alike in its all-consuming self-righteousness.

A small, red-haired man, Judas was destined to become one of the holy dozen of early Christendom, the only member of that group who was not from Galilee and, therefore, an outsider. He became their treasurer and swiftly established himself as a most undependable fellow by creating illusions round the occasional disappearance of their mutual funds. This caused suspicion and doubt to be cast on him by all save those with the illumination to really see him, the Master and his most adept pupil, John the Diviner, he of the Gospel of Saint John the Divine. When the Master's ministry dwindled down to its last days, he gathered his apostles-to-be round him at his cave upon the Mount of Olives outside Jerusalem. There he told them that the end of his earthly ministry was near, but it was only Judas and John the Diviner who could see what he was actually saying through their illumined eyes, for they were the only two of the twelve who had received his inner, esoteric teachings.

The Son of the Sky secretly told Judas that the upcoming events would be so trying on his own time that he would need every moment to accomplish what he wished. Therefore, in order to buy an extra two days, a betrayal plot would have to be enacted so that instead of being arrested at some random hour, a specific time could be set up, ensuring that he would be well-prepared for his seizure and imprisonment. The son of the sicarius readily agreed to his part in this deception, for though his name would be forever besmirched for this act, it was still a small price to pay for his final release from mortal immortality.

There was no need for the Prince of Pax to enact the prophesied drama of crucifixion upon his own body, for he still had secret work to do on Earth in firmly establishing his esoteric teachings here. But since the ShadoWord dictated that he best Death in a race and show humanity its divinity through his transcendence, Jesus chose a substitute who bore a superficial resemblance to himself. This man knew that he would be dying not for the sins of humanity but for its ignorance in not recognizing its own divinity, and so he agreed to the duplicity, recognizing the Master for the master trickster he was and making this personal sacrifice to become more closely bonded with him on a soul level.

All, then, was in place, when the Master reentered Jerusalem and made preparation for his own inner temple and outer church, as his chosen twelve gathered round him in the upper room of a house owned by one of his followers for their last Passover feast together. There, after washing the feet of his disciples and settling who should sit down beside him, the Son of the Sun/Child of the Moon announced that one of their number would betray him.

At this prearranged accusation, Judas left to finalize his presumed perfidy, while the others all sat in shock as their awesome Prince then made his last magical gesture, offering them the wine of his blood, which was secretly drugged, and the bread of his body. Afterward, he led them out to the Garden of Gethsemane. They followed him in morbid procession, all but John the Diviner unable to grasp what was happening, for despite his powers Jesus seemed to have encouraged his betrayal and was doing nothing to stop the inevitability of his cruel death.

As the Son of the Sky fell into prayer, each of the eleven who had served him for three long years dropped off into unconsciousness from the potioned wine they had drunk. While they were consumed with their own nightmares of betrayal, the substitute Jesus appeared and the original Master Runner stole away into the night. With that, Jesus was freed from the demands of his earthly role, save for his resurrection three days later, and was able now to pursue the Word in full force among those secret few who had the illumination to understand it.

Sometime later, Judas appeared with a band of soldiers, hefting both torches and weapons. Seeing that the substitution had been successfully made, he kissed the ersatz Jesus as the sign of who he was and watched as that martyr was seized and carried off for trial. Meanwhile, the eleven, all unaware save for John the Diviner that that was not their master because of their drugged state, allowed their combined sorrows to descend upon them and wept most bitterly at their assumed loss.

His part in the drama complete, Judas was at last allowed to rejoin the illumination whence he had come, and with the Son of the Sky's own blessing of death upon him, he hanged himself and escaped from the world of air into the ethers, free at last from his tainted immortality to become human once again. Though his name would be entwined forevermore with treachery and deceit, his soul would not, for he had acted out of an illumined eye and a body not his own. His sole betrayal was to the illusion of the ShadoWord and its demand for a human entity to conquer Death, even at the price of truth.

THE INNER TEMPLE

While an outer church was created to house the fantasies unleashed by the transcendental magic of Death's defeat, it was his secret inner temple that truly carried the message of the new Master Runner's stay here. The inner temple was based on a four-step progression of faith, belief, illumination, and the Unyielding Light, a process that would take many lifetimes to complete for all who chose to follow this path toward enlightenment.

This, then, was the Master's master plan: that a temple of truth stand inside a church of illusion to ultimately reveal the Word as he had truly spoken it. The church, with its papal authority and rigid orthodoxies and warrior spirit and exoteric secrets, would be the manifestation of the father principle with its egoistic concerns of power and immortality, since that is the patriarchy's vision of spirit and matter. The temple, with its divine mysteries, ever-flowing and ever-changing form, and esoteric secrets would be the manifestation of the mother principle and would remain hidden in the heart of humanity until that time when the two halves of humankind could equally accept one another and allow the world to fully flower under their joint auspices.

JOHN THE DIVINER

Of the twelve original apostles, only John the Diviner was entrusted with carrying on the mystery of the inner temple. The others, save for Judas, would be the cornerstones for the outer apostolic traditions of the church, but Jesus recognized that John had a sufficiently developed inner sense of self to penetrate beyond his exoteric teachings and, accordingly, taught him privately.

When this former fisherman from Galilee had completed his secret studies under the tutelage of the Son of the Sky, the Master gave him an initiation into the secrets of the temple, showing him immortality through mortal eyes. John recorded this event in his own Christian litany, the Gospel according to Saint John, using the name of Lazarus to identify himself.

In ancient Egyptian rites of initiation, in a magic ceremony usually reserved for males about to be inducted into the high priesthood, the initiate would allow his master to place his body in a sarcophagus for several days. He would spend that time dancing with the dead, his body suspended in a dream state of neither wake nor sleep, with all its life force muted to the point of nonexistence. During this time, the initiate would experience a reunion with his higher bodies—the astral, etheric, and mental—and he would be given access to the information therein, a process totally denied most mortal souls constrained to the laws of the physical plane. When the initiate finally returned to his body at the end of that period, he would have made profound connection with the various worlds connected to the earthly realm; once having done that, he would have continual access to them the rest of his conscious life. This was no casual feat, and many an initiate lost his path back to his body following this rite and was forced to abandon it to the frozen fingers of Death because of his unpreparedness for this amazing journey.

With the Son of the Sky as his master, John the Diviner underwent this very same rite at the home of his sisters in Bethany, allowing his body to be entombed within a rock and wrapped in burial clothes as he had been instructed. There in the darkness, his spirit rose to contemplate his own heavens, and he saw all that would transpire twixt him and his fellow disciples. He spoke to the Christ-spirit within, which showed him all that would come to pass for thousands of years hence. As much as he could remember he brought back with him, which became the basis for the Bible's Book of Revelation.

When he returned, the Prince of Peace rolled back the stone to his tomb and commanded him to come forth. To the amazement of his sisters, family, and friends, he did, and he was very much alive. Though this was yet another miracle ascribed to the Son of the Sky, it was actually magic of an entirely different order, for now the Master had a male disciple who was on the same high plane as he, and he knew the Word would not pass with his own passing but would live on in the writing of this mortal who had been shown immortality through illumination.

CRUCIFIXION & CRUCI-FICTIONS

With that preparation, all was set for the finality of the Master's ministry when he rode into Jerusalem for his last week on Earth. Though that week would be recorded in great detail for posterity's subsequent religious rumination, nothing in it happened as it seemed, for there were actually two tales that were acted out during that momentous seven-day span. One would be the basis for a church wherein a holy man was martyred and crucified and rose from the dead to show that love conquers all. The other would be the basis for a temple wherein a holy trickster avoided both martyrdom and crucifixion and disappeared into life to show that love *is* all—the very foundation of life on Earth.

After the substitution of the martyr for the Master was made in the Garden of Gethsemane while the disciples slept following their last supper together, the Son of the Sky slipped away and adopted a disguise as a journeyman from Cyrene. He called himself Simon and invented a family and a life to go with his new name so that he could follow the progress of the mock-Christ from an anonymous vantage point.

At his subsequent judgment before the Roman procurator of Judaea, the martyr remained silent as per his instructions, and of all the disciples, only John and "the rock upon whom the church would be built," Simon called Peter, witnessed his trial, the others having fled into their own sorrow. John knew the identity of the martyr, while Peter had already denied his master three times the previous night as he was told he would and was not about to deny him a fourth time, even if he could see past his overwhelming emotions and guilt that the man before him was not who he seemed to be. Later, on the long walk to Calvary, it was the Master himself who took the cross from the stumbling martyr and buoyed his sagged spirit with the light of his love, healing him so that his wounds would not be as painful as they seemed, nor his humiliation as demeaning.

For the entire nine-hour ordeal upon the cross, the Son of the Sky passed back and forth through the crowd, sending out his Unyielding Light whenever he saw the torture upon the body of his look-alike becoming excessively agonizing. Finally, the spear of a Roman centurion named Longinus ended that poor man's travail and sent him sailing off on bloodied wings to his own heavens.

When the body of the martyred look-alike was brought down from its perch, wrapped in linen and embalmed with oils before being entombed nearby, it was the Master who cast a time-spell over the soldiers on guard so that they would be frozen in the moment and would not see him and his small temple band spirit away the deceased's corpse for a proper burial on the Mount of Olives. Thus was the way prepared for the discovery of its absence and his subsequent seeming mastery over that Old Master Athlete, Death. The Master then assumed the marks of the stigmata upon his own body so that he could reappear briefly before his remaining apostles as a sign of their belief and faith, if not their illumination, and fulfill the prophecy of his transcendence over the forces of antilife, before disappearing to do his real work upon this plane of never-ending illusions.

THE GRAIL

There is a legend about a fallen angel who dared to challenge the heavens for dominion before suffering a swift expulsion from the empyrean for the audacity of that act. As the tumbling angel plummeted earthward to the chthonic halls beneath the surface of this planet, its emerald crown toppled off its head and was rescued in midflight by a contingent of seraphim hovering nearby for that purpose. The seraphim then reshaped the crown into that of a peacock-festooned cup and let it drift to Earth, where it ultimately found its way to a supper of lasting fame, the final meal in which the Son of the Sky bid farewell to his inner ring of outer disciples by announcing his betrayal. After dismissing his betrayer to fulfill his prophecy, he secretly placed a sleeping potion inside that crown-turned-cup and asked all to drink from it, declaring the wine within to be his own blood. Drink they did, only to fall prey many hours later to its delayed power, during which time the Master switched places with the martyr and vanished into his own intense night.

Acting out of a high-hearted mischief, the Master performed his farewell trick with just a magical cup and the slightest of sleights of hand to give his disciples their final unheard message: that instead of searching for the illusions behind his truths, they should have been looking for the truths behind his illusions, for therein lay his true Word. Save for John the Diviner, however, this was not heard at all by any of the outer ring of disciples, and they went on to build an edifice based on their patriarchal fantasies of immortality. In their obsession with that singular facet of the Master, they helped create an institution that would largely ignore its founder's message of life and love in favor of his illusory conquest of the third member of that trinity, Death. Thus, the apostles turned the Master into a deity of the dead, and in their passion for emulatory immortality, they reduced their divinely inspired teacher into a shadowed figure of sorrow, with their successors going on to build great tomblike churches to celebrate humanity's abject fear of the unknown and the immeasurable.

The magical cup that helped bring all this about became a subsequent symbol of illusion and mystery to both the worlds of exoteric and esoteric Christendom. It seemed to hold the key to immortality within its mystic frame, and its quest has provided Western literature with some of its finest secular fantasies.

At the end of the Master's final feast, following the exit of his drugged apostles-to-be, one of his inner core, a man named Joseph of Arimathea, a respected member of the Sanhedrin, or council of male elders of the Hebrews, walked upstairs to where the twelve had just been and grabbed the cup from their still-laden table as a souvenir of that most significant event. Cleaving to his prize throughout the tumult of the following day, Joseph found himself at that sad

Friday's end standing at the foot of the cross, gazing up at the dying mock-Christ, when suddenly a spear came hurtling overhead and pierced that suffering soul in the side, allowing him to take leave of his earthly agony.

Joseph of Arimathea immediately held the cup to the wound, catching the dripping blood of the substitute martyr and, in so doing, transformed that legendary vessel from mere goblet to Grail. Not only had it been party to the illusion of the Master's sleep-inducing final feast, but now it bore direct witness to the decided mortality of the mock-Christ, whose ordinary blood belied the extraordinary circumstances in which his end had been fashioned. Gathering the cup and the spear as well as several other mementos of that momentous occasion, Joseph unconsciously proclaimed himself the first bishop of the inner temple, for he had collected all the relics of its basic mystery and made himself their immediate keeper.

Asking for the body of the martyr after its descent from the cross, Joseph, along with the Master's inner circle, buried it as he had been instructed. As legend has it, he then found himself physically imprisoned for forty years, but to his illumined eye, the time passed in the snore of a sleep-filled night.

Following his release, Joseph and his high and holy band were allowed to leave Jerusalem and travel the ill-charted face of Europe, which they did, permitting their hallowed objects to grace a wide swath of land. After many adventures, in which the relics played a major part, Joseph and his heart-filled crew finally reached the shores of Greater Britain, there to settle on the island of Avalon, where the first temple was constructed in order to house the relics of the Master's illusionary contest with Death.

After Joseph passed from this plane round the year 85 A.Z. (after the year 0), the guardianship of the Grail and spear passed on to his descendants who, in turn, passed them on to enchanted monarchs, who built wondrous castles to encase their power. Ever so gradually, however, all of it—guardians, Grail, and spear—receded from the physical plane into the ethers.

Initially, the relics were placed on public display for any of the temple's pilgrims who infrequently found Britain's shores, but as orthodox Christianity began to invade those isles the holy objects of its unorthodox counterpart began to fade from view. At last they joined the other side of visibility and disappeared into other dimensions, so that only those who knew them to be there could see them. And there they still sit, perhaps to be discovered by a future world that has truly learned to feel the love that can see them; then again perhaps not, for this is, after all, a planet of choice, and all things are possible here.

In the wake of the rise and fall and resurrection of this Son of the Sky, two opposing edifices came into being. One was a temple that payed homage to the humanity that was the underside of the god who housed them, and the other was a church that saw only the deity and not his other aspects. Together, the two would come to be a totality of their opposite parts, one half hidden and one half far more visible than anything else on the horizon in the West for a long, long stretch of the enchanted and oppressive Kingdom of Come's first two thousand years of earthly existence.

And with the Master's passing into the anonymity of ordinary existence, and the founding of his outer church and inner temple, it was once more, as it constantly is in this world of the eternal present, the very beginning of things.

○

T H E
PROFANED
HEART OF TIME

Part Four

CHAPTER TWELVE

Age of Light/Age of Darkness 0-1000 A.Z.

The reader is invited to enter
the first thousand years of our modern world and experience
the profound rifts between the Word and the ShadoWord, the
flesh and the spirit, hierarchies and heretics, Western and
Eastern empires, a third face of the One God, and the com-
ing of Doomsday to once more end the world so that it could
begin anew.

Israel's idea of resurrection had always encompassed its entire self,
so its ruling authority was very resistant to the idea that one of its
own could possibly hold the secret of spiritual immortality for everyone. Thus, when a presumed savior did make his appearance and
begin rousing the rabble to renounce their chosenness for his own
vague Kingdom of Come, he was presenting a great threat to Israel's
own collective sense of having been singularly and separately chosen as the Earth's most special people.

  After three years of his continually provocative presence, a confrontation between Christian Judaism and Mosaic Judaism was
inevitable, for if this rabbi were really a manifestation of the heavens,
then Moses' avenging fire god of the flaming bush, YaHWeH, would

be something else entirely, and Israel's whole empyrean base would be shaken to its core. The existence of each faction, in essence, denied the true existence of the other. So the authoritative elders of Israel were forced to condemn Jesus as a renegade rabbi, and he was handed to Rome to die a political death upon a Roman cross, that symbol of rigid straight-line synthesis. In passing judgment on a man who claimed to be the very soul of Israel, an uncrowned King of the Jews, the elders had passed similar judgment on themselves and their nation, sentencing it to its own curious pursuit of resurrected immortality without a physical body of land to contain it in the wake of the events that followed the spectacular passing of this claimant to the title of *Rex Yehudi*.

The ego supreme of the ruling hierarchy of Rome felt little love for the similarly egoistic nation of the Hebrews, for the two dwelt in the same sphere of individual self-importance and neither wished to accommodate the other's exclusive sense of "I." And so Judaea was allowed to crumble inward, and it did so with a heady passion, as messiahs began to appear in droves, some of them attracting tens of thousands of people desperate to touch upon their own divinity and not particularly choosy about who showed them how.

In 68 A.Z., the Christian-Jewish community left Jerusalem en masse, moving northward and westward, thereby uprooting its home base and pulling it far closer to Western Europe and its eventual citadel there. This act of separation, much in the earlier manner of Abraham and family, would establish Christianity as a religion of its own, as its strong Judaic root gradually got swallowed into different ceremony and structure, thanks to a different focus on the same spiritual obsession of immortality.

Jerusalem fell shortly after the Christian Jews crossed over into the realm of continuance. With its passing, and the destruction once again of the temple, went the spiritual base of the God-granted home of the ancient Hebrews. Israel would once more become a state of mind, an orphan with no place to call its true home, as YaHWeH opened his name to a sometimes-used form, JeHoVaH, and receded from Earth to become a totally invisible presence, never again to so directly assert his will through a chosen vessel. Miracle and divine interference on a mass scale would have no place in the material schematics of the West to come. The Father of the separated self now separated himself from the inevitable consequences of having been brought to Earth by the Hebrews. Of the infinite faces of divinity, the "distant divine" would be the face, in less self-righteous form, that the West would choose as its own to give mortal reflection to what it felt was the true nature and destiny of humankind: to pass uncomfortably through the trials of this world so that it might be judged fit enough to live in passive splendor in the higher one.

Yet another epoch ended and yet another epoch began, as the Hebrews were now asked to act out their lessons of separation to their fullest. They slid most uncomfortably into the exoteric Christian epoch, taking on the role of the hated father of the loved son to see if their specialness would allow them to survive that most debilitating of paternal-filial fantasies. Without an earthly territory to call its own, Israel was once again a bodiless nation and would continue in that stateless state for most of the next two millennia, for a long winter was about to start for this country of the mind that counted its seasons in thousands of years.

SACRED LIBRARIANS

Since the overall theme of the Fifth Civilization is opening up to everyone their fifth e-zones, those of communication, the role of "sacred librarian" has been of paramount importance here. From the first shaman and storyteller figures who gave life to the invisible world of the spirit, the sacred librarian has acted as both a guardian and a channel for the greater story of humanity. As our disunited civilization has progressed, however, our sacred librarians have followed a similar pattern of fragmentation and disconnection, clinging to the wisdom of a singular story or set of stories and denying and denigrating all other librarians who choose a different view of the divine.

The many librarian wars that have ensued, particularly since the introduction of the One God, show the high level of intolerance this calling has come to represent. It is here that those teachers of the separated self, the Hebrews, once again set important precedent, through the condensation of their library into one holy book, the Bible, which, in turn, would be the basis for the One God/One Book/one self trinity at the core of subsequent Western civilization. Through this book, the Hebrews became creators of spiritual history, and for being party to its creation, Israel was granted continuance long after its physical country had scattered and dispersed, testimony, perhaps, to the Bible's unearthly power as a book of immortality.

By 300 B.Z., the full tri-part text of their One God/One Book library was complete. The early books of Moses, the midstory of the Kings and Prophets, and the final tales of the Psalms, Proverbs, Songs, Lamentations, Names, and Chronicles all came together to make up a testament to the power of the librarian here, allowing the Hebrew imagination to augment that with commentaries and commentaries upon commentaries to give secular complement to the divine blueprint of their central masterwork.

Their basic book of Father, fathers, and sons would be amended by four more tales of the One Father and the One Son, epistolary comments, and a book of revelatory prophecy, making sixty-six books in all, along with a whole new host of sacred librarians to reinterpret these Old and New Testaments to the presence of the divine upon the planet. As such, these new sacred librarians would be given unprecedented power in the temporal world, and would show the same absolute intolerance for any word that did not pay homage to their rarified position as ultimate arbiters of faith and knowledge here.

THE CHRIST & THE ANTICHRIST

With the introduction to the earthly sphere of the idea of the Christ, a being who could teach humanity how to touch upon its divine aspects, there came a second figure to balance off the purity and the goodness of the immortal Savior: the Antichrist. Its purpose was to create an illusory draw away from the power of the Master and to offer its own darkness as a gross alternative to illumination.

In order for the Light of the Christ to exist, then, it needed this antithetical force so that it could do battle for the soul of humanity.

Thus the two became very much complementary entities, for neither could truly exist without the other, since if there were no darkness, there would be no need for the Light. Instead of the Judaic idea that evil is but the shadow side of existence, and that it emanates from the same source as good, the early sacred librarians of the church posited a far more dualistic universe, acknowledging the destructive side of humanity as an aberration tinged with sin and perdition rather than recognizing it as part of the much larger process of creation and continuance.

Taking the Hebrew concept of Satan, a figure of limited power, they upped that entity's position in their heavenly diagram considerably and gave it its own title, the "Devil," creating, in essence, two deities, one in heaven and one deep in another earthly dimension. Thoroughly male in its physical and spiritual makeup, with horns and cloven hooves and a great swinging phallus, the Devil was the product of the worst imaginings of the patriarchal Christians, who first conjured up its existence as mythic manifestation of their own secret fears of self.

However, what they did not realize in their creation of a force to counterbalance the glory of their Lord was that they had taken the goat/human/god of the earlier Dionysus resurrection figure and divided it into its separate parts, breaking it down into a triune of impossibly different components that had no desire to resolve one another's conflicts save by doing fierce battle—winner-take-all—in the contest between god and goat for the soul of human in between. Instead of recognizing the trinity of creature, human, and deity as evidence of the unity of existence, they chose to see the divine order of earthly life as having its various parts in disconcert, at war with one another. Because of this, they created a warrior religion round the peaceful teachings of the Prince of Light, failing to recognize the goat inside the human inside the god, for all they saw were the separated levels of existence here and not its unified totality.

In this exoteric Christian trinity of separate creatures, the Devil is the goat, taking on the guise of that beastly entity as symbol of the material excesses of humanity and its continual draw toward degeneration and animal depravity. The Devil's sphere is Hell, and that creature represents destruction without any thought of re-creation for it is an end unto itself, unloving and uncaring with no interests save its own. The Devil represents humanity's selfishness and self-centeredness incarnate, ego unchecked. In the exoteric Christian schema, then, destruction is a dead end: it does not offer its own elements of darkness for the purpose of enlightenment.

By not recognizing the destruction and/or re-creation principles in the continual circular, spiraling cycle of healing and growth upon this planet, the early exoteric Christian fathers created a theologic system that was destined to do continual battle with itself and everything around it. It did not think in terms of synthesis, or bringing things together, but rather in terms of conquest. The Word of the Master, "Love is all," was readily altered into the ShadoWord of his disciples, "Love conquers all," and it wasn't long before the concept of conquest vastly overshadowed the concept of love in its official creed. The Prince of Peace, then, eventually became a crusader of the soul, armed with a cross-hilted sword of light to do endless struggle with the many manifestations of his adversary: the Devil, the Antichrist, the Darkness. By naming evil and giving it cosmic form, early exoteric Christianity created a multileveled scapegoat for humanity's baser impulses, and by making that creature inflexible in its consciousness with no capacity for growth at all, they doomed their own consciousness of good and evil to similarly rigid lines, with little capacity to see where the two meet and reflect one another.

Having defined the light through the darkness and the darkness through the light, and positing that the two could never meet save as victor and vanquished, the sacred librarians of exoteric Christianity also divided all human activity into matters of the spirit and matters of the flesh, with no thought of ever synthesizing the two in celebration. By refusing to see the spirituality in the goat aspects of humanity, they redefined Western consciousness quite radically from its earthy pagan and Judaic foundations. And by placing a stigma on pleasure and a premium on pain, they caused a goodly amount of confusion, guilt, and self-denial down through the centuries for many who thought they were following the one and only path of the Master. Part of their basic humanity had been judged as foul and evil, and the great celebration of life and love that was at the core of the Son of the Sky's teachings was all but eliminated.

Exoteric Christianity was consequently transformed from a turn-the-other-cheek call for pax and soul integration to a clarion cry for endless battle between the forces of light and dark as interpreted by the orthodox authority of the patriarchal keepers of the faith. The goat/devil, once an integral part of all humanity, was now labeled as its adversary, and the sphere of the flesh, which that creature represented, became the uneasy province of temptation rather than an avenue of spiritual expression.

The second part of the goat/human/god triune was represented by the human Jesus. He, too, was both ignored and transformed from a passive-fist, god-fearing communard into the avenging angelic force of all the Western *isms*—militarism, capitalism, and imperialism—in an extraordinary reversal of his basic message. The human Jesus—the pastor of peace, the drinker of wine, the proselytizer against property, the breaker of bread, the litanizer of love—was all but swallowed by his trickster illusion of transcending Death, for it was his demise rather than his life that enflamed the imagination of most of his future followers. He would come to be remembered for the pain and suffering of his spectacular ending rather than for the joy of his living essence. The orthodoxy that would surround the celebration of that essence would focus on his most gloomy aspects, creating an entombed religion of dark cathedrals and dirge chants that would commemorate the crucified spectre of his passage from mortality to immortality but would do little to explore the humanity of the being who took that awesome leap.

Instead of explaining life through the teachings of Jesus, orthodox Christianity would come to be an explicator of Death, an end-of-the-world religion. It would offer its adherents no particular peace on Earth, but a promise of greater rewards in the beyond, should they but conform to the edicts of the authorities who were the intermediaries between the world of matter and *the world that truly mattered:* the eternity of immortality.

So it was that both goat and human disappeared into the god that was the Master, and so it was that only the deity was recognized for

who he truly was, with the other elements of his race against Death
all but forgotten by the officially sanctioned interpretation of his coming and going. So it was, too, that a church was built that came to
embody all the same ironies and contradictions surrounding the
mystery of the Master. This church turned into the antithesis of what
its founding teacher had taught as it progressed down through the
centuries, metamorphosizing itself from the spiritual keeper of the
memory of its Son to that Son's all-powerful representative on Earth,
a bastion of wealth and presence and authority. In its confusions over
the material and the spiritual, and over the goat and the human and
the god that made up the triune of life, the church suffered endless
schisms, attracting both the high and the low alike to its slowly forming halls of power, while its orthodoxy grew ever more conservative
and self-serving.

Thus, an unbridgeable gulf was ushered in by the Christian
epoch between the various unintegrated dualities that make up the
human animal. That gulf has been part of the ongoing story of Western humanity's fragmentation of all its separated parts through divine
intervention in order, perhaps, that they may all one day unite in a
far greater understanding of all our different components, after those
components have been satisfactorily isolated, experienced, and reintegrated into our larger whole.

At the time of Jesus' appearance, the great majority on Earth were
not ready to hear the true message of their Master Teacher—that of
the integration of heaven and Earth—for this next evolutionary step
upward from the separated One God/one self of Judaism had not yet
been given a strong enough base through a sufficient planetary host.
Christianity, instead, wound up serving as a more accessible form of
Judaism, less intellectual and more emotional in its appeal but ultimately with the same ongoing teaching of learning about unity
through separation, before the two could somehow be synthesized.

In its celebratory mystery of the mass, a ceremony where wine
and wafer are offered as magic symbol that the blood and the body
of Christ are within everyone's physical and spiritual reach, the
church was able to touch the secret heart of a wide range of suppli-
cants eager to begin the process of learning how to feel self directly

through the divine. By making sacred many of life's commitments through the seven sacraments of baptism, confirmation, holy communion, marriage, confession, holy orders for priests, and extreme unction for the dying, it also fulfilled a sense of magic and mystery and deep spirit—as well as chosenness—that Judaism had never been able to foster outside of its own people, which quickly gave Christendom the heartfelt imagination of the West for its own.

TWO ISRAELS

From the time of humanity's first etheric presence upon the planet, Israel has been symbol of its larger unity, a world-nation predicated on divine principle where both the divine and the human could live in harmonious acknowledgment of the glory of each other. The Israel of ancient and modern history has been but a dim unrealized shadow of that concept, with the father principle of separation and self unlinked to the mother principle of the connection and collectivity of all beings who share this planet.

The recorded story of Israel after the second destruction of the temple in 70 A.Z. focuses on those who went east from Judaea to join the established mid-Eastern communities of earlier exiles, there to add to the chronicles of separation that would mark the spiritual continuance of displaced Israel. However, some also went west, to serve as teachers and healers and builders. These wanderers would disappear into the larger Israel of the planet, disavowing their heritage of separation so that they could serve and assimilate into the much greater community of humankind.

Many of the latter had been initiates in the Jewish mysteries, and when they went into exile they took their schools with them, reestablishing themselves in southern Spain and southern France well before the fall of the second temple. By 100 A.Z. they were teaching the arcana of architecture and science in both places, while offering refuge to those exiled Hebrews who did not wish to play out their lives to the rhythms of separation that their host culture had so eagerly embraced. An unrecorded "Age of Light" dawned in various pockets of southern France through their auspices, as the relatively primitive Gothic tribes who dwelt there were drawn into this magical spectacle to become, eventually, master architects themselves. These two cultures of teachers and students connected and absorbed one another's wisdom for nearly a millennium, until the militant armies of Christian orthodoxy began to bring this area back into the folds of control and "disenlightenment" after the year 1000 A.Z. They successfully aborted the Age of Light, founded on both Christian and Judaic esoteric tradition, and the self-absorption of God the Father would never be so seriously challenged on such a large scale again.

HOLY WHORES

In the earlier epochal story of the White West, in the river-worlds of Mesopotamia and Egypt, as well as in Greece and several other previous civilizations, there existed a phenomenon called the "temple of the revered prostitute." When men went off to war, and befouled their hands with blood, they were considered divorced from the deities who watched over them and had to have their bodies cleansed in order to return to the grace of the gods. The mode of cleansing they employed was through sexual union with a priestess of this temple, who acted as a channel to help these temporarily defiled warriors regain the purity of heart they had first brought into battle.

The "revered prostitute," then, was considered a gateway to the ethers, and the physical act of sex was part of a reunion ritual that united four of the divided elements of humanity—male/female and heaven/earth—into the oneness from which we all come. This was a time when the Goddess was still seen as a conduit and unifier of the many dualities that govern this sphere, particularly that most vexing and perplexing dichotomy of the mortal/immortal rift that separated humanity from its eternal self.

The early patriarchs of the Israelites saw these sacred prostitutes as highly threatening to their own position as earthly vessels of God and condemned them most bitterly. This rejection opened the way for their later priestly brethren to complete the process of ending humanity's female linkage to the heavens by making the spiritual connection between the higher and lower worlds solely a masculine province, despite femaledom's magical ability to make spirit into flesh and maledom's total inability to do the same.

With the transformation of woman from high priestess of the heavens to slave of procreation and slattern whore, humanity came crashing down to the planet, divorcing itself quite thoroughly from much of its higher potential, and the act of purifying union between the two sexes quickly slid from the sacred to the profane. An impossible rift was thus created within the divided soul of humanity, and the Christian fathers, thanks in large part to their epistle-obsessed apostle, Saint Paul (ca. 3 A.Z.–64 A.Z.), and his traditional patriarchal dismissal of all things female, helped imprint this rift indelibly on the minds of Western man and, sadly, woman as well. The Christian epoch would cement the gulf between the various unintegrated dualities that make up the human animal, and that gulf would be at the heart of the separation and fragmentation that has determined the subsequent course of Western civilization.

SAINT PAUL

It was Paul more than anyone else who would give earthly personality to exoteric Christianity, spreading its ShadoWord in a manner so driven as to verge on the superhuman. A small, extremely homely, bandy-legged man, he was born a Pharisee in the Asia Minor city of Tarsus and bore the name of the first king of Israel, Saul, a rather possessed figure in his own right.

Coming to Jerusalem to study under the rabbinate, he proved to be a most apt and dedicated student, likely becoming a rabbi himself. As a zealous persecutor of early Christians, he was on the road to Damascus, where he intended to put a stop to that upstart sect there, when he was blinded by his own internal light and heard the voice of Jesus, whom he had never met, question the pathway he was on. A conversion soon followed, and when he had regained his sight, he changed his name to Paul, immersing himself in his newfound belief. From that point onward he spent the rest of his life crisscrossing Asia Minor preaching communal salvation, until he was eventually beheaded near Rome. A traditional Jew at heart, he nevertheless recognized the Master's message of world integration through spirit and saw the cross as a linear road to draw everyone into Israel's embrace. His ultimate fate, however, the separation of his head from his body—the divorce of the mind of Judaism from the heart of Christianity—would be the powerful and subtle legacy he would leave Christendom. This disunion of the mental and the spiritual from the physical, which was further underlined by his firm belief in the imminent end of the physical world, would give that religion its basic cast for the next two thousand years.

HIERARCHIES & HERETICS

After the death of Jesus, a host of diverse groups claimed to be the Master's true inheritors and roundly denounced one another to support their own claims. Because of this, early Christianity would have surely splintered itself into unrecognizability had its inherent schema of a master teacher and twelve apostles not held within it the seeds for an enduring political structure. It would be the apostles, rather than the Master, who would become the foundation for exoteric Christianity. They would create a hierarchical organization of bishops who would claim their authority directly from the outer circle of the Master, in accordance with Jesus' own biblically recorded dictum that his earthly church would be built round the anchor apostle of Peter, who became the first bishop of Rome and the inaugural chairman of the "Chair of the Fisherman"—the original pope.

The Papacy was a direct outgrowth of the formal religious structure of the multideitied Roman world, transforming the titular pontifex maximus of pagandom into its own pontiff, or earthly Father Supreme, and transliterating many of the earlier visual trappings of that highly stylized office into the splendid panoply that the "house that Christ built" was eventually to become. The earthly duality of Virgin Mother and Visionary Son, which was the physical core of Christendom, needed a counterbalancing patriarchal force to complete its familial trinity and give representation on Earth to the will and wisdom of the heavens as viewed through the canonical eye of the church fathers, and the institution of the Papacy gave perfect form to that. Although initially subject to much martyrdom by the antagonistic forces of the larger apostate world, it would prove to be the enduring material focus of Christendom when the dire predictions of its first proselytizers that the end of the world was coming did not quite come to pass. Anything that menaced its continuance served only to harden and rigidify the outer church even more, as it slowly established its territorial presence over the first three centuries of its existence amidst periodic persecutions from its greater Roman host.

With each threat that rose to challenge the absolute authority of the outer church, cries of "Heresy!" could be heard from its hierarchical librarians, and vigorous suppression and opposition would ensue. The word *heresy* is derived from the Greek word *hairesis*, which means "choice." Those who represented orthodoxy, however, insisted there was no choice as far as they were concerned. Just as the "chosen people" looked with less-than-loving eyes on all who lived outside their God-inspired realm, so did the church fathers deny there was any choice upon this planet of choice save the one they represented. Thus, the Prince of Light came to be usurped by an edifice of material darkness, and despite the high level of many of the church's early postulants and theoreticians, the exercise of its earthly power became its overwhelming concern, with all else subservient to that.

GNOSTICS, DUALISTS & ARIANS

Three of the church's most troublesome heresies were represented by the Gnostics, the Marcion Dualists, and the largely Aryan Arians.

Gnosticism was a synthesis of many of the beliefs of the ancient world, deriving its name from the Greek word *gnosis*, which means "knowledge." The Gnostics felt that to know oneself at the deepest level was to know God, and they saw Jesus as a bringer of spiritual enlightenment and a humanistic force who allowed humanity to open up to the potential of its higher self. To them, God was a dyad, a dual presence who was both father and mother, and they saw YaH-WeH, the Hebraic Creator, as a force of evil and separation, a false

god solely interested in control and submission. In essence, they
were a thinking and feeling person's brand of Christendom, eschewing earthly hierarchies for the freedom of self-exploration through
inner knowledge. In their religion of union of all the disparate parts
of humanity, both men and women could touch on the male and
female within, and their various sects ranged from extreme asceticism
to orgiastic carnality as expression of this. However, their librarians
were no match for the bookkeepers of orthodoxy, and they were
swallowed up by history after several centuries, not to be directly
rediscovered until 1945, when some of their scrolled writings turned
up in a cave near Nag Hammadi, Egypt.

Their dualism of two gods, the true one of the New Testament
and the false one of the Old, was also propounded by the Mar-
cionites, who felt faith rather than gnosis was the key to understanding the divine. To them, *love* rather than *law* was the divine law, and
Jesus was considered but a phantasm of the Father and had never
really existed in bodily form. A powerful church rose out of this philosophy after their prime apostle, Marcion (ca. 80–ca. 160 A.Z.), was
excommunicated by Rome. It, too, was eventually suppressed, but
the combined animosity toward the singular self-righteousness of
YaHWeH that Gnosticism and Marcionism released would be heavily
felt by Israel throughout the rest of the long Christian era.

The third apostasy, that of Arianism, was introduced in Egypt by
a theologian named Arius (ca. 256-336 A.Z.), and it would give the
church a far longer run for its monotheistic money, not to die out until
well after Rome had fallen. Arius taught that Jesus was neither
human nor divine but somewhere between the two—a demigod—
and that the Father alone represented the true power of the heavens,
while the supernatural son was well below him. This reduction of the
Master's status would be adopted by many of the Christianized
Aryan barbarians, who found it a far more palatable brand of
Christendom. Though condemned by the church, Arianism would
serve to solidify that orthodox body's beliefs by forcing it to convene
many subsequent councils to unify its doctrines, and it did not die
out entirely until the seventh century A.Z.

TWO ROMES

As the exoteric church dealt with all these apostates in heavy-handed fashion while building its own territorial empire, the all-consuming might and majesty of Rome began to falter and wane. In 312 A.Z., the Roman emperor of the time, Constantine (288-337 A.Z.), vanquished his enemies at the gates of Rome and marched into that city eternal with a cross upon his shield, subsequently giving Christianity his benediction so that it became the official belief of his domain within fifty years of his lifetime. His pagan predecessor had previously destroyed all the Christian documents he could find, so Constantine commissioned new versions of those writings. The custodians of the church were thus allowed to edit and rewrite the whole orthodoxy of Christendom according to their tenets, solidifying Jesus' position as soldier of the cross, as well as their own powerful position as his sole official interpreters. This was the century where books began to replace unbound documents, uniting the scrolls and parchments of the past into one accessible work. It was now that the New Testament of the Bible took its final shape, since none of its nearly five-thousand early full manuscripts exists from before this time.

In addition, Constantine moved the capital of the empire to a city he had built especially for that purpose, Constantinople, in Asia Minor, giving, in effect, the Eternal City to the church, which it quickly made synonymous with itself. Thus did Rome and the church and the sword and the ShadoWord become one. Though it took centuries more of political maneuvering to solidify that process, still it was a miracle that it happened at all, for in the beginning Rome was the mightiest empire the world of present memory had ever known, and opposite it was a single, solitary logo, a tiny little word—"love." Though misheard and misspoken and misunderstood, that word still had the power to overwhelm that vast material entity with its own will to conquer through humanity's abject fear of the unknown.

As the centuries passed, the word transformed itself into the Sword of the Lord, as the smell of burning libraries filled the air. Rome fell prey to the barbarian Germans, and those hairy warrior hordes also became worshipers of the Runner who mastered Death and added their pragmatic nature to the pomp and ceremony of the Eternal City to give exoteric Christendom its subsequent Aryan face and theosophy. The unity of the empire would move east to Byzantium, with its representative capital at Constantinople, while the West would be allowed to grow in fragmented isolation, separated from itself through changing territorial designations so that it could truly experience the darkness of unconnected self.

MONASTICISM

As part of that process of separation, a movement called "monasticism," from the Greek *monachos*, meaning "solitary," started in the Egyptian desert during the third and fourth centuries A.Z. It saw the especially devout of the Christian world disavow any and all connection to the physical sphere in order to follow ascetic lives of prayer, simple labor, and self-denial in what they felt was the true spirit of the Christ: outer material impoverishment to bring out the richness of the spirit within. They were the inheritors of the tradition of the Essenes, the original spiritual progenitors of Jesus, and they flocked to the desert in droves to slake their deep thirst for the divine.

Communities came to be formed around these desert hermits as the movement spread north and east and west, with a host of sainted figures giving it both personality and focus. The earlier extremes of self-flagellation and excessive isolation gradually gave way to orderly, regulated monasteries that did much to keep learning alive when all else around them was plunged into the more immediate concerns of dealing with a wayward and rather violent world. Although eastern monasticism would continue to reflect its unscholarly and separated Egyptian root for a long time to come, Western monasticism would come to be an important arm of the church, and the various orders that arose from it would act as both primary preservers and promulgators of the sacred library of Christendom.

The monk with his shaved crown e-zone would come to symbolize the separation that the church's form of spirituality had to make with materiality in order to properly express itself. As a result, those two realms on the planet would feed ever further into the process of fragmentation that the One God/one self of monotheism had introduced to the West.

JUSTINIAN

In the late fifth century, the Roman Empire in the west finally fell to the warrior forces of fragmentation, and some fifty years later in the east, a Byzantine emperor arose who would complete the process of closing down the ethers to Western consciousness. His name was Justinian (483-565 A.Z.), and though history has given him a beneficent place in its archives despite his aberrant personality defects, he was a force who would do much to perpetuate the West's ignorance of its true connection with the divine.

In the tradition of many of his earlier over-the-edge Western predecessors, the emperor Justinian existed on the inner edge of his own madness, craving neither food nor sleep, only order, amidst bouts of violent outburst and sullen withdrawal. This he brought about by standardizing the law of the burgeoning material Kingdom of Come he had inherited. He also successfully expunged the doctrine of reincarnation from Western exoteric Christian thought by having it officially decreed that there was no preexistence of the soul, thanks to the machinations of his mistress and empress, one Theodora (508-547 A.Z.). Because of their efforts, all allusions to reincarnation were eradicated from the early Gospels, and a centuries-old battle between the shapers of the early church twixt the humanity and divinity of Jesus was effectively ended.

Through the auspices of Justinian, the straight line of life and death formally replaced the spiraling circle of immortality that is our true human legacy and "church 'n' state" were indelibly wed as the supreme arbiters of life on Earth. In addition, the humanity of Jesus was denied through his all-encompassing divinity, thereby reducing both the Master's presence and his message considerably, by effectively removing him entirely from human experience and putting his teachings instead solely within the province of a hierarchical priesthood.

Justinian succeeded in politicizing the considerable course of exoteric Christianity even more, while widening the already unbridgeable chasm between heaven and Earth, so that no pathway in the Christian tradition could possibly be employed to unite the two. With him came the final obliterating darkness of orthodoxy that would deny the immortal ethers to the imagination of the West and place all power in the hands of those mortals with the muscle and earthly might to maintain it.

ALLAH: THE THIRD FACE OF THE ONE GOD

After the followers of the Immortal Son had completed their monotheistic separation from their father, Judaism, a third divinely inspired force began to stir in the East as a counterbalance to the aggressive wedding of the sword and the cross that orthodox Christianity had become. This force appeared in the guise of the prophet Muhammad (570-632 A.Z.), an archetypal combination of the forces of the earlier earthly patriarch Abraham and the lawgiver Moses, who telescoped their teachings and trials down into one forceful lifetime, for now was the time for the essence of each to appear together, united in one being. Muhammad, a one-time Arabian shepherd and merchant, had a vision at the age of forty in a cave and was called to preach, naming his credo the "Submission to the Will of God," with Allah, the god, as its supreme deity and Mecca, a western Saudi Arabian city and his birthplace, as its sacred earthly abode.

This third face of the One God of monotheism would be composed of *Al* (the masculine principle) linked with *Lah* (the feminine principle), and like the other two, it would give flower to an overt patriarchical ordering of life on Earth and a more hidden esoteric tradition as well: Sufism. While emphasizing a disciplined orderly structure through its outer practices of daily prayer, diet, and behavorial control, internally it kept alive the unity of mystery that is the connective link between all earthly religions. Islam was introduced as a needed balance to the aggressive face of Christianity and the isolated face of Judaism, using the two principles of male and female united in one god as its focus: a god of both submission and will as well as mercy and compassion. This linkage, however, would be played out under the same dominating patriarchal aegis as the rest of its monotheistic fraternity, with similar fragmented results.

Detailing its own story in a biblical work called the Qur'an, or the Recitation, Islam excited its followers into a period of incredible conquest covering the century following Muhammad. When this equal force to the aggressive drive of orthodox Christianity had ended, yet another horde had scaled the diminishing gates of civilization and a Muslim empire stretched from western Europe to eastern Asia, and yet another host of sacred librarians had risen to reinterpret this sphere through the ideas of one god and one book. It was in the Islamic world that the light of culture would remain dazzlingly alive in philosophy, art, medicine, literature, mathematics, and science, while those same disciplines stood at a temporary standstill on the western frontier, subordinated to more myopic and immediate concerns.

The One God heaven of the combined forces of monotheism had a trio of faces now: Jehovah, Allah, and the Christian Lord. However, the sacred librarians of all three ultimately showed a remarkable lack of tolerance and respect for the other two, little realizing that all three were the same face of spiritual separation in different guises looking for the ultimate synthesis that each in part represented through its exoteric and esoteric traditions: male and female, heaven and earth, and selfhood and divinity.

THE AGE OF FRAGMENTATION

The years between 500 and 1000 A.Z., give or take a century or two, are generally known as the "Age of Darkness" in the White West. During that time, all record of the West's rich interior life virtually disappeared, as life grew more isolated for most concerned and Europe stood in many fragments of its greater whole, allowing its multitude of regions to evolve unfettered by any more than a vague sense of the entire continent. The glory that was once Rome was inherited by a trinity of benefactors: Byzantium, the church, and Christian Western Europe, which was now an Aryan stronghold, the end result of that former Atlantean warrior race's barbaric curiosity to see what lay inside the closed gates of civilization.

In the year 800 A.Z., the Frankish monarchy of northwestern Europe allied itself with the western church under the designation of the Carolingian Empire, which considered itself a successor to the suspended Roman Empire. This progression, in turn, fed into a successor German state a century and a half later that eventually came to be called the Holy Roman Empire, which would last until the beginning of the nineteenth century. Though it ultimately wound up as neither holy, nor Roman, nor even an empire, it did give earthly validation to the imperial forces of secular rule in their wedding and struggles with the church over who really held sway over the minds and hearts of the sodden mass of humanity under their combined aegis.

Thus, as missionaries spread the shadow of the Word to all parts of the continent, they found an increasingly more receptive populace for their tale of The Man Who Had Outraced Death. Because a vast range of mortals were now evolving their sense of "I," and with it also their fears of the inevitable death of that "I," this tale of promised immortality was given an eager ear. The idea of individual male self-importance, which was spiritually introduced to the West by the Hebrews, secularized by the Greeks, and then spread about the continent by the Romans, was now about to be let loose for most of male Europe to experience in the guise of a religion that promised the eternality of the self to all who embraced it.

Prior to the lowering of the curtain of darkness over the White West, the tradition was established that the pope was the vicar of God in all things spiritual, while kings and emperors held sway over the temporal world. Empires came and empires went, while the church grew ever stronger. The various territories of Western Europe coalesced into identifiable divisions, each giving birth to a highly noticeable character that would soon take on a national identity, woven as it was from the hidden spirit of the land and the personality it attracted to reflect its life-giving powers. As the land lost its hidden magic to ownership and property law, so did the temple, that secret underside of the church, grow ever more invisible, manifesting only in the imaginations of its adherents and remaining unseen by the larger consciousness of patriarchal exoteric Christianity, which was growing ever more intolerant of any belief that threatened its own monopoly of the spiritual truths of this plane.

THE KNIGHT & THE LADY

During this time, there came into being a romantic fantasy that gave measure to both the exoteric and esoteric tenets of Christianity. It was personified by the male and female figures of the knight and the lady, and was morally guided by a code called chivalry, which demanded a mastery of the earthly plane by its male adherents and a similar grip upon the stellar spheres by their female counterparts. Though this was the stuff of ideal far more than fact, it gave voice to the separated dualities that have plagued this planet since the introduction of physical consciousness. Together, the knight and the lady became, in their own ways, the physical manifestations of the church and the temple, a wedding of strong moral purpose and the manly arts of conquest with truth and beauty incarnate and the womanly arts of wisdom intuited and knowledge subtly revealed. Although this marriage was achieved rarely among the largely besotted crew who inspired it, it did come to flower in the mythos and legends that grew from their imagined deeds, and it is in those tales that a spark of light comes out of the darkness that pervaded Western orthodox Christian culture at this time.

During the decline and collapse of the occidental Roman Empire, there came upon the landscape of Europe an onrush of Germanic tribes from the hinterlands, who easily hacked their way through the frontiers of civilization to establish themselves as the direct forebears of many of the subsequent nations of that still-primitive continent. This was the second-to-last Aryan wave, in essence, to sweep across the Fifth Civilization. Though united only in language and general custom, they were to dominate the fifth epoch of consciousness of the White West in the same way their diluted predecessors—the Persians, Greeks, and Romans—had made themselves known through three of the previous four. In their swift evolution, they moved from loyalty to kin to loyalty to king and then to emperor, quickly adapting their brutish ways to small kingdoms in which the mass majority of their citizens were labeled as subhuman and were made to do the bidding of a raucous, strong-armed minority who, in turn, served as their protectors from others of their ilk.

Because of this power structure, the precepts of exoteric Christianity did little to assuage the numbing realities of the unlanded. Though some clung to it in the hope of better worlds beyond this one, many turned to superstition and tales of fear to explain away the unexplainability of their miserable lot, saving the lessons of the cross for the future when their egoistic souls would be more attuned to the "I" within and thus more open to promises of immortality.

The pagan folklore of the feudalized slaves of Dark Ages Europe took on an irreal life all its own, peopled as it was with ogres and dragons and enchanted castles. It entwined the mythos of yore with the spirit of the shadow of the Word to create a second Kingdom of Come, this one etheric in nature. This pre-Christian and Christian melding of fancy turned the Runner Who Outraced Death into a star-crossed Quester, making his implied message of the universal search for love here a far more aggressive one in the interweaving of the order of the Christ-force with the disorder of the warrior ethos that supported it.

Thus, both the powerful and powerless alike dreamt of conquest through the crucifix. It was their combined imaginations that conjured the knight and the lady as the purveyors of Christian perfection in a highly imperfect civilization where the few were born to rule over the many, who came here only to mindlessly serve.

The knight and the lady also helped introduce the concept of romantic love to the heart of the later West. Heretofore, partnership had largely been either of expediency or of survival. By acknowledging the human heart as a connective link between people here, romantic love would greatly open the fourth e-zone to its larger possibilities and place the divided sexes on a far different, and potentially more healing, footing with one another. Myths would become actualities, and the deep, rich interior of humanity would be made accessible to itself again.

Many of the mysterious tales of the knight and the lady centered round the Sangreal, the Holy Grail, which Joseph of Arimathea had carried with him from Jerusalem to the Isles of the Britains. As legend has it, however, one of the holy men who had been entrusted with the guardianship of the Grail and spear looked upon the loosened robe of a voluptuously chaste pilgrim kneeling before him and asked, with a droplet of desire upon his beatified brow, "Dost thou ever wonder what we wear under these cassocks, m'dear?" But before she could give her shocked reply, the spear fell upon him, rendering that question academic by inflicting a deep cut into his pulsating groin.

Both Grail and spear disappeared from the earthly plane shortly thereafter, but all who came to be the guardian of their magic powers also came to suffer that monk's shameful injury. Therefore, they were bestowed with the title of "Sinner King," acting out the role of a dying impotent god awaiting the salvation of an innocent quester who would recognize his wound, express compassion, and heal it, just as the Master had done when he walked upon this spiritual desert and gave it the life of his death.

After the holy relics of the inner temple, the spear and Sangreal, disappeared into other dimensions, these artifacts multiplied throughout the West, occupying many a castle in the legends of all the Western European cultures that had adopted Christendom. They came to symbolize a mass search for the perfection within, as exemplified by that ultimate of hero-seer-healer seekers, the newly knighted "master," now armored and stallioned with the truth as his sword and the light as his guiding shadow. The "lady" was usually entwined with the object of his quest, a motivating force with the promise of enlightenment behind her. She was, however, much less defined than her male counterpart, being a party to his drama, rather than his being a party to hers. The Grail was as female in its ephemeral essence as the spear was male, the two representing the aggression and receptivity of their knight and lady counterparts and an attempt at integrating some of the basic dualities that lie at the core of the long, chaotic story of life upon this curious plane called Earth.

RHYTHMS OF CIVILIZATION

There has been a definite rhythm to the development of patriarchal civilization in the White West, which has followed a flow of three—tribal, feudal, and royal—before breaking down into its fourth stage of multiplicities: democratic, socialistic, or communistic. Because recorded civilization has yet to move past the stage of mul-

tiplicity, it is difficult to see what the next step will be, since it will be
a return to the trinity on the wheel of sevens. However, our own Fifth
Civilization is still in its developmental stages, and that trinity might
lie somewhere in the unseen future.

In the first stage, tribal, a unity based primarily on blood connections is established within a set of people who see, through aeons of
common territorial purpose, that they have the ability to maintain
themselves as a group. On a most primitive level, they are also different extensions of the same person, the tribe being a collective soul,
sharing a common memory and experience as a host of earthly neo-
phytes slowly work their way up (or is it down?) to an individual consciousness on the part of each of its members.

After a tribal presence establishes itself, sooner or later it is going
to confront another crew of similarly disposed souls, and if it follows
the usual patterns of territorial aggression prevalent on this sphere,
one side will ultimately emerge victorious over the other. Once a tribe
learns it is more talented in the manly arts of "self-defiance" than its
neighbors, it isn't long before it is the dominant force in its area. This
situation, in turn, makes for a two-headed state of affairs, conquerors
and conquerees sharing the same space. However, as time progresses
and civilization advances, this shared space devolves into feudal
realms, with a superior force presiding in lordly fashion over its
acknowledged territory and an inferior force, bred from those tribes
that could not withstand their will, serving them.

Eventually, all the feudal realms within a much wider boundary
are either coerced, conquered, or seduced into uniting under a common territorial banner, which is wielded by an ambitious noble
obsessed with the dominion of kingship. Thereby is royalty created,
based on a patriarchal trinity of king, knight, and countryman. And
that is how the European theatre populated itself with governments
and, along with them, a hungry spate of monarchs dreaming of the
next enfoldment in the advancement of political consciousness,
empire, and its ultimate of male fantasies: total and absolute and
complete earthly power over all.

In the evolution of Western material consciousness, there was
also another element in all of this: the church, which followed that

same flow, beginning as a tribe comprised of the small band formed round the teachings of a master who had seemingly defeated Death. That tribe then went out and selectively conquered a vast territory, which was eventually divided amongst a score of bishops, who ruled their little spiritual feudal realms in highly divergent fashion, allowing, in its beginnings, a great separateness to the Kingdom of Come. Eventually, the Western church came to recognize the royalty of Rome and pledged its allegiance in that direction. A powerful rulership thus came to exist within its own demarked territory, the Papal States, which dreamt of empire as well and eventually became the largest landholder in the domain it served, as worldly and mindful of power as any kingdom formed in its shadow.

All during the Age of Darkness, however, the church was also the singular force keeping Western literacy alive, although in its tight, paternal manner it carefully controlled what was writ and what wasn't, creating an autocratic dictatorship of the mind and soul that could be challenged only at the risk of both martyred life and burning limb. For most of the wretched souls scratching their survival from land they did not own, life was not worth thinking about, and if someone else wished to define theological doctrine, that was fine by them. In the same way, their blood-drenched masters were too busy wallowing in the crudities of their unholy trinity of fighting, feasting, and fornicating to question the whys and wherefores of their existence.

DOOMSDAY

As the year 1000 A.Z. began to loom on the horizon, a very real fear spread throughout Europe that the Last Judgment and the end of time was, at last, at hand. Gloomy prophets abounded with the dire warning that Doomsday was imminent, and the West nervously prepared to meet its Maker, for there is something about even demarcations of time that brings out the most pessimistic in people. Our own approaching millennium, the year 2000 A.Z., has also born witness to the same expression of foreboding sentiment, based on similar fears of galloping change. Christianity, which had first gained popular acceptance as an end-of-the-world religion and then went on to recast time in relation to the birth of its premier prophet, lent itself quite readily to the Doomsday hysteria, and there was much collective breath holding as that ominous year came and went without apocalyptic incident.

Though the world did not quite end in the manner speculated, in a sense it did, for just before the millennium, around the year 996, a most telling device, the mechanical clock, was invented. This machine would, indeed, spell the end of natural time and the beginning of technological time, as a whole new world awaited everyone, making it once more, as it had been so often before, the very beginning of things.

◯

CHAPTER THIRTEEN

The Muddled Ages
500-1500 A.Z.

The reader is invited to spiral
through the Middle Ages and the rise of sorcery and the
necrocracy to meet the growing demand for capital, resource,
control, and knowledge, as the Crusades reconnect Europe,
the Renaissance gives that continent a rebirth, and Europe
goes to on reconnect with the rest of the globe, as worlds
within worlds once more collide here on planet Earth.

The period between the fall of the Roman Empire and the White
West's discovery and immediate exploitation of the New World of the
Americas is loosely known as the Middle Ages. Though there is wide
disagreement over the exact dates of this era, 500 to 1500 A.Z. serve
as convenient numbers to loosely demark the long period of fragmentation and the equally long period of reconnection that they
span. Those thousand years have a strange, spiraling symmetry to
them, for the Age of Medievalia was ushered in by pagans and
heretics, bringing an end to a longtime civilized Christian empire,
and it was ushered out by civilized Christendom, wreaking similar
havoc on the many longtime nations and empires of American
pagandom.

209

In the millennium that bridged those two world-altering events, the continent of Europe found its separated face, giving distinct personality to a variety of geographic territories that eventually coalesced either into countries or parts of shifting empires. After the tribal weave of Western Europe had undergone sufficient incursion, invasion, and Christianization, kings and emperors rose to give identity to large land masses, and a loose chess-board order fell over things, based on might and wealth and the ability to both defend one's boundaries and offend the boundaries of others. England, France, Spain, and the Holy Roman Empire of Italian and Germanic states all took forceful shape during this period, to give secular complement to that last direct vestige of Rome, the Church, which continued its domination over the soul, if not the body, of Western humanity.

SORCERER ETHICS

Long ago, when humanity and the natural world lived side by side, the very first instrument that came into popular use for transcending the physical world was the stone-headed spear. With it, you could send a symbol of yourself at a speed far greater than human, and when it arrived, moments later, all your warrior-hunter essence arrived with it. This highly portable projectile, which sped up the process of covering space and foreshortened time while doing so, would go on to give its more adroit and aggressive users the possibility of altering reality. The first adept spear-launchers learned how to accurately project themselves into several places at once, and it gave them the sorcerer's power of simultaneous manifestation. Those who came to use this skill in order to kill dispassionately from a distance learned how to steal into virtually anyone's space at the mere magical flick of their wrists and rob them from time if their aim was true. With this lethal ability, the ethos of the sorcerer was born, which would come to be the dominating factor in the creation of our subsequent Fifth Civilization.

Since Earth is continually subject to the laws of manifestation, this is and always has been a magician's world. Those who master the art of manifestation here are those who make their presences felt the strongest; in turn, they are usually recognized, revered, or feared for their skills, as they become archetypal extensions of the powers of the planet. All who come here, on some level, do so to give expression to their internal magician and to see how they can give voice to and ultimately integrate their own special magic with the larger realities of the planet. Magicians come in all sorts of guises: mage, merlin, enchanter, illusionist, sorcerer, sorceress, necromancer, wizard, and wicca, to name but a few. Each seems to operate from quite different principles, creating a world—our own—where the magic of light and the magic of darkness are continually vying with one another. While wizards and wiccas and their ilk work for the most part on integrating worlds here, necromancers, sorcerers, and sorceresses do their conjurations out of the fragmentation of supreme self-interest, and it is their combined power that seems to have prevailed in giving the outer story of our civilization much of its fractured scope.

Sorcery prizes its own will above all others, and it sees power totally in terms of control and expression of will. The projectile-launching warrior societies that eventually grew out of this expressed will became in time, by continually stealing space, the force that violently united much of humanity. Those who proved the most willful in this process were accorded positions of leadership and were imbued with deitylike powers over life and death. Though their power-magic was based solely on the tenets of dominance and submission, they created an unbroken legacy of the blind worship of might and will that has been at the core of earthly consciousness ever since.

The invention of the wheel, some five thousand years or so before the Common Era, was to spiral this whole process upward greatly, giving rapid rise to the Age of Metals in order to properly harness that new shape's circular genius for easing the strictures of gravity. The wheel, in turn, became the gateway invention to all the machinery that would ultimately redefine the laws of the physical world. Humanity's worship of secular might was further enhanced by the weaponry and devices all this development stimulated, as will and control came to be the planetary definition of power, while invention was turned into an endless war machine to serve those sentiments. By the time those ultimate purveyors of will, the

Romans, became masters of their known world, the West had become an out-and-out sorcerer civilization, bowing to whoever held the evolving machinery of power.

In the first century B.Z., Rome adopted the Julian calendar, which officially took measured time out of the lunar cycles that had governed the temporal consciousness of most of the ancient world and placed it in the rotating realm of the sun. Time had finally been taken away from the mysterious night world of the Goddess and given over to the day world of the war gods of technology and invention. There it would stay for the next two thousand years, bending the majesty of the natural world to suit the unnatural desires of might and mastery that are the keynotes of sorceror civilization.

The straight line of the spear and the circle of the wheel would rejoin as the mechanical clock, which first showed its face at the 1000 A.Z. mark. This new device was the first information-launcher, thanks ultimately to its colossal shape and its loudly pealing bells. It added a whole new concept in weaponry, for information had the same controlling force that projectiles and swords did, with far less effort expended. With the mechanical clock's mass introduction over the next several centuries, our modern denatured world began, for now time was a servant of progress and the day could be ordered and regulated. The systematic containment of nature that that progressive invention brought wound up divorcing its host civilization from the greater realities of its collective imagination, allowing the world to grow smaller through a concentration on the mundane and the practical, while dismissing all mystery that science and technology could not answer.

As time became successively more ordered, and the centuries began to add to twelve, thirteen, and fourteen, so did mystery slowly begin to disappear from the imagination of medievalia, and the invisible world that had long existed in the faerydoms that dotted the plowed landscapes of agrarian Europe receded ever further. Western civilization became far less enchanted than it had been in the innocence of its earlier brutal isolation and ignorance. The tales of the grandfathers and grandmothers faded into the solar flow of the seasons for many of the young, eager to unhook from their dirt-encrusted pasts and step into the bright-lights, big-city future toward which this process was inevitably leading.

It was during this time that humanity's long tradition of public tricksterdom began to peter out, its last incarnation being the Feast of Fools, begun in mid-twelfth-century France, where clergy and laity alike mocked the greater pretensions of both secular and religious authority. This festival gave tremendous release to the strictures of their beliefs, much in the manner of the Saturnalia of ancient Rome. The coming world would have no place for such festive mockery of its failings, nor would it be able to countenance the absolute abandon that some of these fests inspired. Public display of this nature would become progressively more contained as the centuries climbed in number, for fear of tapping into an emotional-ecstatic root that was no longer appropriate to the serious, stolid face of the rising self that the One God/one self ethos of monotheism had created.

CABALA & CAPITALISM

All during this period the land of Western Europe was being staked out and passed on from father to son and given definition through the name of its owners. As a result, great power was bestowed upon all who could hold title over a piece of Western European earth and lay claim to the "I" of ownership.

Through this wandered the spiritual fathers of the White West, the Hebrews, strangers in an estranged land. Though they were welcomed at the beginning of the Middle Ages into many of the enclaves of both Islam and Christianity, they were never allowed to forget that they were a people apart. With their reverence for scholarship and their fascination with the preternatural, the sages of the Jewish world began to organize and record during this period the magic of names and numbers through the study of the Cabala, a mystical work based partially on the secret teachings of the Bible via its letters and digits. This system, which dates back to ancient Israel, allowed the Hebrews to learn the esoteric meanings as well as the practical application of figures, so that by the time the civilized world around them was about to plunge into the murk of capital and distributed wealth, they knew both the higher and lower implications of dealing with the mathematics of exchange and easily became adepts in finance and transaction.

Displaced Israel was allowed to exist outside the feudal world of medieval Christianity, with its freedom for the few and entrapment for the many. Because of this, many of its members gravitated toward the slowly building cities, to become merchants and moneylenders, the latter trade being forbidden to Christians, and to act as communicatory links between the isolated outposts of civilization, as well as to teach others the magic of numbers and all that their mastery can yield in terms of wealth, possessions, and sense of self-importance. Number magic would be the basis for that secular celebration of the material world, capitalism, and its worldly veneration of the powerful, separated economic self, so that in their ongoing teachings, the Hebrews once more fed into a vehicle that would give expression to the evolution of individual identity.

The concept of capitalism, which would be many centuries in the forming, is, in its essence, an economic system of production, distribution, and exchange of goods or services between a buyer and seller geared toward the profit of all parties concerned. The subsequent story of the White West has been a variation on that simple theme, with the added variable of a perpetual floating war thrown in to separate the true exploiters of human misfortune from the merely acquisitive and greedy. War and the maintenance of an ongoing military machine, in fact, would be a prime factor in the development of capitalism, creating much industry, purpose, and activity that, in essence, would produce absolutely nothing save for devastation, though it would manage to stave off the unfocused economic lethargy that intermittent peace always seems to bring. In addition, conquering nations and empires would wind up spending themselves out in maintaining their landed conquests, guaranteeing a continual shift of power so that no one in the West would be able to maintain controlling dominance for more than a couple of centuries at best. This would insure no more long-term Romes and the inevitable history-eating "barbarians at the gates" that that unchecked phenomenon seemed to have a habit of inspiring.

THE NECROCRACY

The prefix *necro* means "dead," and it well describes the death-producing economic, or "necronomic," war-machine philosophy behind the development of our modern age, as well as the "necrocratic" triumvirate of government, science, and industry that derives its power from that machine. The necrocracy has been with the planet since the Atlantean apocalyptic sorcerer wars some 850,000 years ago, achieving its fullest flower in the ancient world through the god-emperors of Rome before transferring its focus to the exoteric church. By continually moving its seat of power from one rising empire to the next, it has managed to cast its funereal pall over the length and breadth of Western civilization without ever having to acknowledge its presence here, for it is less a collection of personalities than it is a larger-than-life force, and most who rise to rule here fall prey to its decisions and designs without fully grasping that they are its mere servants.

As the technological world continues to obliterate the natural world, so has the necrocracy grown in might and strength, for it feeds off naked will and the desire to control and subject all life to its extraordinary appetite for Death. The paternal authority of the Muddled Ages directly abetted this process by grounding the temporal world in the illusionary pursuit of material wealth, while keeping the spiritual world a place of judgment and ignorant submission to its earthly orthodox authority.

As the necrocracy reasserted itself throughout medievalia following the fragmentation of the West, it was the institution of the city that would give commerce and capital its reinvigorating impetus. Land came to be equated with money, allowing a great demand for both to stimulate trade and monetary circulation, as well as the intense sense of competition and self-interest-above-all-else that is the hallmark of sorcerer civilization. Merchants began to repopulate earlier abandoned urban areas to follow the flow of their goods, and craftspeople and others soon joined them. By 1100 A.Z., the face of Western Europe was starting to become well-pocked with both cities and towns, and some in northern Italy became self-governing small republics in the thrall of powerful ruling families.

An incredible inequity existed between those who were landed and those who were not. However, with self-importance on the rise, those who had little began to proliferate in great optimistic number, and their offspring began to gather together in considerable quantity wherever work or study was offered, swelling the walled cities with their presences over the next few centuries. With them, came the meeting of many disparate minds and the exchange of much diverse information, making the European continent a sudden repository of ideas and invention, when heretofore it had basically been the reserve of the carnalizers and the carnalized.

In the cities that housed houses of higher learning, the students grouped together in organizations called *universitas* to protect themselves from both their professors and the townspeople. Through this process the university was born and, with it, a gradual challenge to the church as the sole librarian of the truth as perceived from the lowly perspective of planet Earth. In addition, a cult of the Virgin Mary began to blossom in the twelfth century throughout Western Europe. It was the first time a woman was given a place of individual spiritual honor in the exoteric Christian schema, signaling a return to the feminine principle of interior spirituality that heretofore had been quite absent. The European Dark Ages had been a denial of the inner person, and with Mary's resurgence, the inner life of the West was resurrected as well.

ZERO

The Middle Ages would also see the concept of the number "zero" enter into the West's mathematical vocabulary for the first time. It was introduced by the Islamic Arabs at some unknown date during this period and filled a void, both literally and figuratively, that had been absent from Western thinking. The year 0 of the Common Era is actually missing from the Western calendar. 1 B.C. is immediately followed by 1 A.D., which is why this almanach is dated by the invisible link connecting the two—as symbol of the invisible, nondenominational circle that draws all time together here.

If the number 1 may be looked on as the male principle—the singular self, the one visible world, the one male god—then the number 0 is its female opposite. It is the unseen self, the link between opposing worlds of positive and negative numbers, the Great Mother who draws life from the void and sends it back there again.

The idea of zero would profoundly augment both practical and abstract thought and ultimately serve as yet another subtle reminder of the duality of the sexes and their equal, albeit different, roles here. But first, the West had to link up with itself again, after so many centuries of fragmentation and "zero" internal growth, and this it did in the only way it knew how— through swarming, aggressive, bellicose activity.

THE CRUSADES

As Western Europe began to expand its separate secular horizons, its greater sense of spiritual whole still lay in the church. Even though the mortal world was beginning to hold within it a far greater potential, the immortal world was still ubiquitously represented by a high-profile clergy that was well-integrated into virtually all aspects of public life.

In a ringing exhortation in 1095 A.Z., the chairman of the Chair of the Fisherman initiated a librarian's war to recapture Jerusalem from the Islamic Arabs who had long since occupied it. The promise of both heavenly reward and high spiritual adventure stirred all of Europe, as knights and rag-tag retinues alike banded together in locustlike armies to wrest that symbolic city from the infidel whose presence now defiled it. This first crusade, named after the Latin word for cross, *crux*, succeeded in its overt objective, creating a Latin Kingdom of Jerusalem. This conquest would allow the warrior-librarians of Islam and Christianity to play necromantic Ping-Pong with one another over the next two centuries, as the former took its initially lost territory back piece by piece from the latter.

There would be nine official crusades in all to various parts of the Middle East, as well as a pathetic children's crusade in 1212, in which a goodly portion of innocents would either be sold into slavery or die from starvation and disease. Despite the fact that all its sound and fury wound up signifying little, the Crusades effectively began the process of reintegrating the fragmented continent of Europe through

the sheer force of the movement and aggressive interchange it generated. Its one big loser was the displaced nation of Israel, for Hebrews
were indiscriminately slaughtered by the thousands throughout
Europe as well as the Holy Land in its fervor, and their tenuous presence in the West was totally undermined. In 1290, they were expelled
from England; in 1306, from France, although some remained in the
light pockets of the south; and in the fateful year of 1492, from Spain.
Thus ended yet another long season in the continuance of that eternal nation, whose civilized pockets of asylum in the West were now
urban walled ghettoes, separating these exemplars of unity-through-
separation even further from the rest of humanity.

The Crusades also gave the church another arm with which to
crush all apostasy. This it did most ruthlessly, bringing an end to the
"Age of Light" that had existed in southern France, while destroying
the final vestige of its earlier heresies, the Catharist sects, throughout Europe.

The Cathars, from the Greek *katharos*, meaning "pure," were the
last upholders of the dualistic traditions of early Eastern Christianity, as well as of the tenets of poverty and antimaterialism that they
felt Jesus exemplified. They were the champions of the feminine
principle, looking deep within for their spirituality, and both rich and
poor were welcomed to their nurturing bosoms. They saw no spirituality in either the sacraments or the hierarchy of the exoteric church,
viewing this world as an evil place that only pure ascetism could
overcome. The threat that they posed—of an integrated humanity
operating on both inner and outer levels—was definitely not in keeping with the military might of orthodoxy. They were, therefore, exterminated with a vengeance, and with their passing in both the West
and the East by the fourteenth century, so did another light of the
Prince of Light go out. The dark eyes of dominance and control could
now see clear across the spiritual horizons of the West without anything impeding their view.

ORDERS OF THE CROSS

While the Papacy attracted some extraordinarily forceful personalities to its long list of chairmen to give some sense of form and

reform to that institution, its lesser clergy also manifested several larger-than-life figures during the Middle Ages to give itself diverse order. Three in particular—Saint Benedict (ca. 480–ca. 547), Saint Dominic (ca. 1170-1221), and Saint Francis of Assisi (ca. 1182-1226)— stand as strong symbols of the wide range of character that could find its commonality in the church.

Saint Benedict was born to a noble Italian family, studied in Rome, then retreated to a hermit's existence for several years, garnering the reputation of a holy man. This practice attracted other solitary souls to him, whom he ultimately organized into twelve monastic communities, based on an orderly rule of communal prayer, study, and work, which would, in turn, become the basis for Western monasticism. The regularity of existence that Benedict introduced eventually created a highly controlled clockwork world where everything was ordered by time, leaving no room for anything that lay outside of routine and devotion. Because of this rigorous adherence to routine, the Benedictines could be trusted to serve as the preservers of sacred texts, keeping the various libraries of learning alive, even if most of them did not or could not use them themselves, for they were the passive linkers of many worlds. Saint Benedict, then, represented the submissive community of God, giving over its body for the greater good of all while sacrificing personal freedom to the safety and sanctity of repetition and routinization.

Saint Dominic was a Spaniard noted for his learning and his missionary zeal, particularly among the heretic Catharist sects of southern France. Before he was born, his mother had a prophetic dream that he would found an order that would become *domini canis*, the "watchdogs of the Lord." Just as Benedict mirrored the passive receptivity of benediction or blessing, so did Dominic reflect the active assertion of dominance and control—the Order of Black Friars he created became the church's most tenacious arm in uprooting all heresies.

A reverence for the mind as a spiritual tool of God would be the legacy of the Dominicans. Their preaching, teaching, and writing would have a profound effect on medieval theological thought, for like all the monastic orders, they dwelt in both the astral and physical worlds with equal conviction, considering themselves masters of the magic of thought and its integration into spiritual physicality. They were the most feared magicians of medievalia, for their inquisitional skill at providing burning evidence of evil on Earth left the European landscape cowed and quaking at their accusatory presence. They took their sacred librarian role all the way up to that of grand inquisitor, that curiously YaHWeH-like archetype of the supreme, uncompromising judge of all humanity, who, ironically, helped hasten the presence of Judaism from Western midsts. Saint Dominic represented the aggressive community of God, as well as both the light and darkness that vigorous belief is capable of manifesting.

Saint Francis was the son of a well-to-do Italian merchant, led a dissipated youth, became a prisoner of war, and suffered severe illness. Deeply moved by those experiences, he then decided to dedicate his life to helping the poor. Disowned by his father and renouncing the material world, he adopted the pathway of poverty as his mode of spiritual expression. Told to "go herd pigs" after his first ill-kempt meeting with the richly accoutred pope, he returned covered in pig dung, and his sanctity as well as his unquestioned allegiance to Rome were recognized.

An exact contemporary of Saint Dominic, Francis met his fellow saint in Rome, and both founded active evangelical orders at the same time, which would continue to work in complementary concert with one another down through the centuries. If the Dominicans were the proselytizers of the mind, the Franciscans were the preachers of the heart, and though their rigorous poverty would suffer several schisms, these Gray Friars felt they were the direct inheritors of the apostolic tradition of early Christendom. They were the midpath of the preservers and the provocateurs, linking both by subtly reflecting aspects of each. Saint Francis, then, represented the integrative community of God, working on the level of the heart to bring spirit to a world that is impoverished from both within and without.

The trinity of supportive body, inquisitorial mind, and suppliant heart that these three sainted figures stood for would symbolize the

Christian ideal of medievalia. But ideal differed greatly from actuality in the necrocratic schema of this muddled age as yet another prophet, that of profit, was fast capturing the imagination of the temporal world, and it would soon leave everything else behind in its acquisitive wake.

TROUBADOURS, BUILDERS & TEMPLARS

While exoteric Christianity found ever more order through its monastic orders, its esoteric and mysterious side was forced into further and further isolation, unable to withstand the all-pervasive arm of orthodoxy. All through early medievalia, the written word and the spoken word were two separate languages, and most people had access to and familiarity with only the latter. The spoken word or the vernacular, then, was the means of communication for most, and the sung word was the highest and most universal method for ideas and ideals to be passed among a largely illiterate public. Western civilization had a long bardic tradition, singers of the sacred and poetic mysteries of pagandom, and they would find their medieval counterparts in the troubadours. These poet-musicians operated on many levels, including aristocratic chivalric knights and nobles, who counted several kings among their number. Others were more attuned to mystery and mysticism, and were far more heretic in the wisdom they sang, dedicated as they were to changing the world through the revelation of ancient truths. The troubadours flourished in southern France, Italy, and northern Spain between the eleventh and fourteenth centuries. With their passing, the last oral link to the earlier Age of Light passed with them, yet another victim of the displaced crusader zeal of control, conformity, and orthodox convention.

The singular manifestation of ancient mystery that was allowed to continue was in the realm of architecture. This period saw an incredible spate of cathedral building in the Gothic style: light, airy, soaring edifices that well reflected the spiritual teachings of the mystery schools that had been kept alive in southern France during its Age of Light and in secret, repressed form elsewhere during the earlier barbarian invasions. Many of the traveling Freemasons who spread the fruits of their skills throughout Western Europe were members of lodges and guilds that had re-formed during the Middle Ages to act as visible channels for the invisible majesty of the divine. The various Masonic orders they created remain as one of the strongest bridges between the hidden world of the past and the overt world of the present, testimony to the power of the builder as a primary synthesizer of inner and outer worlds here.

The third force of mystery present during this time was the Knights Templars, an order initially formed in 1118, following the first crusade, to keep the roads safe for Christian pilgrims in the newly created Latin Kingdom of Jerusalem. Tradition has it that they were first quartered on the site of the long-destroyed Temple of Solomon, and they became the warrior manifestation of mystery—disciplined soldier-mystics who were equally adept in both spheres. Although sworn to poverty, chastity, and obedience, the order soon grew worldly, wealthy, and powerful, attracting a host of highly skilled young nobles to their ranks, so that their expertise ranged from warfare to banking to international diplomacy. The splayed red cross upon a white mantle became their symbol, and all worlds were accessible to them: commercial, philosophical, political, Christian, Judaic, and Islamic alike. Secretly pledged to the idea of one eternal world religion, they were a force of physical, spiritual, and mental integration. Though subject to excess and corruption, their power was deeply respected, feared, and resented, for they were beyond the control of the secular world and yet moved easily through it. Because of this, a systematic campaign of persecution was instituted against them by the king of France in 1307 with the reluctant compliance of the pope. By 1314, they were no more, as their last "grandmaster" was burned at the stake, while correctly predicting that both king and pope would follow him off this plane within a year.

With the demise of the Templars, mystery lost its most assertive chivalric champions, and it would now fall into the realm of astrologers, alchemists, cabalists, and occultists, a hidden force whose only accepted outlet would be through the subtleties of the arts and architecture. Although mysticism would continue in various lay brotherhoods and the writings of several Germanic theologians, its greater ancient sense of mystery would be absent: the idea of co-creation, the ability to do as the gods and manifest immortality here. But just as everything is always subject to death on this mortal sphere, so is it subject to renewal, and by the mid-fourteenth century, the White West was poised for still another rebirth, which would come in several forms.

THE AGE OF HEAVY METAL

The Age of Metal, which had lasted some five thousand to six thousand years, was coming to an unofficial close, after having given the inventive soul of Europe the ability to organize its resources and remove itself from the thrall of the natural world. In its stead would rise the "Age of Heavy Metal," that industrialized, amplified, electric sound of machinery everywhere, filling our aural and urban theater with the music of production and progress, until nothing else could be heard in its insistent, incessant wake.

If the Age of Heavy Metal were to be given an opening date, it would be in 1346, at the Battle of Crecy, during the Hundred Years' War between England and France. The English, using a new invention called the longbow, found that they could pierce the armor of the opposing nobles of the French from a considerable distance, thereby elevating the warrior status of the ordinary English bowman while reducing their enemy's knights to clumsy, superfluous figures. In so doing, they permanently changed the face of warfare from the singing swords of the Age of Metal to the superhuman barrage of flying projectiles that modern battlefields have become. Crecy would begin the process of changing the chess-board dynamic of medievalia from its larger archetypal pieces of king, bishop, knight, and castle to their lesser and more varied components, thereby cluttering the political and martial games of the age with many more pieces that now could be empowered with some of the former strength and reach that had been exclusively reserved for its major players.

The Age of Heavy Metal, then, would be the great equalizer of humanity. It would give power to any and all who mastered its simple mechanical principles, while de-personalizing all it touched by reducing life to the three dimensions of the present. This steady erosion of temporal and preternatural consciousness would evolve from the order and rationality that would be needed to control the power it unleashed. The necrocracy could now place its presence everywhere. As if to underscore this, an epidemic called the Black Death, which was transmitted by fleas that were carried by rats aboard Italian trading vessels from the Far East, entered the world of the eastern Mediterranean the year after the Battle of Crecy and from there spread across the continent. This plague would go on to wipe out 30 percent of the population of Europe and an equal proportion of the Middle East, returning again and again over the next century as an odd reminder of the vulnerability of humans when their own alien cultures, in this case Far Eastern and Western, have any kind of direct intercourse.

THE RENAISSANCE

During this long "dance of death," a second phenomenon, that of *renaissance*, which is French for "rebirth," rose to complement it. The Renaissance would offer the necrocracy a rational foundation for placing its entire emphasis on the realm of the material, which was far easier to manipulate and control than the constantly schismatic sphere of the spiritual. The idea of the separated self could now permanently separate itself from the hierarchy of medieval institutions and stand alone, for it had numerous secular models upon which it could be patterned: men of power and accomplishment and importance, who would inspire an equal sense of individuality in their emulatory if less-successful lessers.

The church had already passed its peak of absolute authority and control, and because of its deep immersion in affairs of the material, it was now subject to the same power struggles and corruptions as everything else, with the added onus of a rigid inability to change with a vastly changing world. Later in the century, this inflexibility would send the Papacy fleeing from Rome to southern France, creating two popes and a nervous populace who no longer felt they were protected by paternal authority. All through the fourteenth century, black satanic masses, flagellant orders of self-punishing priests, and diabolical ceremonies in graveyards were used to counteract the spiritual, social, climactic, and plague-ridden disorder that was now being visited upon the West. If its sacred librarians no longer had the answers for all this chaos, perhaps its renascent secular librarians did. The death knell for magic had been sounded, and this period was a last-gasp mass invocation of supernatural forces to stave off the coming of the modern world.

Like the plague, the White West's Renaissance was channeled through the Italian city-states of the mid-fourteenth century, in large part because of the success of the flourishing urban centers there and the wealth of travelers, trade, and information they attracted. It was here that medieval emphasis would begin to shift back to the Earth sphere, for the boomtown riches in abundance there were far more of an imaginative inducement than the vague otherworldly promises of a church that seemed equally, if somewhat hypocritically, drawn toward the same kind of material display as its merchant and princely cohorts.

In addition, the past stood in magnificent ruin in the Italian city-states. This awesome decay became far more intriguing to the young scholars of the time than the Christian mythos that had long over-ridden it. Thus, a connective link was established with earlier ages through the wholesale study of Greek and its emphasis on the individual as manifestation of the higher glory of the heavens. The Renaissance, then, was a reopening of old channels: a reconnecting of ancient pagan civilization with its Christianized present and a reintroducing of the separated secular self of Greece and Rome to the One God/subordinated-self world of medieval monotheism.

This wedding of two worlds would produce a secularized worship of all things human among the elite who fostered this reconnection, and the educated few who thoroughly embraced it and began to costume and comport themselves exactly like their ancient forebears were well mocked by the populace at large. But the spirit that was inspired by the relatively free friction of unfettered minds rubbing together swiftly spread to the north and west, as journeying students imparted what they had learned to their receptive friends, who were eager to shed their clodhopper medieval consciousness for the sleek new style of pointy-toed thought coming out of Italy.

In 1453, the Byzantine city of Constantinople fell to invading forces, and this, too, served as a means for disseminating and spreading the past. The walled fortifications that had long preserved the artifacts of ancient civilization were now being asked to share in their bounty through the chaos of territorial self-interest, as the greater world sensed the ending of a great age and the beginning of another through this mass rebirth of the past and its reintegration into a greatly expanded sense of the present.

However, although the smell of burning libraries gradually receded from the larger landscape through this new reverence for knowledge, the stench of burning bodies did not. Fear of change and fear of power continued to be visited upon those whose true potency was suspect, particularly witches and wiccas, in a last attempt at limiting the ancient power of women that did not fully end until the early eighteenth century.

The Italian Renaissance was ushered in, more or less, by the plague and ushered out in 1527, more or less, with the sack of Rome by French, German, and Italian mercenaries. In the interim, an astonishing host of artistic beings decided to incarnate en masse in that country of city-states to take advantage of the patronage that abounded there. Soon, such masters as Michelangelo, Leonardo, Raphael, and Donatello were chiseling and stroking and hammering out a body of work that proclaimed humans just short of the angels in the divine order of things. As art bloomed, so did science and invention blossom, although the natural sciences deferred to the weighty speculations of the ancient Greeks and were not truly unbound from their spell until sometime later.

The Renaissance successfully transformed Western thought from an infantile dependency on unquestioned patriarchal authority to a focus on personal inquiry. In the process, however, humanity was left in further isolation on the planet, separated to an even greater extent from its divine origins and left to muddle over its rightful place in the universe totally on its own. With the sack of Rome in 1527, the central importance of Italy in the European schema, save for the independent papal states, began to fade, as the rest of the continent absorbed its rebirth of the human spirit and experienced its own separate golden age of literature and art later on in the century. This renewal would be an indication of the West's successful passing through the absolutism of its Middle Ages and into the relative freedom of what would soon be its "Old Ages": a gasping, choking planet barely able to breathe through its ruined and heavily exploited body.

THE OLD WORLD MEETS THE NEW WORLD

In 1492, a trinity of ships set sail from Spain under the command of an Italian navigator to try to find a western passage to the riches of the East. Though this voyage of discovery did not accomplish its original objective, it wound up linking the two hemispheres of our planet by touching down on an ancient site of Atlantis, the islands of the Caribbean Sea.

The immediate offshoot of this joining of disparate worlds was yet another plague, this one occasioned by the sexually transmitted disease of syphilis, which was carried back to Europe by the sailors of this expedition and then quickly spread about the continent by the "brotherly love" of the combined armies of Spain. Since syphilis was unknown in Europe, there was no resistance to it. It quickly reached epidemic proportions, spreading as far as Russia and Africa, until it finally lost its initial virulence sometime during the next century, although its plaguelike presence would rise often in succeeding years.

The dis-ease with which the alien cultures of our planet often unite speaks volumes on the fragile nature of our connections here. Syphilis was a fitting epitaph for medievalia, for that epoch began with the penetration and violation of a longtime civilization by relatively primitive forces and ended with an equal ravishment of another ancient way of life by the transformed civilization that had grown out of that earlier rape of the West.

And so, with the violent end of this millennial-long Muddled Age, came the promise of a whole new era, unlike anything the world had ever quite seen before, and with it, just as in so many times previously, it was now once more the very beginning of things.

○

The Age of Information, Reformation & Transformation, 1500-1800 A.Z.

The reader is invited to explore earthly time and space before the Reformation and the Counter-Reformation do battle with one another for the hearts and souls of Western humanity, as the Messiah once more returns to Israel and enlightenment brings revolution and the advent of the modern political state.

Around the year 1455, "heavy metal" entered the lexicon of European letters through the introduction of movable type and stationery paper to the West. The first full-blown manifestation of this new form was the book of law and love, the Bible. Its printer, an inventive but unoriginal German goldsmith of the mid-fifteenth century, wound up going into debt and exile for his troubles, thus ignobly ushering in a communications revolution that would speed up the "Age of Information" to which the clock had steadily been giving rhythmic order throughout Western Europe.

The Age of Information would allow a totally different kind of sorcerer to rise to power in order to give complement to the controlling dominance of the secular and spiritual warriors of church 'n' state. This would be the "datamaster," and like his fellow patriarchs, he would re-create the realities of earthly existence in accordance with his own proscribed view of things, turning the concept of time into an exclusive measure of material productivity, with the simple formula of T=$: time is the exclusive preserve of money.

The datamasters of the late Muddled Ages were able to see the global weave of what was needed, what had to be organized in order to supply it, and how to best use time as not only a controlling factor, but as an actual resource in itself. By doing this, they put Western Europe on "merchantime," slowly transforming a work force that had been frightened off the seasonal sweep of the land by the disease-ridden chaos and upheaval of late medievalia into a numbed extension of the growing machinery of progress. Though the machine was still centuries away from becoming the dominating force of modern life, it had already begun to turn its tenders into abject slaves of time, attuned to a consciousness that made the past irrelevant and the workaday present a dull and deadly means of staving off the uncertainty of unknown tomorrows.

Merchantime, with its overweening emphasis on trying to control the future through the manipulation of physical and temporal resources, would finish the process of taking Western civilization out of the deep spirituality that living in the eternal present moment entails and would place it, instead, in the illusionary realm of striving for future-time material security. This shift, more than anything else, would deemphasize the role of the divine in the Western schema of things. Now that life was a marketable commodity and safety from the unknown could be bought and sold, the mystery of this sphere became less and less important; material mastery could be achieved here, at least by some, without having to acknowledge any force higher than one's own skills at profitably playing with secular information.

Since merchantime needed more and more data about Earth-space to properly exploit it, the previously unshakable marriage between the church and Truth began to be questioned throughout the sixteenth century, albeit not without considerable jealous resistance from Truth's insistently monogamous mate. This rift was widened in 1519, when a navigator with "mage," or magician, prominently displayed in his name, Ferdinand Magellan (ca. 1480-1521), set off from Spain to find a western passage to the Spice Islands in the Pacific. Though he sailed off into the ethers during the journey, one of his ships completed the girdle-the-globe trek in 1522, proving empirically that the Earth was round, rather than flat, while giving some sense to its ocean-separated landmasses. The Earth, in effect, had reconnected with itself, and its multitude of resources was now at the mercy of its datamasters.

Then, in 1543, a Polish astronomer, one Nicolaus Copernicus (1473-1543), wisely waiting until he was on his deathbed, published a treatise that mathematically placed the sun in the center of our solar system, with Earth and the other planets revolving around it. This apostasy against the long-held view of God and self standing in the very center of the universe, with everything else subservient to that dynamic, was bitterly and rigorously opposed by orthodoxy; nevertheless, a telling blow had been struck against a belief that had lingered from pagan times. The universe could now be coded and ordered through mechanical law, and that order could be transferred to political and social institutions as well. The unknowable was no longer the virgin province of faith for it had been violated by reason, and the potential for humanity to master this sphere was becoming apparent with or without the blessings of its official spiritual fathers.

In 1582, the solar calendar, which had been steadily gaining time since the adoption of its Julian version by the Romans in 46 B.Z., was put on Christian time by the pope in order to regulate the date of Easter. Ten days in October of that year suddenly disappeared, much to the outrage and resistance of many, and the Gregorian Calendar, named after the pope—Gregory, part XIII (1502-1585)—was insti-tuted, although it was not fully accepted by all of the West until the twentieth century. Despite keying the calendrical clock to the immor-tal mystery of the Resurrection, a further mortal order fell over the invisible province of time. In the scientific spirit of the age, it had finally been given the measurement that most accurately reflected Earth's true journey around the sun, even though that journey would not be officially accepted by the church until 1922. Time and space were now the properties of those who best knew how to exploit them to maximum material advantage, as the Sacred World, from which they emanated, could no longer lay predominant claim to their magic and mystery.

THE REFORMATION

With the advent of printing and the accessibility of paper a century previous, the holy writ of Christendom started becoming accessible to the populace at large. Now that it was written in their own spoken language, they could judge the worth of their brothers of the cloth by directly reading or listening to their canonical scripture without having to have it interpreted for them through the narrow suspicious eye of scholastic orthodoxy. Thus, well before Truth had named science as a "corespondent" in its separation from the church, a crisis of consciousness began to erupt in the Germanic states over that longtime exclusive and abusive marriage.

During the time of the Renaissance popes, the practice of indulgences, or bribes paid by mortals to insure their immortality, had become big business. People were exchanging hard cash for a papal promise that their place in the heavens would be secured once they were evicted from the sphere of the living by that supreme landlord, Death. Though the church itself was horrified over some of its own excesses and began a modest movement from the top down toward reform, it took an angry, constipated cleric who was prone to much outhouse rumination, one Martin Luther (1483-1546), to fire the shot in 1517 that officially started the war that was to cleft Christianity in twain, although that war had been waged on a sectarian level in pockets of Europe for several centuries.

Thanks to the miracle of movable type, however, Luther's official challenge to orthodoxy—ninety-five theses against indulgences tacked to a church door—would dramatically escalate the conflict. Within five years of that act, a knight's rebellion of noble German disclaimants, aflame with the zeal of reformation, seized upon his call for secular authority to override spiritual abuse and grabbed a great deal of church-owned land in their divided country, thereby bringing his movement of protest into political being. An even more brutal peasant uprising followed, and Germany, along with the rest of the continent, was suddenly plunged into secularized spiritual chaos.

Luther, who was excommunicated for refusing to recant his heresies, advocated a direct relationship between God and humanity through the auspices of the Bible rather than through the intermediaries of a highly self-indulgent clergy, whom he urged to marry and live like everyone else. Salvation, said he, was a sole and soul matter of faith alone, instead of the various trappings of works and exaggerated humility that the church encouraged. Denying any freedom of human will, he also felt that secular rulers should be supreme in matters of the spirit. In keeping with these beliefs, Luther proposed reducing the sacraments that lay at the base of Christian ceremonial mystery from seven to two, baptism and communion—cleansing and connection—for the world that he envisioned was simple, pragmatic, and devoid of any of the superstitious magic that had so often led to abuse and exploitation. The Reformation, like the Renaissance, was a call to return to roots—in this case, the original unadorned Christendom of the Gospels and Epistles.

Because he believed so fervently in the basic depravity of humanity, Luther spearheaded a movement that was far more political than it was religious. This freed Germany's capital for its own growth instead of the church's, which allowed that splintered nation of separate states to give expression to its own material needs rather than serving a corrupt but centralized spiritual authority. It subsequently divided evenly along Protestant and Catholic, or universal, lines, with princes dictating the choice of their states, while the nominal head of all of them, the Holy Roman Emperor, retained his loyalty to Rome, since that relationship was the basis of his title.

COMMUNITIES OF GOD

While Luther addressed himself primarily to the Germanic states and their separate rulers, other forceful souls spread his movement throughout Europe. Co-equal with him in importance was John Calvin (1506-1564), a French priest and lawyer who, like many influential religious figures, experienced a sudden conversion and let the world know of it in 1536, when he published in Latin his "Institutes of the Christian Religion." His cold, lucid prose limned a sphere totally in the thrall of God, with an elite picked before birth for salvation and the rest, even if they did their damnedest, still destined for eternal damnation. The trick, according to Calvin, was to know if you were among the elect and then to act accordingly, resisting any and all temptation along your pathway to dip into the abundant degradations available to all who were not already chosen. This view of yet another chosen people would see a Protestant Rome ultimately set up in 1541 in the city of Geneva, nestled high in the alpine country of Switzerland. The no-nonsense figure of Calvin would be its driving impetus, in accordance with his further dictum that only a purely theocratic state reflected the true governing tenets of the Bible.

Grimly denying any outward display of anything that did not smack of work and devotion, Calvinism became a prime necrocratic force in controlling earthly and earthy excess, while wedding its adherents to the rising ethic of capitalism by stressing the religiosity of labor and the bedevilment of all else. Its uncompromising puritanical stance gained audience in many parts of Western Europe, for the idea of being superior and chosen on a planet of choice has always been appealing, even when couched in thoroughly life-denying form.

When the Reformation hit England, it found the king, one Henry, part VIII (1491-1547), far more worried about the lack of a male heir than the spiritual welfare of his subjects. Thus, for entirely political reasons, he wound up giving his blessings to a reconstituted Church of England, which, in turn, allowed him the serial freedom of a half-dozen wives, who ultimately produced one short-lived son and two daughters. They alternately embraced Protestantism, Catholicism, and Protestantism again, before the latter was finally adopted in 1559, although internecine struggles of a religious nature would continue to occupy that country for another 130 years.

PROTESTER HIERARCHIES

Because the Protestant church splintered almost immediately into various sects and had no central authority governing them all, as did the Catholic church, the problem of power had to be resolved within each denomination. John Calvin, with his gift for organization and control, instituted the form of Presbyters, from the Greek *presbyteros*, meaning "older." These Presbyters were a combination of teaching and preaching ministers and lay church elders, and together they formed the ruling office of their church.

Presbyterianism was derived from the apostolic model in the New Testament, which, in turn, drew its inspiration from the spiritual hierarchy of the Jewish synagogues. Rather than being an innovation, it was an interrupted continuation of ancient practice and, as such, found favor all over the European continent.

The alternate form to this was Episcopacy, from the Greek *episkopos*, meaning "overseer." Episcopacy maintained the hierarchy of bishops and stayed closer to its Catholic root, becoming a blend of the reformatory schism of Christendom, with the northern Lutheran countries and the Anglican Church of England, among others, adopting its governing tenets.

THE EMPIRE STRIKES BACK:
THE COUNTER-REFORMATION

To counter its growing loss of control, the Catholic church proposed its own Counter-Reformation, calling a trinity of ecumenical, or general, councils in the imperial city of Trent around the midcentury mark to redefine its absolutes in the wake of this freely willful continentwide rebellion. In the process, the church clearly spelled all of its doctrinaire positions, including salvation through works and faith; the upholding of the seven sacraments—especially the mystery of the mass; the maintenance of a separate celibate priesthood; the joint tradition of scripture and church history as the true foundation of Christendom; and, after much political maneuvering, a reaffirmation of the pope as its titular and singular head, all of which had been challenged by Protestant apostasy.

Earlier, in 1534, the Society of Jesus, or the Jesuits, were formed by Saint Ignatius of Loyola (1491-1556), a Spanish soldier who, after being seriously wounded in battle, read the life of Christ and traded in his sword to enter the spiritual army of the Master. His order, stressing the loyalty that his name unconsciously evoked, wedded strong mind with stout heart to serve as the missionary and teaching arm of the Counter-Reformation, as its scholar-soldiers eventually became confessors to kings and headmasters of the Catholic ruling classes. In their continual dealings with power, the Jesuits were also deeply involved in various political intrigues and were deeply resented by both sides of the great Christian schism, so that they had to go through many struggles merely to maintain their order, much in the manner of the higher order of the church they served.

During this period, the countries and empires on the European continent with the most autocratic traditions maintained their religious ties of old, while those that granted their citizenry the relative freedom of incipient capitalism opted for the ethic of Protestantism. The latter saw this more secular and less mysterious brand of Christianity as a better pathway through which they could compete in the growing world of ownership, possession, and individual self-importance.

From 1560 to 1648, Protestants and Catholics engaged in a near century of incessant combat over the relative merits of the West's dual interpretation of the Master's long-ago presence here. When the great librarian wars of Christendom finally spun themselves out across the battlefields of Europe in 1648, most of the north was in the Protestant camp, while the southern part of the continent still adhered to their original faith, albeit in a world that was far more conscious of the various elements that comprised its totality. Europe was now rife with a host of fierce librarians, both sacred and secular, to share the burden of the Truth's multiplicity of beliefs, since no singular discipline could now hold continental sway.

ROSICRUCIANS

Along with the wars of intolerance that marked the outer history of this period, there were many secret societies giving voice to its inner story. One of these was the Rosicrucians, an alchemical brotherhood whose mythical founder, one Christian Rosencreutz (1378-1484), wedded the rose of perceptual and awakened knowledge with the cross of mysticism and spirituality, through traveling, teaching, and healing. This union of the divine and the mechanistic worlds drew from both the ancient mysteries and modern science to create a hidden "kingdom of illumination," dedicated to using the tenets of rational and irrational wisdom to draw together the deeply sundered spheres of heaven and Earth. Both utopic and apocalyptic in its scope, Rosicrucianism eventually surfaced in 1614 through the writings of one of its members and briefly captured the European imagination, for it posited a blending of the many diverse worlds here, with all working for the ultimate good of humankind.

In 1619, a short-lived buffer state between Catholic and Protestant Germany was organized with Rosicrucian principles as its basis. However, the political alchemy needed to maintain it was not there, and it reverted to the ways of the rest of Europe the following year with the defeat and deposition of its king. The West was far from ready for its hidden traditions to meld with its overt story, and the Rosicrucians returned to their previous hidden imaginative stance, awaiting a more conducive time to marry spirit with matter in an evolved world with the capacity to see the illumination in both. Science, which they saw as a vehicle to uplift humanity, was now free to further the advance of industry and weaponry without feeling much of a moral imperative to do otherwise.

THE MESSIAH RETURNS

The displaced nation of Israel, which had been systematically driven out of Western Europe prior to and during all this time, was the singular nonrecipient of the wealth of violently shared wisdom of the Renaissance and Reformation. Moving into the feudal realms of the eastern part of that continent, Israel stepped sideways through time as everyone else moved forward. Settling in Poland, Lithuania, and Russia, the Hebrews repeated the process of making themselves useful to an emerging international economic consciousness, only to find themselves target for the misplaced zeal of the citizenry of those countries once that consciousness had been partially forged, unloved teachers that they were of the magic of names and numbers and the separation of self from all save the embrace of God.

After the Jews had been expelled from the last of their Western European strongholds in 1492, they began to add the old concept of Messiah to their secret doctrines, demanding that one should appear after all this time. They probably got exactly what they asked for, several centuries later, in one Sabbatai Zvi (1626-1676), a troubled soul given to alternate bouts of ecstasy and melancholy. A student of the Cabala, Zvi eventually read himself personally into it and became a wandering rabbi, making his way to Gaza in Palestine, where he met with official benediction to his exaggerated claims of being the long-awaited deliverer of his people.

In 1665, Sabbatai Zvi announced his messiahdom to a rapt Gaza and appointed a dozen apostles in fine Christian-Judaic fashion. His legend then grew to near hysterical proportions in the Hebraic pockets of the European continent, which eagerly clutched at the possibility that divine intervention was at last going to free them. This erratic rabbi, inspiring both ecstasy and condemnation in his wake, sailed on to Constantinople, long a Muslim stronghold, to prove his power and wound up being unceremoniously tossed into jail nearby. Nine months later, a very depressed Zvi was given the choice of Islam or death and took the former, accepting a comfortable pension from the government as a converted Muslim for the last decade of his life.

His followers, unable to countenance this ultimate of embarrassments, slowly buried their disappointment, but the entire travesty served, coming as it did on the heels of Christianity's "librarian's truce" of 1648, to thoroughly bury Judaism's long-hoped-for wish of YaHWeH's miraculous termination of its displaced wanderings. Unlanded Israel thus turned its defeated head back toward the material world for a resolution of its endless problems of continuance and survival. The false messiah had delivered his people from the self-defeating Jewish joke that the Messiah has always been for Israel, and though an occasional self-proclaimed deliverer did appear from time to subsequent time, that extraordinarily self-destructive fantasy was put to final rest. With this ending came a far greater acceptance of the temporal world by the separated Jewish nation, whose only strength now lay in its own hands and hearts and not in direct supernatural force. This opened the way the following century for a prophet of the divine within to step forth and found a movement called *Hasidism*, from "Hasidic," meaning "holy."

The original Hasidim had appeared around 175 B.Z. They had been a force of purity, giving birth ultimately to the Essenes, in whose midsts the Master had first appeared. Hasidism was a reaction, in its second incarnation, to both persecution and false messiahs. It was a product of the heart and mind of a man born in southern Poland under the name Israel, who took the title of Baal Shem Tov (1700-1760), "Master of the Good Name," from the traditional role he played as herbalist, exorciser, and physician without degree. Poland had been the repository of much of his displaced nation when it wended its way eastward to escape the displeasure of Western Europe. The northern half of that country was to see the culmination of the rabbinic civilization that had held Judaism together ever since the time of the Diaspora, or dispersal, when the temple first burned in self-destructive rage over the arrogance and materiality of its worshipers.

While leading a life that curiously paralleled that of the Master, without its dramatic and preternatural ending, Baal Shem Tov taught that religion should be joyful, and he encouraged both music and dance, as well as prayer and humility, as expression of spirituality. In so doing, he found an extremely receptive audience among many of his people, who took to his simple belief in the ubiquitous presence of God in a way they had never taken to previous orthodoxy. The movement was to remain a staple of Judaic life, and its male adherents, with their black hats and coats and long, curled *payess*, or sideburns, were to serve as a visible testimony through modern times that the Biblical Hebrews of long ago still persisted and survived in uncompromising fashion. In so doing, they gave living breath to the immortality of continuance that their covenants with YaHWeH had so long ago promised.

THE LAW OF THE GRAVE

In 1687, an English mathematician and physicist named Isaac Newton (1642-1727) published his *Principia Mathematica*, a library work to rival anything ever writ by human hand. In it, among other things, he postulated the laws of motion and gravity, showing mathematically how everything in the material universe is affected by the attractive force of gravitation, from the motion of the planets to the relationship of all physical bodies to the Earth. Gravity, then, brought both a different kind of knowledge thundering down to Earth and a far less thunderous deity to preside over it, as befitting a Lord who directly reflected the newfound rational order of the physical universe.

The old "law of the grave"—"Nobody gets out of here alive"— which had been the very basis of patriarchal monotheistic Western civilization, now lost some of its hard edge. Though the Earth still drew all life back into it, that process was far less mysterious and chaotic now that humanity had the rational means for filling the space between birth and death with its own rapidly advancing power over nature.

Gravity also brought with it a new seriousness of purpose on the part of the necrocracy, for now that everything had the potential for material and mechanical explanation, control was of the utmost importance. Those national states that could centralize their political, economic, spiritual, and aristocratic authority around the strong personality of their ruling monarch were the ones who emerged at this time as the dominant powers. The European White West would now have a great deal of the planet at its disposal, thanks to its wedding of science and weaponry, and, as the eighteenth century progressed, England and France stood more and more as the two preeminent spheres of influence upon the continent.

Part of their dominance was due to a two-and-a-half-century process of migration round the globe that had begun about the year 1650, after the separate factions of Christendom had agreed to war under auspices other than religious difference and then channeled part of their redirected aggression into sweeping across oceans and continents in a wave that surpassed their earlier descents. The wealth of a wide swath of the Earth was thus exposed to anyone with the heavy-metal mettle to control, secure, denature, and colonize it. A brave new soon-to-be-denuded world now lay open to the might of rationality, as the West expanded its earlier continental concerns to include the entire globe in its desire for dominance.

AGE OF ENLIGHTENMENT

While the European necrocrats and datamasters continued along as always, its secular librarians began to turn their philosophic attention toward a reexamination of the social systems that had brought them to their current status. They now employed the new concept of rationalism in thrashing through the ancient earthly problem of those who had and those who had not and how to bridge the strange and terrible gap between the two.

As royalty of the French persuasion danced to their "last absolute waltz" in the person of one Louis, part XIV (1638-1715), who claimed to be part sun and part king, an incipient revolt of the mind began to brew that was desirous of reforming the basic fabric of authority. Spurred by the rational order that Newton had bestowed upon nature and the writings of John Locke (1632-1704), a fellow Englishman who saw humans as a blank page upon which anything they desired could be writ, the rationalists of the eighteenth century saw that the destiny of humanity lay totally in human hands. Henceforth, free will would become a factor in social evolution, and all that stood in its way, most notably the autocratic control of church 'n' state, would be roundly razzberried in their well-reasoned writings.

Enter the Enlightenment, which was begun in the salons of Paris and was furthered by the foremost and most formidable intellects of the day. Based upon a belief in humanity's free-will potential for utopian perfection, this outgrowth of Renaissance thought, with the added impetus of scientific discovery, led to a reevaluation of the heretofore unassailable position of God. The result was the philosophy of Deism, in which the Prime Mover of the heavens was given credit for inaugurating the process of biological life, before gracefully stepping aside to let the laws of nature run their natural course. The duty of humanity, then, was to discover these laws through rational investigation and apply them to all the disciplines of civilized existence: religious, political, social, and economic. Banished from the realms of serious investigation were alchemy and wicca-work and astrology and a host of other odd disciplines that did not conform to the strictures of organized knowledge. In their stead stood science and technology and the empirical truth of the five acknowledged senses.

The patriarchy's great fear of the hidden power of women, which had come to frenzied fruition in its ongoing witchcraft trials, had been progressively soothed by the ever-increasing advent of heavy metal, that great equalizer of the high and low. With its full-fledged introduction in England by mid-eighteenth century, no occult power seemed as mighty as the machine, for the unknown could no longer inspire trepidation in the torpid wake of science and industry's ever-growing presence.

Eschewing the superstitions, bigotry, and restraints of their church- dominated predecessors, the new rationalists of the White West precipitated two active revolutions by the eighteenth century's end, one in the Old World and one in the New. These were to bring the collective consciousness of humanity into its fourth epoch of political development: that of multiple rule by the people, an experiment that had been partially implemented by the ancient civilizations of Israel and Greece.

For most of the better-born of France, the Enlightenment was a time of all-out partying in preparation for the soggy deluge to come, for the day of an all-powerful aristocracy that ruled society from every level was fast drawing to a close. The egoistic consciousness of universal self-importance began to embrace an even larger segment of the male populace, who were beginning to take violent umbrage at their second-class citizenry. As the White West moved ever deeper into its own mind, it felt that the answers to its earthly problems lay not in its peaceful capacity to love but in its angry ability to act. The light that flowed from the Enlightenment, then, was one of a purely cerebral nature, which reinforced the ever-widening gulf people felt between body and mind, and heaven and Earth. It addressed the social injustices these divisions had created by moving ever deeper into the material world to try to find the key that would bring humanity back to the unity it once sought through its innocent, unlettered heart.

This focus on the physical would not be lost on the organized sacred world. The seemingly irreversible shift to materiality would shake Protestantism loose from its church-bound moorings and give rise to various evangelical sects who actively spurred revivals and re-awakenings to counterbalance the lost spirit of mystery that necro-cratic technology had so easily replaced. One such sect was the Methodists, initially named for their methodical approach to all things spiritual. They brought a simpler, more direct faith to the wan-ing heart of modernity and found a surprisingly open audience for their brand of salvation through faith rather than ritual. Protest, how-ever, was not restricted to matters of the spirit, as the secular world, too, wished to test the will that had been freed from the absolute strictures that had so long held it in thrall.

REVOLUTIONS OF TIME & SPACE

During the century numbered eighteen, the shift of European power moved strongly toward the British Isles, thanks to their rational and effective policies of colonization, conquest, and trade. England had a long tradition of relatively shared power, for it was a relatively small landmass that was very conscious of its own sense of both space and conduct, a warrior society that tempered its reined-in emotionality with a highly rational sense of overall order. Piece by piece, down through the centuries, it had allowed power to gradu-ally manifest in a number of different hands dating back to century thirteen, when the barons, bishops, and commons had first united to limit the singular authority of their blood regent.

In the period prior to the Enlightenment, the English had exper-ienced a highly "uncivil war" that saw their reigning monarch and his head part company and a brief Puritan republic replace him. Fol-lowing the restoration of the crown to its rightful pate in 1660, the king was made responsible to a political corpus of gentlemen called Parliament, which had evolved down through the centuries into a segregated, double-headed organ of highborns and commoners. This duality further divided into two opposing factions, one calling itself Whig, whose concerns were "life, liberty, and the liberal pur-suit of property," and the other claiming the title of Tory, whose credo was "king, church, and status with a heavy emphasis on the quo."

That ultimate bastion of celebratory democracy, the political party, was thus reborn, and the structured antagonism of its rival revelers has been the mainstay of Western republican government ever since. Political parties have created an orderly visible framework for public dialogue that its participants can then privately manipulate toward their own ambitious ends, in a system of checks and balances forged from the uneasy partnership of democracy's basic law firm, "Corruption and Idealism." The constant tensions twixt those two have been at the core of much of the West's subsequent social progress and regress, as both have continually played off one another with a mutual respect for the inherent wiles and reach of each. With the added dynamic of an independent press reporting its triumphs and failings, a certain illusion of power has been successfully passed down to those whose votes control the visible actors in the various legal dramas to which this system has been party. With it, a greater sense of separated self-importance has been visited upon all who live under the banner of democratic republicanism.

By the year 1763, the English were the singular most potent force in the Western world, supplanting their longtime foe, the French, for that distinction, thanks, in part, to their cunning exploitation of the Second Hemisphere. Some dozen years later, the New World was to throw all this exploitation back in their superior, triumphant faces, in a revolution of space and property. However, that is a tale reserved for later, as its reverberations were felt throughout the Old World, particularly in France, which of all the countries on the continent was now the ripest for revolutionary reevaluation.

THE FRENCH REVOLUTION, PART I

During the time that England's various estates began encroaching on royal power, France's royalty was increasing its hold at the expense of those very same groups. Thus, they unconsciously laid the groundwork for a totally different consciousness of power that would come to full flower a century and a quarter later in Russia: the multiple rule of the masses through a singular all-encompassing state.

By the late eighteenth century, the authority of both God and king could no longer be effectively invoked in France, for the former had manifested himself in a church far too material in its concerns to inspire spiritual awe, while the latter had shown himself to be a rather insensitive dullard.

In 1789, cries for greater reform gave way to angry action, and the red flag was first raised as symbol of this action, forever correlating red with the radicalism of new social order. The countryside suddenly found itself afire with the blazing embers of the toasted homes of the rich, while the estates of the second estate, the clergy, were consumed by the flaming passions of those who had gone so long without outlet to their incendiary grievances. Many factors fed into this violent upheaval of the symbols of church 'n' state, which had reigned supreme during the transitional centuries between the disparities of power of the Age of Metal and the great equalization to come through the auspices of heavy metal. One of the French Revolution's primary causes was the necronomics of maintaining a superstate status through a well-armed war machine, which, in turn, depended upon heavy taxation sans representation from its beleaguered citizenry. This imbalance, coupled with a starving countryside from recent poor harvests and lack of work, was more than enough to turn empty bellys into bellicose mobs, unleashing the sheer rage and frustration of their powerlessness without any ideological current behind it, save for naked release and revenge.

Though the blood-drenched, terror-filled sacrifice of a fair part of the upper tier of French society did little to immediately assuage this incredible and overwhelming anger, it did create a revolution of both time and numbers that would have far-reaching effects, particularly through the four-dimensional analysis of class dynamics and working-time values that it would inspire in the social thinkers of the coming century. With the renaming of the months and the declaration of the revolution as synonymous with the year 1, notice had been served to the European continent that the endless cycle of time had reached another of its culminations. French culture was now beginning anew, under different rules and a different order, with a Declaration of the Rights of Man (if not woman) as its basis in raising the self-importance of France's ordinary citizens. In the revolution's excesses, however, it began moving backward in time, with its barbaric cries for more and more blood and its orgies of paganlike release in the countryside as well as its peasant uprisings. Finally, a decade after the Terror had bled itself out, the government went all the way back to the concept of emperor, allowing France to enter the nineteenth century with that ancient symbol of ego supreme at its head.

In its disruption of the temporal political order of things, however, the French Revolution did give voice, if not total actuality, to the ideals of fraternity, liberty, and equality. Its ultimate legacy would be the modern political state with its similar high tolerance for "governmental violence in the name of public good" and its nonspiritual religiosity of ideologies and ideals, which, in turn, would produce a similar low tolerance for completely opposing viewpoints. Also, for the first time in modern history, women would be an active and violent political force, and this factor would not be lost on the rising consciousness of the power of sisterhood in the coming decades.

Thus, the eighteenth century saw the White West refocus its primary view of existence thoroughly within the limits of the earthly sphere, rather than the greater universe that surrounded it. In doing so, that integrater of all worlds here, as personified and deified by the spirit of the Christ, receded ever further in importance from the realm of inquiring speculation. Though the Christ-force remained potent in the hearts and imaginations of those who still wished to see spirit remain alive here, his immortal power had been usurped by more temporal, secular concerns. As the possibilities of material existence on Earth grew ever greater for one and all, so did the process of fragmented individual consciousness continue to rise, moving people ever farther away from their deep-seated connection to the unity of all life and into the isolation and separation of the disconnected "I" of self and self-interest.

And so, as the ages of Information, Reformation, and Transformation drew to their eighteenth-century close, a depraved new world awaited everyone, and just as it had been so many times before, and just as it would be so many times after, it was once again the very beginning of things.

The Age of Fragmented Unities
1800-1900 A.Z.

The reader is invited to fully enter the modern world, with the rise and fall of Napoleon, a further revolution named Industrial, the first of the Marx Brothers, sisterhood's emergence, Darwin of the Apes, the return of the Roman Empire, and a prolonged visit from the World of the Dead, all packed into a century that would bridge memories of medievalia with modernity.

By the early 1800s, the spiritual soul of the White West had put its credence in its full pockets rather than in its enfolded palms, choosing to limit its vistas to that which could be physically seen, felt, and touched now that it had permanently moved upward from its irrational heart into its far more ordered head. As part of this process, the Bible, which had been the unquestioned sacred-library source of the creation and continuance of humanity, lost its singular authority over time and truth. The two now began to be examined on a far greater scale outside its literal story, much to the fundamental displeasure of those who refused to dip into its brilliant gift for figurative metaphor and clung, instead, to the straightforward surface of its narrative.

Christendom had taken a long time truly separating itself from its Judaic root, and the relaxation of the Bible's power over the secular and scientific libraries of the West during the eighteenth and nineteenth centuries was the signal that this separation had been completed. Since the two beliefs in the One God shared different stories that were bound together in the same sacred book, with each taking its version as an absolute, this separation had been long and tortuous, with the master storytellers not only divorced and denounced by their students but actively persecuted as well. The Christian student tale of a singular spectacular resurrection had been a highly personalized condensation of the original story's collective immortal sweep, and while both had the unmistakable hand of the divine about them, each, in essence, denied the full power of the other. This had caused the Christian librarians of the far more accessible and personal tale, the story of the Master's mastery over Death, to drive their original Judaic teachers into as deep an exile as they possibly could, for fear the two tales might one day reunite, with a set of newer and even more powerful librarians to contend with through their reunification.

With the rise of commerce and science, this sacred-library work lost some of its all-consuming importance. As the West grew less Catholic and more ethically Protestant, its Jewish presence started to grow more tolerable again, for the daemonic magician image long associated with these ancient absolutists was now the dying relic of a superstitious age that had finally spun itself out. Old resentments still simmered and upon occasion exploded, but the displaced Israeli nation saw that if it relaxed some of its absolutes and took on the outer trappings of its surrounding world, it could achieve a far greater degree of assimilated acceptance; it was now looked on only as a displaced nation of aliens and intruders, rather than a direct channel of the Devil.

Although many of the tribes of Israel refused to compromise on their distinct dress and traditions and continued to suffer the stigma of isolation for it, others superficially altered their outer separateness in order to submerge themselves in the secular spheres of commerce and trade. Though they were still resented as a race apart, the world was once again begrudgingly opened to them. So it was that these founders of individual self-importance, who were so vigorously vilified for that conceit, now found that the rest of the White West had finally caught up to them. They were permitted to coexist with most of the rest of the continent, save for Eastern Europe, amidst much demagogic grumbling and one last symbolic trial and judgment in France at century's end. The master storytellers had returned, and part of their story now was to reweave themselves into the complex tapestry their students had created out of the tales of separation they had first woven.

NAPOLEON BONAPARTE

The 1800s were officially inaugurated by an obsessive little chap, one Napoleon Bonaparte (1769-1821), who acted as symbol of both individual and empire, two political considerations that would be heavily emphasized over the next hundred years. In November 1799, the Directory, which had been the nominal head of France, was overthrown, and a dictatorship was set up with Napoleon as first consul. So began the Napoleonic Era, which was to see him crown himself emperor in 1804 and set his family on the various thrones of Europe, while he rewrote the legal codes of society in order to give order and uniformity to the empire he was to forge through martial will. Two years later, he officially ended that last vestige of medievalia, the Holy Roman Empire, as he continued along his pathway of European dominance. Until the year 1809, he seemed invincible, a blazing whirl of energy who was everywhere at once, superhuman in both his drive and his detail of attention to all that affected his ambition.

However, this incredible expenditure of blood and sweat, if not tears, was to take its toll. By the time he had reached forty, he was once more an ordinary mortal, and his empire, built totally around the shining light of his being, began to crumble. This demise happened slowly at first and then in waves, beginning with his sacrifice of more than a half-million men to the idea that the eternal steppes of Russia could be conquered by an invasionary land force. It ended finally with the Battle of Waterloo in Belgium in 1815, which ultimately saw the defeated and now corpulent former little corporal shipped unceremoniously off to the south Atlantic isle of St. Helena. There he was to grow ever fatter and more lethargic as he pondered his shattered career, till his release from that life in 1821, under somewhat suspect circumstances.

Napoleon's name reflects the Greek god of unity and light, Apollo. However, read backward, "noelopan," he is a combination of Christian beliefs ("noel"), the "great circle" (0), and pagan lore (Pan). That trinity would influence his ultimate effect, impelling a far greater idea of country in each of his enemies by drawing their sense of identity with their land (pagan) together with their growing One God/one self sense of self-importance (Judeo/Christian). Through his auspices, a great circle (0) had been completed and the West would no longer need a solitary emperor to show it the way to itself. It had, at last, found political voice for its desire for unified separation and would henceforth demand a far more complex pathway to unity than mere military genius could bestow.

Characters like the Emperor Napoleon exist on numerous levels, for in addition to their effect on the world of actualities, they serve as fantasies for the lives of all they touch, and thus many became a part of them. They are the emperor within, that mythos each of us secretly carries if we were but allowed to exhibit our absolute power. For the many who lived at that time who could barely abide their miserable existences, being Napoleon, at least in their minds, made for a more tolerable mode of thought. Thus, a curious legacy was passed down to the unhinged in mental institutions for generations to come, as the delusion of being Napoleon became the cliché for mental derangement of the highest order, which served as a fitting epitaph for the insanity of the dream of absolute control in a world as fragmented and out of control as our own.

The year 1815 marked the end of the Napoleonic Era, and a congress was called in the Austrian city of Vienna to reassess the havoc that France had unleashed on the continent over the last twenty-five years. Although the Congress of Vienna looked backward in all that it did, it unconsciously precipitated a great leap forward in political thought and feeling. The Western world now realized that whatever happened within the borders of each of its separated countries profoundly affected what happened outside their borders as well, for the world, thanks to Bonaparte's retreat from it, had come quite a bit closer. Though it chose to rigidly define itself in terms of enclosed geography, it was now totally dependent on its many parts in order to maintain the level of civilization its denizens expected for themselves. Despite a regression back to the governmental forms of the eighteenth century, Europe was now bursting with nationalistic spirit and chafing to express it, as a revolution called Industrial began to drag its adherents ever deeper into the material world and ever further away from their interest in anything that was not of that plane.

A REVOLUTION NAMED INDUSTRIAL

The "revolution of industry" began in England in the 1750s with the emergence of the "machine," a monster that could do the work of ten, then twenty, then a hundred and more, never complaining of its lot, or dissipating itself in drink, or asking for political equality. It merely functioned as it was asked, and then sat quietly until asked to function again. As the machine grew ever more complex, it was housed in its own quarters, called factories. Soon, the elements that always had been the juice of life—the wind and the water—were no longer satisfying to its rapacious appetite for energy, and the earth had to be stirred and dug for metal to lace its sides and for food to shovel down its craw.

Suddenly the machine was everywhere, singing the reverbed screech of heavy metal, twanging and spinning and whirling and clanking as the cities throbbed to its deadening drumbeat and people came from all over to serve it, building shanties and slums around themselves so as to insure their captivity in its all-consuming sound. They multiplied and drenched themselves in misery so that they could fully appreciate the sonic power of this cold, hard creature who knew but one song, though it was such a compelling tune that few could resist its mechanical howl. It ate its audience alive and it poisoned their garbage-strewn quarters with its excess, reshaping the planet with its clawing, scraping, shoveling, tunneling need for ever more fuel to keep its smokestack mouth aglow.

THE INSECT WORLD

By 1830, heavy metal had utterly transformed England from a nation of isolated villages to one of cities thick with people competing and battling with one another for work and narrow space, as the rapacious datamasters who controlled this process began realtering their urban model around one of the alternate realities on this planet. The inventiveness of humanity throughout its dual metal ages has always reflected the form and brittleness of the insect world, with the tool-makers among us creating mechanical creatures that superficially mimick those odd biological beings that swarm and sting and crawl in outrageous numbers over the humid and temperate zones of Earth.

Many have been here in the same form for the last two hundred million years, so that they are a direct biological bridge between the archaic Eden of Earth and its lost paradise of both remembered and unremembered history. Their hard-shelled durability and devotion to instinctual task has been imitated in the mechanical wonders we have developed to transcend the limits of our natural world. These insectlike inventions have gone on to inspire in the cities subsequently redesigned to house them an equally unconscious indebtedness to the hive and colony mentality, which allows a great number of busy beings to live in close proximity with one another.

Not only did the apparatus of the machine come to take humanity into a totally alien culture, it also re-created that culture on a much larger scale in the honeycombed layout of our many-leveled modern cities. This transposition of a complex, interdependent, life-filled world to a lifeless replica of it would be accompanied by a befouled, sulfurous, barely breathable environment and a further reduction of the work force needed to stoke and maintain it into dronelike automatons completely subservient to the all-encompassing, thoroughly alien, and thoroughly alienating hum of mindless and compulsive progress.

As men left their homes to serve this mechanical blight, women began, en masse, to take their first steps toward their own realization of self-worth, much to the consternation of their confused sexual counterparts. These latter still felt that self-importance was strictly a male province, but because of the deadening distractions of serving the machinery of technological advance they were less able to consistently maintain this posture. In addition, the long tradition of working in concert around the home and in the fields had been broken, and this, too, would further alienate the sexes.

In projected reaction to the "insectization" of urban humanity, a movement dubbed "romantic" began to dance across the imagination of the European continent at the end of the eighteenth century. Romanticism glorified nationhood, self, and heroic death in its masculine guise and praised nature, emotion, and sensual life in its feminine. The Goddess, so long absent from the West, save in her secret worship by the very few, began at last to return in loose disguise to prepare humanity for the acceptance of its hidden half.

Thus, a triune of *isms*—romantic, liberal, and national in its masculine form and emotional, egalitarian, and identity-based in its feminine—pervaded the thought of the continent all through the first half of century nineteen. The air became laced with ripostes of revolution everywhere save England, whose orderly and rational use of debate and enacted law countermanded any calls for violent upheaval, despite similar dissatisfaction expressed over its own inequities of power shared. These *isms* finally came to full head in 1848, and the Goddess in liberty guise was called to the barricades in a host of countries, as a mass emotional cry for equity and identity went up all over continental Europe. Though much of it was quickly stilled by force, the voice of the people had definitely been heard, and that voice would soon grow ever more shrill.

THE FIRST OF THE MARX BROTHERS

In that year, a revolutionary pamphlet was writ called "The Communist Manifesto," and the reverberations of the ideas expressed in it are still being felt nearly a century and a half later. Its author was the first of the "cosmic" Marx brothers, Karl Heinrich ("Karl-o") Marx (1818-1883). Though his act was largely a single, he was a very serious comedian and one of two secular storytellers supreme who would totally rewrite the tale of humanity during the 1800s.

His manifesto roughly limned society as a two-sided affair that operated around its economic aims, with two classes—one dominant, the other recessive—in a continuing struggle for power round the labor that is produced by the dynamic of their antagonism. The dominant, or "drooling," class, called so for its avarice, greed, and general unconsciousness to everything but profit, was now, according to Karl-o, completing its cycle of power, since it was partially occupied by the *bourgeoisie*, that sober, acquisitive midclass of data-gatherers. The *proletariat*, those uprooted workers who had to leave both land and town to follow the machinery of progress and who were the only true producers left in society, were about to begin their own ascent to authority, for their cycle had just started.

Marx took the traditional tri-part rhythm of thesis, antithesis, and synthesis—or entity, its opposite, and a resolution of the two (unity, duality, and trinity)—and ran the evolution of economic consciousness against it. He thus created a story of exploiter, exploited, and revolution of one against the other, which in turn, creates an entirely new story of exploiter, exploited, and revolution of one against the other, until at last it is resolved in a worker's paradise of unity, where there is no need for either of those two catalytic roles to be enacted any further. In envisioning his impending perfect state, however, he didn't realize that the two classes of oppressor and oppressed would once again be created by his ultimate order of rule by the proletariat and that the process of thesis, antithesis, and synthesis would have to start all over again, with his new state as the beginning premise for this process rather than its end product.

If Karl-o hadn't been so primed for revolution, he might have realized that the two basic processes of politics—revolution, with its emphasis on upheaval and new order, and evolution, with its emphasis on reform and gradual change—rarely resolve themselves on their own, for life on this planet is far more than an economic affair. Most revolutions are fought with the idea they are the end product of this process of threes, when in actuality they are only the catalyzing party. Thus, the real revolution becomes a far longer affair than the brief span usually allotted it, for inherent in its process is a score of revolutions, evolutions, resolutions, and revelations to come, sometimes centuries and millennia apart, since they are by their dialectic nature a continuing process rather than a resultant one. The concept of communism, which he envisioned as the theory and practice of communally shared wealth, is still very much an evolving, revolving procedure, as it awaits the proper consciousness, both individual and mass, to truly understand its precepts; it is a process of evolution that will probably take many more revolutions to reveal.

The first of the cosmic Marx brothers went on to lead a life of spectacular gloom—an alien wherever he beetled his dark brow. Though he had a visionary's view that could sweep the entire stage of human economic development and a sense of humor so high it was beyond laughter, the last laugh was on him, because in the final several decades of his life he could not see how to support himself and so had to live off the capital beneficence of friends.

This myopia says reams about Karl-o, for in his master utopian vision, little shrift is given to the individual or the mundane concerns of the worker: he or she is merely an anonymous part of a much greater whole. Though he understood the processes of social evolution as few before or after him ever have, still he could not turn them to his own personal and spiritual benefit. Denying his own simple needs of heart, family, and home, he was forced to suffer greatly for his genius, for he allowed none of it to guide his own welfare.

The absence of direct spirituality in his writings has gone on to create an equal absence of direct spirituality in the various states that have subsequently embraced his theories, atheistic economic theocracies that most of them are. Therein lies half the tale of the twentieth century, over whose twisting corridors his shadow still heavily hangs.

SISTERHOOD EMERGES

In 1792, the same year as the French Revolution's "Declaration of the Rights of Man," a unique library work was published in England on behalf of humanity's other half. Written by one Mary Wollstonecraft (1759-1797), it was called the "Vindication of the Rights of Women." Though little mass heed was paid to it at the time, it was the "emancipation proclamation" of a long-enslaved cross-cultural segment of our race and signal that the sacred and secular libraries of the West would now have another highly unpredictable force scribbling over and defacing its sacrosanct texts, a prospect fraught with grim consequence to the upholders of the library's pristine all-male traditions.

Sure enough, within a couple of decades, their worst fears were realized when the honored role of teacher was returned to European women, after so many millennia of denial. From the teachers came Teachers, powerful public personalities who knew how to articulate the deep slavery that women had been cast under so that their brothers of the "I" could have the relative freedom to develop their separate selves. This was yet another fallout of the loss of social power of the Bible, for though it had long held the separate and collective world of sisterhood in mighty check, a whole new world, that of female emancipation, had been opened by that good gray book's partial closing. The freedom from patriarchal servitude promised by this liberation would continue growing in strength throughout the century, as a political rather than a personal force, but one that would eventually open up the primarily male preserves of self and self-interest to the rest of still highly segregated humanity.

Mary Wollstonecraft died ten days after giving birth to a daughter of the same name. That daughter, Mary Wollstonecraft Shelley (1797-1851), went on to live a romantic and tragic life, while producing a most extraordinary mystery tale, *Frankenstein*, which gave odd prophetic complement to her mother's text. In it, a student of the world of man and science and reason gives life to the dead, but in his alchemical ability to co-create, that student produces a monster that cannot be loved and therefore extracts a dire retribution on its creator. "Frankenstein" would become an apt metaphor for the excesses of scientific reason, and a cautionary, if unheeded, projection on the inevitable consequences of unthinking and unfeeling science, two patriarchal considerations that the succeeding epochs would be uncomfortably playing with more and more.

THE NINETEENTH CENTURY, PART II

The second half of the nineteenth century saw the earlier triune of *isms*—romantic, liberal, and national—synthesize down into a singular concern: realism. This methodical approach to problems brooked neither fantasy nor high ideal, looking as it always did for the "real" road, the one least odious to the most people in power.

With the advent of the machine and its spread of urban insect consciousness to the continent, the tempo of life picked up considerably. The processes of social evolution speeded up, as information previously won over lifetimes was now spread in minutes through the various miracles of telegraphy and print. Through this immediate dissemination, the beloved cry of country began to supersede all concerns, as the fragmentation of separated self now dictated that everyone within its secular grasp have a sense of belonging to some sort of unified national whole.

The old Holy Roman Empire's two former enclave territories, Italy and Germany, were, at century's middle, divided in twain, with the north of each representing rule for the entire land and both subject to Austria, the seat of a modest mid-European empire still clinging to its medieval ideal of church, monarchy, and paternal authority. The architect of Austrian policy through most of the first half of the century was Klemens von Metternich (1773-1859), a highborn minister and diplomat who liked strong authoritarian states. Though no global war was fought during his long political supremacy, no peace could be had anywhere either, and the forces of change were finally to erupt at the halfway point of the century everywhere that Austria, the last European gasp of the ancient way of the West, lay its archaic hand.

The original European seat of all this turmoil, France, after a brief try at a second republic, settled in under the aegis of a nephew of Napoleon (1808-1873), whose same name, with a III affixed to it, allowed him to assume the mantle of emperor in 1852. After eighteen years of monarchy, the emperor was suddenly caught without his clothes upon the battlefield during a territorial war and suffered the ignominy of being captured. This event precipitated three momentous events in 1871: the return of Rome to Italy and its subsequent complete unification; the uniting of Germany around the militaristic state of Prussia and its subsequent nationhood; and the return of France to its idea of republic for a third time.

The papal states, left unprotected by these events, suddenly found themselves reduced to a city of 110 acres inside Rome. Thus, despite much unholy grumbling by the pope, the church was forced to accept the indignity of no longer being a landed force in the European schema of things.

DARWIN OF THE APES

Haughtily sitting above all these changes was the British Empire, the largest mass of earth ever recorded under one banner, which was ruled in form, if not substance, by one Victoria Regina (1819-1901). Under Victoria, dullness was raised to mythic proportions as the widowed monarch cast a somber pall of manners and double-edged morals upon the high-spirited nation over which she sat for an incredibly long sixty years. She set a tone of sobriety that would make the epithet "Victorian" forever after synonymous with prudence, propriety, and the suppression of all things prurient.

Since England's strengths in relation to its surrounding world far outweighed its discernible weaknesses during the time of Victoria, Britain was able to occupy a rather unique position in the affairs of the world. Engaging as it did in both imperial fantasy over the non-white civilizations of Asia and Africa and industrial dominance over its similarly hued but less advanced neighbors, it looked upon a great deal of the globe as its separated province. This dominance over their presumed lessers was to generate a secular storyteller who would rival Marx as the top comedian of the century, one Charles Darwin (1809-1882). In several strange ways Darwin paralleled his fellow philosopher of ascending and descending humanity, limning an English theory of evolution that would stand right alongside his compatriot's German theory of revolution.

Darwin proposed in two book-length treatises, *The Origin of Species* in 1859 and *The Descent of Man* in 1871, that humans had evolved from lesser beings, as had the other complex creatures of this planet. Although this was a most intriguing proposal from a scientific standpoint, it was met with a public revulsion that only the theories of Marx had been previously accorded. It was read as a direct linkage

between the exalted superiority of humanity and the degraded inferiority of the great ape, a concept so anti-Victorian as to be regarded
as the apostasy of a luridly perverted mind.

Because he had dared reveal the possible primitive nature of
humanity to a people who were trying to transcend the loathsome-
ness of their primordial senses, and because his ideas conflicted with
the Book of Law's lingering story of creation, "Darwin of the Apes"
was ultimately forced to retire to his modest estate. There he was to
morbidly hang on the long tendrils and vines of his thick-leafed
mind while brooding in melancholy reflection for the rest of his days
over the irony that his own species was not only unwilling to accept
the possibilities of its origins, but it had unmanfully descended to
insult and name-calling in its resistance to the simple gift he had
tried to bestow upon his fellow sapient Homo sapiens.

Ironically, Marx was much entranced with the political possibilities of the theory of evolution and sent him a copy of the second German edition of his *Das Kapital*, but Darwin politely demurred at this
expression of intellectual solidarity, feeling he had enough troubles
of his own without incurring further wrath for befriending a fellow
genius-pariah.

A century later, many of Darwin's theories are being seriously
challenged by further findings from the bones of antiquity, spurring
the belief that humans are just as much a product of revolutionary
adaptation, in which they instantly pop up in proper form to meet
new environmental circumstances, as they are of slowly evolving into
them. In not seeing the process of revolution in the evolutionary
process, an oversight dictated by the limited material with which he
had to work, Darwin's unfolding vision of the evolvement of humanity curiously paralleled that of Marx's myopias, who, for similar reasons, had failed to see the full possibilities of evolution in his own
revolutionary process and had therefore deemed it an end in itself.
Thus, the theorists of evolution and revolution wound up misread-
ing their incomplete data and suffering mightily for it, when in actuality their diamond minds had discovered two philosophic lodes that
would take considerably more plumbing before their true yield could

surface, four-dimensional thinkers that they were in a world rapidly reducing itself to 3-D.

THE MECHANICAL EYE OF HUMANITY OPENS

Contributing to this process of dimension reduction was the invention of the camera, which seemingly captured life exactly as it was in its unique gift for turning light into image through the miracle of absorptive paper. This opened the globe to its own odd assortment of physical wonders, for now there was photographic proof positive of realities that heretofore could only be symbolically re-created through pictographs and pictorial language. The planet could now tighten its view of itself through the vicarious intimacy of photography, while bringing its collective imagination far more down to earth.

The first war ever recorded under the auspices of this new invention was fought in the Russian Crimean peninsula in the 1850s, and the sacrosanct arena of the battlefield, that peculiar province of male initiation into the survival dichotomy of the quick and dead, lost much of its grim mystique to the intrusion of this unblinking eye. The West thus began to prepare itself for the industrialization of aggression soon to come, where armaments would be measured by the ton and the human fighting factor, save for body counts, would become more and more negligible. The ubiquitous machine, which could spew out both cold information and hot death—and create the mechanical apparatus to do each—now had the capacity to draw in information as well. This ability would revolutionize dimensional consciousness, for the alchemical magic of co-creation, that ancient mystery that enables humans to play directly with nature, was now pictorially available to the West through a machine.

The magic of photography was a giant sorcerer's step forward for the forces of control, for the seemingly irrefutable reality of pictures could be manipulated as potent weapons in themselves by the datamasters and necrocrats, who profited most from the reassessment of political, social, and economic information that had reshaped Europe during century nineteen. In similar manner, at the century's midpoint, a full half of the Western European continent was illiterate and therefore beyond the reach of anything outside their immediate experience. However, through determined governmental effort in expanding elementary education throughout Europe, this situation was speedily amended. By late century, a proliferation of print, newspapers, and periodicals was subtly and blatantly shaping public opinion, reaching into the minds of the many to give them the illusion of intelligent choice, as power could now assert itself through a host of different avenues with a far more accessible citizenry to manipulate at its behest.

Thanks to the continuing rise of a highly acquisitive midclass of consumers, who reveled in the magic of manifestation that the new masters of materiality could now produce, the last quarter of the nineteenth century saw Europe imperially colonize and exploit its undeveloped fellow continents in unprecedented manner, a process that would finally end in that ultimate necrocratic nightmare, world war, early in the next century. For the moment, however, a goodly part of the material world lay prostrate at the feet of the states of Western Europe, whose intense rivalry with one another seemed to hold within it the future for everyone for centuries to come. Empire and individual, those two Napoleonic considerations, had been democratized and capitalized all through the nineteenth century, and by its end, no force on Earth seemed capable of halting Western Europe's resounding dominance of world affairs. The unified mantle of Rome, lost in the long ago and then reborn in the church, only to see that edifice steadily reduced and compressed, was now seemingly shared by several highly competitive nation-states that had once known the outer reach of that empire and secretly desired to recast the world similarly in their own image. The real Roman Empire, however, was still very much alive, and it would emerge in the twentieth century as an unacknowledged superpower, with all its old sorcerer will and control still very much in evidence.

THE ROMAN EMPIRE NEVER DIED

When a phenomenon as awesome as the ancient Roman Empire hits a planet, it does not just disappear into the bloodied archives of oppressive memory when its exit on the timepike of history finally hoves into view. Rather, it alters form to blur its true identity and then continues on in lumbering disguise until an entranceway back onto that temporal highway has once more been cleared for its continuance.

The Roman Empire was an epochal sorcerer civilization based on the expression of pure will. Though its potency was ultimately blunted by those eternal eaters of history, the ever-accommodating barbarians at the gates, ancient Rome never completely died. Well before the Renaissance came to flower, it began to look for an appropriate vehicle in which to rise phoenixlike once again and found it on the island of Sicily, which was separated from Italy proper by a narrow strait of water and had, through its long story, been unable to defend itself, allowing a series of foreign forces to occupy it from pre-empire days on down. A long tradition of absentee ownership ensued, so that its interior ultimately became managed by those among its lower orders who could secure order through the sheer force of their will. As a result, this peculiar island evolved quite differently from the rest of Europe, pivotally placed as it was along trade and warfare routes and yet vulnerable as it was to continual alien encroachment.

Christianity had had little initial impact on this former Roman colony, and so an ancient disregard for life taking flourished here far longer than in any of its European neighbors, thereby keeping this repository for the new empire medieval long after the rest of the continent had passed into modernity. On both the Sicilian coastline and in its interior, pure force was the prevailing mode giving expression to power, and *il uomo inteso*, the strong man, that relic of patriarchal power fantasies, became the ruling core of the many estates of this feudal realm.

Sicily was finally liberated in 1860 from more than two millennia of foreign rule, and during the decade that followed, just prior to the reunification of Italy, a secret society of political power-brokers and brigands came into being there. They were known as the *Mafia*, the true inheritors of the will and the force that was once ancient Rome. Products of a social system that time seemed to have sidestepped, they were given further opportunity to develop along their singular lines by the neglectful central government of their united mainland. The consciousness of dominance by any means whatsoever was thus allowed to thoroughly determine Sicily's codes of development and behavior. The controlling dons of this classic sorcerer's underworld, along with their feudal armies, would rise to prominence within short order as the urban insect lust of heavy metal began to cry out for escape from its denatured entrapment. The necromasters of this new empire were now given ready excuse to supply the sorely oppressed world of commerce with illicit stimulants and depressants, as well as gambling apparatus and other heart-pumping diversions for those whose tastes ran beyond the range of legitimacy.

THE OVERWORLD, THE UNDERWORLD & FREE ENTERPRISE

Our planet is a place where light and darkness have always lived side by side. The daily cycle of the moon following the sun tells us that this is a world of endless dualities, where opposites have to learn their common connections in order to recognize and deal with one another. The day-and-night dynamic that shapes our lives gives power to illumination as well as ignorance, and both dwell together in virtually everything on our world of cyclical light and dark.

Because of this phenomenon, wherever there is a powerful ruling "overworld" here, there is usually an underworld to reflect it and give shadowy complement to its excesses. Although our popular conception of the underworld consigns it to the realm of the criminal, it is a far more complex and convoluted domain than that. All of our definitive spheres of earthly power have their own underworlds with which to contend, hidden spheres where social and spiritual apostasies are acted out in defiance of accepted authority. The underworld is here in part, then, as a mirror of those elements in the human spirit that are not allowed to flower in the light and yet seek compulsive expression somewhere. Instead of dealing with this sphere as an integral part of our slow evolution as sentient beings who are equally affected by both the dark and the light, the underworld is looked upon as a total social aberration, something that is completely divorced from our collected civilized presence.

Over the last several centuries, most of the overworld of Western commerce has adopted a system called "free enterprise" to give order to its material cravings. The basic idea of free enterprise is that anybody is free to be enterprising about anything that has a potential marketability. Although all this is theoretically constrained by commercial law, in actual practice this system recognizes no boundaries, and anything that falls outside the law falls prey to the enterprising underground entrepreneur.

The basic nature of free enterprise seems to dictate this duality, for it encourages profitable exploitation of whatever can be exploited, regardless of the consequences. Anytime a desired commodity is made illegal, its marketing channels are merely altered to accommodate this condition, and an underground network is created to facilitate its distribution. Inherent in the structure of free enterprise, then, is an enormous potential for criminality. Because of this possibility, the Mafia dons, those teachers of the power of pure will, have become yet another controlling force in the economic sorcerer hierarchy of the White West. Though the self-interest-above-all-else philosophy that they so willfully represent is looked on by many with ethical repugnance—and with secret admiration by others—they are, in fact, a direct mirror of the overworld of commerce stripped of its surface politeness, as well as a continual reminder of free enterprise's failure to recognize its social and moral obligation to create a mature-enough marketplace to deal with the freedom of choice that marketplace truly entails.

As long as arbitrary standards of legality and illegality are imposed over commodities, there will always be a commercial underground to reflect the disintegrative excesses that the unconscious exploitation of resource without any thought other than pure profit always seems to engender. Both the underworld and the overworld of commerce have come to reflect different sides of the same whole, operating as they do out of the same credo of supreme self-interest. Both have helped as well to deaden the greater spirituality of the West through their venal competition for its material soul, although only one, the underworld, has borne universal condemnation for this.

THE WORLD OF THE DEAD

In the momentous year of 1848, which marked a considerable turning point in White Western planetary consciousness, some mysterious table-rappings in a house in the northeastern part of the far-off United States, belonging to a family with the beast-name of Fox, began a transcontinental fascination with the world of the dead. In England, the titular head of state, Victoria, had spent most of her long reign in mourning her prematurely departed husband, Albert (1819-1861). The British Isles were thus particularly ripe for the mediumistic explosion that followed shortly after the Foxes were let into the coops of the public imagination and allowed to run wild under the name of "spiritualism," a movement that spawned an orgy of misinformation via the unclear-eyed channels who exploited it.

Despite its fraud and flummery, however, spiritualism provided a release for many women from the grasp of orthodox patriarchal religious institutions. In the sances they attended, they found a freedom of spiritual expression and independence that would be translated for many into all other aspects of their lives. It is no accident that the rise of spiritualism coincided with the rise of women as an active political force. Through it, a power long denied by medieval witch hysteria had returned, and this time that power was here to stay.

Nineteenth-century mediumship was a final attempt by a world in the process of reducing itself down to its three-dimensional planetary essence to try to keep its larger vision of itself alive. However, little did the spiritualists of that time realize that the world of the dead with which they were so eager to open communications was coming directly down to the planet through the channel of the denatured squeal of heavy metal and all the antilife force it brought with it in its insect efficiency.

As a result, the dead came in great numbers to share quarters with the living through both suburban séance and slavery to the machine in the urban hives. And ever more of the magic of existence, of the natural world, of the higher planes became lost to the clarion clank of humanity's inventive need to contain and control the elements.

In the process, the Earth completed its post–Middle Ages collective life transition by moving inexorably into its "Old Ages," its body now toxic and scarred, with its necrocratic forces of will and power and dominance in total command of its machinery of opinion and progress. The nineteenth century ended in the Occident's First Hemisphere with the living and the dead living side by side with one another, neither knowing who was who nor much caring that there was a difference. In its individual and collective striving for self-importance the West had finally lost all of its ancient magic, and now only its naked and deadly ambition remained in the many fragmented unities that made up this world so strangely connected and yet so deeply isolated from itself.

And so, as the despiritualized West prepared itself for a century in which, for the first time in a very long time, it would confront its very real and possible collective death, it was once more, just as it always is, the very beginning of things.

○

CHAPTER SIXTEEN

The Age of Relativity 1900-1990 A.Z.

The reader is invited to re-experience the War-to-End-All-Wars, parts I and II, the French Revolution, part II, sisterhood's continuing rise, the Einstein/Frankenstein duality of modern science, the birth of the atomic Antichrist child, Israel's reemergence, the Cold War, the explorations of outer and inner space, and the coming of Doomsday, part II.

As the clocks of the White West chimed in the new century, the twentieth since the Kingdom of Come had come and gone, all the worlds that had come together under the aegis of heavy metal—the overworld and underworld of commerce, the insect world, the wedding of science, industry, and weaponry, and their combined legacy, the world of the dead—were now poised for a hundred years whose collective likes had not been seen since the worst of the sorcerer excesses of ancient Atlantis.

Over the last several centuries, the mantle of rotating dominance had passed steadily from one European empire to the next: Spain, France, England, and now Germany in noticeable cyclic order. Each conquering nation wound up deflating itself from the necronomics

266

of military expenditures to keep up its battlefield empires, allowing the aftermaths of their various competitive conflicts to dictate the real winners and losers, while insuring a continual shift in power through this illusionary system of territory combatatively won and then economically lost.

Two of the central groups in this ongoing conflict of superiority of the national "I," the Aryan Christians and the Semitic Jews, those eternal nemeses from Atlantean times, now occupied the polar extremities of power in Europe. The former exercised diluted dominance over the rest of the continent, as well as a goodly part of the globe, while the latter were finding only compromise and assimilation as their most viable avenue back to a position where they could gain the power to become landed again.

By the nineteenth century's end, a movement called "Zionist," a name symbolic of Jerusalem and the Promised Land, began to foment among the greatly separated tribes of the Hebrews, with a goal of reclaiming the birthright promised it by YaHWeH in the long ago. The secular timing seemed propitious, for now that the White West had incorporated Israel into itself, through its own brand of chosenness and its own unity through separation, the real Israel was far less of a threat. In addition, Israel's sacred library had been pillaged and sacked and stolen so often by science and spiritual amendment that the fear of the Jews' secret power that had so long plagued the creators of Western spiritual history was considerably diminished. Highly vocal elements in both France and Germany still blatantly clung to that medieval fantasy, and a forged document outlining a plan for Hebraic world domination called "The Protocols of the Elders of Zion" further fed into it. However, the rest of the West, save for Eastern Europe, felt, more or less, superior to these magicians-turned-peddlers who seemingly had been abandoned by their god through all their endless adversities. Anti-Jewish feeling persisted, but it was less a fear of unknown power than it was a fear of those who are different.

And so, in the late 1890s a trickle of settlers was allowed to return to the desert that had so long ago rejected them. There they joined those who had never left and those who had emigrated there in the

1820s and 1830s, when the return unofficially began, to begin the process of re-creating a landed testimony to their specialness. Israel had always been a combination of those who had stayed behind and those who had departed in every country in which it had ever existed as a bodiless nation, so that those who returned this time had finally come full circle to interlock with the shadows of their once and future nation, where ego had first raised its collective head so many thousands of years ago.

THE WAR-TO-END-ALL-WARS, PART I

The Aryan drive for imperial dominion everywhere reached its apex between the years 1870 and 1914, when Europe dominated most of the world's financial, cultural, industrial, and commercial pursuits. Sorcerer civilization had reached a competitive impasse, for each separate expression of its fragmented face had designs on as much of the world as it could possibly swallow, and now that much of that world had been staked and claimed, it only had itself to turn in on. It was inevitable that empires would eventually and angrily collide, and thus it was in 1914 that a shot "hurt" round the world was squeezed off, this one into the weighty corpus of the heir to the Central European throne of the Austrian Empire, one Francis Ferdinand (1863-1914). The necrocratic powers-that-were, who were fairly salivating to try out their stockpiled weaponry on a mass scale, proceeded to go at it nonstop for the next four years, in a conflict that was mostly fought in well-dug trenches. This was a gravedigger's war, in which its participants sat submerged in the ground, ducking flying metal and trying to survive against an enemy made totally anonymous by industrialized warfare.

The longtime warrior tradition of battle, in which combatants broach one another from the distance of a cudgel or sword-length, has over time been supplanted by weaponry that requires neither the heft of a strong arm nor the courage of a brave heart to wield. Warfare has turned into an individual contest of being where the tiny sailing projectiles that carpet the air of every battlefield are not, making luck far more than skill a prerequisite for survival and, in so doing, making the modern warrior the helpless target of fate.

Because of the basically bellicose nature of this planet, war has always served as an intense transference of information between opposing forces, with the heightened awareness of imminent mortality making its participants that much more receptive and alive to the extraordinary particulars of a learning experience as primal as this one. With the advent of modern industrialized warfare, where direct confrontation with an enemy-teacher has been reduced to long-distance lessons, an even more curious form of spirituality enters into the art of battle. Since the face of Death can no longer be seen at close range and personalized, it is present everywhere as an overwhelming depersonalized reality, allowing the imagination to take over in conjuring who and what the individual is fighting, which, in actuality, is only that warrior's will to survive and the fears of the heart surrounding that. The modern warrior, basically male, winds up doing battle with only himself, isolated and separated as he is in the no-man's landscape of advanced heavy metal weaponry.

The brutalizing effects of all this are profound, and the overabundance of spiritual information received on the battlefield, where the astral and the physical intertwine and where life and death are one, usually results in the warrior being exposed to far more than anyone can hope to absorb. This overload creates a nightmare syndrome that the wretched scholar of battle must then carry with him the rest of his life, with no place to put it save in his own heavily scarred psyche. Many worlds collide in life-and-death situations, and the harsh lessons they teach need special processing and separation or else, as this century has repeatedly taught us, they become all consuming.

By revving up battlefield time to the far-faster-than-human tempo of advanced heavy metal, the War-to-End-All-Wars, Part I, also erased the final warrior vestige of medievalism from the European continent. Germany had had a long tradition of aristocratic feudal lords, called *Junkers* ("young men"), who made up the bulk of its officer corps. Living in their isolated castles amidst the militaristic splendor of their ancestors, they whiled away their nonfighting time drinking, fingering their dueling scars, and muttering about the degradations of the post–Middle Ages. They, in essence, were the last of the old knights, out-of-time absolutists from another epoch whose compulsion to show their martial superiority and genetic chosenness fed heavily into beginning the war. However, by its end, their world was over as well, for the machine-paced rhythm of modernity had no place for anyone who did not move and think at a similar speed. Like them, the rest of Europe's landed aristocracy, long its primary source for leadership, lost a goodly part of its overt direct influence as well in a world whose midclass would now set the style for both rule and national personality.

When Germany finally cried *"oncle"* in November 1918, Europe found that in just four short years it had been forced to surrender a world supremacy it had nurtured over the preceding twenty centuries. As it licked its wounds, buried its past, dipped off into depression, and tried to accommodate itself to the grave new world its power demise had created, its sceptre was slowly passed to two rising heirs, the U.S. of A. and the USSR, who would come to represent the dualities of individual and collective self-importance in the "Age of Rule of the Multiple Mass." First, however, the latter of the twin towers of the twentieth century's West had to undergo a revolution that would formalize once and for all the great economic schism of the commerical church of the West.

THE FRENCH REVOLUTION, PART II

At the beginning of the 1800s, Russia was still a fairly medieval enclave, repressively ruled by a tsar, a "moon king" who operated out of a tradition of Oriental despotism that had only in the past century been tempered by exposure to Western ways. As a result, a channel of political consciousness had been created that would eventually allow the French Revolution to be acted out to its completion in a monarchical realm ripe for class restructuring. For the entire nineteenth century, the governmental philosophy of "Russia—love it or get leveled by it!" was put to constant test, as the force of ideals continually rubbed against the might of orthodoxy; nevertheless, by the turning of the twentieth century, little had really changed in the social order and the equity of power shared. The Jews provided a convenient scapegoat for this inequity and were segregated and unmercifully persecuted, but even that could not begin to allay Russia's economic and social malaise.

The revolution that had begun in France in 1789 to accommodate the rising self-importance of the mass consequently translated itself into its second phase, its antithesis, the Russian "Revelation," or unfolding, of this process, with all the same archetypes doing an encore performance to a far more obedient audience. The stage was now set in 1894 for the ascent of one Nicholas, part II (1868-1918), as tsar of Russia. Nicholas, in turn, bore a remarkably similar personality and disposition to the French king Louis, part XVI (1754-1793), who had previously acted out his country's body-and-mind duality by dignifiedly dancing with the sharp blade of Madame Guillotine.

By 1900, several political factions had emerged in Russia. One of them, the "Social Demogogues," another repeat link with the earlier political parties of revolutionary France, the radical Jacobins and the moderate Girondists, split in twain as their predecessors had. These two groups were now calling themselves Bolshevik, meaning "majority," and Menshevik, meaning "minority," with the former demanding total revolution on all levels according to the principles of their high comic mentor, Karl-o Marx.

THE HEAVIEST MARX BROTHER OF THEM ALL

The foremost idealogue of the Bolsheviks was Nikolai ("Neppo") Lenin (1870-1924), a man of razor sensibilities, who, like many century-shakers, seems to have been a combination of many beings, all come together in one forceful soul to rewrite the reality of their time. Originally politicized by the death of an older brother for "revelationary" activities, he read all of Marx's routines, amended them slightly to fit his own stand-up style, and took his act to the people, who were so impressed with it he had to be sent to the frozen wastes of Siberia by the nervous authorities to cool out his rising appeal. In 1900, with his Siberian exile ended, Lenin exiled himself even further to London, where in 1903 he officially formulated the tenets of Bolshevism. This political philosophy advocated a small, disciplined elite, far above the petty avarice of the drooling class, to act out the authoritarian fantasies of the proletariat, or new breed of industrial workers.

In March 1917, a small strike in a small factory was all that was needed to effect this sledgehammer reformation. When the smoke and dust and rhetoric had cleared by near year's end, the USSR was suddenly a worker's paradise, in theory at least, as its former aristocracy hurriedly high-stepped it out of town, many heading for Paris, which had previously rejected their French antecedents a century and a quarter earlier, but now was far more amenable to their toppled company.

By the fall of 1918, a reign of terror once more reared its ugly head. Among its many victims were the tsar and his family, who were inelegantly executed in the ignominy of a cellar earlier that summer in a literal underground performance that had none of the overworld public ceremony of the earlier disenthronement of the monarch of France. Within two years, the spirit of the Paris communards and revolutionary theorists of old now ruled supreme in Russia under the authoritarian auspices of Lenin.

A total disbeliever in democratic processes, Lenin made the Communist party the singular organ of state, with a small group within it, the Politburo, acting as its ruling voice. This was not exactly what Marx had had in mind, but Lenin, being a far more improvisational comedian, felt he had to have center stage for this run of that show in order to give it the flexible order it needed to survive. When theory did not quite cover practice, and he could see that his routine had to either play to a world tour or be amended somewhat to suit his current audience, he threw in a number of crowd-pleasing capitalist one-liners to his new act, called it NEP, or "New EcoComic Policy," and watched in serious satisfaction as the people ate it up. The merriment, however, was extremely subdued with Lenin as host of the party, as Russia struggled with privation, seemingly insurmountable problems, and a recalcitrant clinging to its old ways.

When his body began giving out on him in 1924, Lenin was forced to exit this plane, most reluctantly and prematurely, for if single figures can affect centuries, he was certainly the one for the twentieth. As he left, he whispered in dying gasps, "Nyet...on brother Joe...takink over act...no...sense...of...(gasp)...humor."

But as fate would have it, the twentieth century was wrenched from Lenin's dead grasp and placed at the behest of a far more base comedian, one Joseph ("Gouge-o") Stalin (1879-1953), another archetypal collection of many beings. This one, however, was solely interested in the pure necrocratic principles of power at any cost, with the conveniently departed authoritarian figure of Lenin to serve as his own model of absolute control.

By the late 1920s, Stalin, with his peasant cunning and shrewdness and crude political wile, had solidified himself as a genuine "emperor of the dead." He proceeded, over the next decade, to purge some twenty million less-than-enthusiastic members of his national audience as a reminder to the rest of the country of what a good time they were all having despite what they read in the heavily censored papers.

Thus, Russia got back one of its most oppressive archetypes, the tyrannical all-powerful tsar, this time presiding over a state that was totally politicized, so that not only did he have that autocracy of old with its huge military to back him up, but he also had the very minds of his people within his grasp. Their revelationary consciousness had been expanded to see their place in the much greater whole of shared social wealth. This concept was a wonder at first, an act of God on Earth, to the deeply spiritual Russians, who were told that the deity no longer exists, only the state does; and they came to see Stalin as the very embodiment of that sentiment.

The "man of steel" was given a power of immortal proportion, as strong people marched off to execution and imprisonment at his mere whim, obeying their gray emperor without question. The USSR became a passive, cumbersome machine geared to the collective goals of economic statistics, which violently ignored any and all expression of individual will that stood in the way of that. The world of the dead now had an entire empire within its direct grasp, through the invocation of Stalin into its highest halls of power, and the depressed state of affairs throughout all of Europe during the 1930s allowed him the luxury of time and space to poison the planet with his extended vampire presence.

SISTERHOOD, PART II

As the great equalization force of heavy metal continued to foment confrontation on the European continent between the old and the new throughout the first several decades of the twentieth century, so did sisterhood become more aggressive in its demands, particularly in England. Using street theatre, civil disobedience, arson, sabotage, and hunger strikes, women attempted to claim their proper place in a world whose machine rhythms had considerably reduced the discrepancy between size and strength that had heretofore totally segregated the sexes. The Goddess, who had been invoked in the secular persona of Liberty the previous century, was now focusing all her power around the liberating right to vote, or suffrage. This effort would be met with fierce resistance by the patriarchal defenders of this fairly exclusive male rite, but with the loss of much of the power of tradition that the War-to-End-All-Wars had wrought, this bastion of denial gradually fell too, and women's suffrage became a serial reality on the continent over the next several decades.

Having given women the outer empowerment of accepted citizenry, the Goddess then turned her attention inward, to disappear and to be internalized for awhile before reemerging in the second half of the century. A multitude of channels now acted on and conveyed her graceful power to a rapt, as well as rejecting, audience of men and women alike trying to see themselves anew through the eye of the "I" of their long-hidden female side. While separation and fragmentation were primary keynotes of this period, so was reconnection sitting subtly behind it all, awaiting the appropriate consciousness for people to see and feel their true complexities and their deep and all-abiding linkage with one another.

EINSTEIN & FRANKENSTEIN

In the year 1905, a German theoretical physicist, one Albert Einstein (1879-1955), who believed deeply in the absolute of the ancient One God of the Hebrews, published a planet-shaking library work that redefined the connection between time and space through the concept of relativity. Relativity, like gravity, according to Einstein, is another great planetary connector. Anything within its scope is constantly changing and altering itself through its connection to everything else around it, so that not only do all things exist and operate in coordinated and discordant fashion with one another here, but they are related as well, part of the oneness that is beyond the measurable design of nature. In positing this as a physical truism of our planet, he also gave the West indirect metaphysical permission to take all absolutes here and recast them in relation to one another, creating a far more fluid relativistic reality on all levels. This shift allowed twentieth-century science to reclaim the creator principle from its unearthly origin so that it could have its own godlike power over the mechanics of existence. Relativity would help clear a pathway into the inner worlds of the atom as well; there the secret of planetary destruction would be revealed, allowing the human race to raise itself to the power of the divine, but without divine consciousness to guide it.

The name Einstein, which means "one rock" in German, became the rock upon which the twentieth century's church of physical science could be built. He stands as symbol of both the divine brilliance (Einstein) that humanity can manifest and the loathsome darkness (Frankenstein) into which that brilliance can be easily transformed.

Two profound lessons resulted from this Einstein/Frankenstein duality. The first was the direct assertion that relativity, not absolutes, governed physical law. The second was the sad truth that the good doctor, the monster-maker himself, had not yet learned: that whenever science slips off into the absolute of discovery without thinking of how that discovery will relate and integrate into the larger world around it, it creates monstrosities, planet-devouring devices that know only the absolute of absolute destruction.

This dual lesson would hang over the Earth for the entire second half of the century. Though it was channeled and inspired by Einstein, a wise and gentle God-loving man, in the great teaching of opposites that this planet always employs it would bring the planet face-to-face with its most terrifying deity, the Dark God, the Raging Destroyer, in the form of nuclear holocaust. With that divine's ascendance, thanks to the unthinking assistance of science, the absolute of total apocalypse has come to reign here, while the heavens have receded ever further from Earth, lost in the long shadows of a far more fearsome ruler.

RETURN OF THE HOLY ROLLER EMPIRE

As Europe recovered from its first bout with the groundwork laid for this dark god, its northern and western coastal countries managed to stay democratically, albeit depressively, afloat, while its former central powers, shades of the old Holy Roman Empire, were all listening to an obsessive call of state as represented by one or a small group of individuals—a fallout, perhaps, of the cult of personality that Lenin had instituted in Russia.

In the early 1920s, Italy fell under the dictatorial spell of one Benito ("Il Mousse") Mussolini (1883-1945), who presented an illusion of power that was difficult to resist, as he helped coin an *ism* that would put the state at his behest. That *ism* was appended to the Latin word *fasces*, which meant a bundle of sticks or rods that Roman rulers and later magistrates bore in their discharge of office. "Fascism" thereby came to symbolize a unity of belief in the power of authority, particularly when that authority had the necessary bundles of sticks, rods, and weapons to back itself up. By extension, the term has come to mean a system of government that expresses such a deep caring for the welfare of its citizens that it is interested in every single aspect of their lives. This total governmental concern for its constituency is also known as totalitarianism, a mouthful that says it all in its first five letters: the state, through the coercion of force, is everything, and the individual is nothing, save, of course, for the usual individual at the top. This is unity, then, without any individual consciousness, a dictatorial rule for those most insecure at heart, who like having their lives shaped to the echo of constantly marching boots.

Fascism, in its strange way, was like a shadow-Renaissance in Italy: a repudiation of all humanistic values, a killing of the spirit of creativity, and a reduction of the extraordinary aesthetic of that country to the blowsy pomp of empire dreaming, a sad joke that would ultimately see its human embodiment, Il Mousse, hung upside down in a public square by his heels. Following the same pattern as the Renaissance before it, the shadow-Renaissance of fascism passed up through the old Holy Roman Empire from the united states of Italy to the united states of Germany. There, it subsequently came to global attention under the *nom de totalitaire* of Nationalsozialistische Deutsche Arbeiterpartei, or the Nazi Party, yet another celebration of the growing world of the dead here.

After the end of the War-to-End-All-Wars, Part I, the well-ordered consciousness of Germany grabbed onto the trappings of social democracy to form a republic. However, such was the diversity of political opinion that only coalitions of disparate views could engender sufficient support to stay alive, and none of these could stay together long enough to have much effect, through the recent European practice of moving-target authority. In 1923, workers could literally carry home their weekly wages in wheelbarrows, so wildly did the basic unit of currency, *der mark*, inflate. In that same year, a wild-eyed revelationary, one Adolph Hitler (1889-1945), made an unsuccessful attempt at a revolt in Munich and got tossed into jail for his efforts, there to put his struggles on paper and earn an early rebirth from his five-year term, after serving only a highly symbolic nine months.

HELLO, HITLER

While an art student in Vienna, Hitler had become very aware of an ancient Christian relic there, the spear of Longinus, the legendary weapon that had pierced the side of the mock-Christ upon the cross and had been passed down from a host of rulers all the way up to Napoleon; it now rested in a museum, awaiting yet another conqueror to reclaim it. Following a stint in the Great War, where he was gassed and blinded and later suffered a similar "blinding light" conversion to that of Saint Paul, albeit to the icon of the twisted cross—the swastika—this second "little corporal" buried himself in his two favorite pursuits, "politricks" and magic tricks. Gradually, he began to touch back on the Atlantean origins of the Aryans and the consciousness of a master race that had been espoused so many aeons before. Adopting the Atlantean symbol of the above-mentioned swastika, which was also used by the early Germanic tribes and was shaped like a dual cross with four right-angled feet running off each of its edges, Hitler purposely chose to make his symbol face the left. He thus made it run counter to its normal avenue of benign solar grace and reflect instead the madness of the moon and its call toward enlightened darkness.

As beer-hall putsch turned to shove, this little fellow with the big hypnotic voice underwent various initiatory rites to make himself an adept of the dark, and when they had been completed, he and his Nazi party rose to rewrite history in their own image. With their uncomfortable blend of mysticism and martiality, the Nazis would go on to stage a four-dimensional opera designed to show humanity what its story would be without any spiritual heart behind it.

Most of the tale of Western civilization has been waged under the idea of conquest and unity via racial and martial superiority: the power of common blood as dominating will. The Nazi obsession with people who did not meet their genetic standards, however, was a deep aberration from all that, for they were the first to assume god-like judgment over their victim's biological heritage, deciding capriciously who was to stay here and who was to go. Their unity was built on totally separating themselves from the forces of physical evolution and replacing them with a world reconstructed on every level by a single earthly race of masters. Here was the West's One God/one self taken to its extreme, a master race of gods on Earth, stripped of their heavenly hearts and their earthly humanity in order to show the world what life would look like here without any love, save for the love of power.

This latest conceit of chosenness didn't take long to win *der herzen*, "the hearts," and *der geisten*, "the minds," of *der Herrenvolk*, the German master race, particularly with its penchant for huge auditoriums draped with red and black effluvia and ablare with martial music. These strident symbols formed the backdrop for its star performer and his favorite trick of transforming his unimposing dark-haired hamburger form into a tall blonde Aryan/Nordic presence, all with the spellbinding cant of his voice, allowing him, through the miracle of microphones, to blast his fantasies of superiority and destiny into the highly receptive ears of a mighty nation. Despite his unsettling presence, the datamasters and necrocrats of the rest of the world's business sphere saw him as a potentially convenient enema to flush out their lingering constipated depression and so did little to halt his greater ambition.

In 1936, the Axis was formed through the shadow-Renaissance partnership of Italy and Germany, along with *der Herrenvolk* of the Orient, Japan. In March of 1938, Hitler marched into the Viennese museum that held his prize, the spear of destiny, and took it for his own. He had now been empowered by the forces of imaginative history, for the spear was the symbol of world domination to those who believed in its magic, and in his liberation of it, he knowingly became the full incarnation of the Dark God come to Earth.

THE-WAR-TO-END-ALL-WARS, THE SEQUEL

Thus was the War-to-End-All-Wars, the Sequel, officially proclaimed in September 1939, giving all its participants a huge necronomic boost as depression gave way to industrial elation. Its two sides, the Axis and the Allies, proceeded to slug it out over the next six years, in what would be the apocalypse of the master races, with Germany and Japan representing the old-style consciousness of that ancient conceit in national form and Russia and the United States of America, their Allied enemies, representing its newly evolved poly-cultural manifestation.

Underneath this greater conflict of master races, an even more depraved war within a war was also secretly fought on the European continent. In the sorrow and the pity of that struggle, twelve million souls—six million of them Jews and six million of them Slavs, gypsies, political opponents, as well as the sick, the retarded, and the unwanted—were sacrificed to the swastikaed judgment of the Third Reich. Rounded up, deported to concentration camps, and there starved and incinerated, the victims of this atrocity were part of a soul purge that defied human comprehension. Although genocide had been an ugly heritage of previous manifestations of sorcerer civilization, it had never quite taken this cold, methodical, distant form before against such an unwarriorlike foe, complete with depraved medical experimentation as part of its subhuman demon dance.

The War-to-End-All-Wars, Part II, was, in essence, the last and maddest of the European Crusades, bringing that millennial old story of absolutist intolerance to its cyclical close. The "Crazed Crusaders of Nazidom," in their fear and loathing of the magical powers of Israel, brought to an end the globe's economic and territorial near-domination by a European world that had collectively risen in large part through the mechanics of the original armed marches on Jerusalem.

In this ultimate of separations, Israel would complete one of its cycles and rise phoenixlike out of its own ashes, its promised land soon to be returned to it. It would become a unity once again, with the memory of persecution and intolerance deeply seared into its immediate memory and yet oddly unlearned in its own subsequent dealings with the wandering, homeless Palestinians in its midsts. Those who had died in the concentration camps, Jew and non-Jew alike, had taken it upon themselves to absorb all the horrors committed in the name of the One God on the European landscape in order to sear into the collective vision of the West the repercussions of mortal law and order when there is no higher consciousness behind it.

Israel has always been symbol of far greater realities than its own. In its extraordinary ability to survive even in a world periodically disconnected from the outer light of the divine, it has always been a teacher and storyteller of the importance of keeping that light alive, for without it, this is a place of never-ending darkness. Yet in its separateness and chosenness, and its unwillingness to see the divine in anyone else's beliefs, lesser Israel also has many unlearned lessons to teach itself. The degradations and dehumanization of the Nazis all served as gross reminders of the failure of both Israel and Western history, which it helped create, to integrate with one another. This failure would find a totally transformed planet by war's end, when the darkened heavens of humanity were lit by the terrifying illumination of Frankensteinian science.

By April 1945, the fighting had finally come to the streets of Berlin, the capital of Germany. And at that month's near-end, Adolph

Hitler, who had recently lost his *heilige lance,* his spear of destiny, to erratic safekeeping, decided to end his incarnation of the Dark God in his subterranean accommodation in that besieged city. Bidding farewell to his people through communiqué, he manfully offered them their own generals as excuse for his failure. Then, placing a gun in his supermouth, he scattered his brains about his bunker, as his recently betrothed mistress daintily bit into a capsule of cyanide by his suicided side, and together the two were cremated in a Viking funeral pyre. The spear, shortly thereafter, fell into the hands of the Americans, who initiated the "Atomic Age" while they held it. Eventually, its power-enshrouded presence was returned to the Viennese museum that had previously displayed it, making it once again a curious magical relic of a long-dead world.

The immense chaos that Hitler generated, the depradations of the soul that were engineered in his name, the extermination of millions deemed racially and ethnically inferior—these were hardly the singular responsibility of one unloving human being. Hitler was not a random element, but one welcomed by a significant element of a powerful country who actively brought his fantasies to flower. Once those fantasies became known to his neighbors, they, in turn, did little until they had no other choice but to try to stop him through force. Like the mad magician he was, he had been invoked by the spirits of power and authority, by the world of commerce, looking for order, stability, and control—those keynotes of the ruling necrocracy and their subject world of the dead that have come to so thoroughly dominate our modern machine-driven world. Forces like Hitler, Stalin, and the other emperors of the dead that century twenty has conjured up are no accidents of the fates. They are the shining weaknesses of humanity—the yearning for chosenness, for specialness, for superiority—brought into bodily incarnation, and they will continue to be invoked until we learn to properly deal with their more-than-human but far-less-than-divine political energy.

On May 8, 1945, the ceremony of German surrender took place in Berlin. The war, which had lasted more than 5½ years, was officially over in Europe, as was that continent's supremacy. Two new master races now stepped forward to claim the world as their own, the U.S.A. and the USSR, allowing a curtain of gold and a curtain of iron to come down and divide the White West into its two ideologic halves.

THE BIRTH OF THE ANTICHRIST CHILD

In the same month that *der Fuhrer* bought his own bullet, the president of the United States was mulling over the choice of whether or not he should give the OK on an as-yet untested atomic "device" and thereby speed up the conclusion of the war in the East against the Japanese, whose ferocity and single-minded warrior ethic greatly frightened his own fighting force. The atomic bomb, the device he was contemplating, had been the result of humanity's extraordinary genius for self-destruction, as a group of Allied physicists in a project called Manhattan figured out how to make an explosive that would react with the atomic particles of its target to blast it and everything around it into universes unknown.

Although many of the participants in that project were to suffer great remorse over what they had wrought in the name of pure science, the deed was irrevocable. With its first test in July 1945 over the southwestern sands of the United States, a totally new and horrifying choice was suddenly given humanity. It now had actualized the possibility of destroying itself, and that prospect would loom larger and larger as the century progressed into its second half.

In unintended irony, the code name wrapped round the bomb was "Trinity," giving that religious symbol a whole new symbolic twist, for here was a force that could take out half the planet with a few simple push-button prayers. Its first utilized offspring, dubbed with equal ironic unintent "Little Boy," was yet another manifestation of the Antichrist itself, born out of a love of power that would see the United States forced to stare down into its very soul in the decades to come and to wonder by century's near end if it could spiritually survive what it had let loose decades earlier during the primitive dawn of the Atomic Age. The president, one Franklin D. Roosevelt (1882-1945), opted to sidestep the direct responsibility of all this, even though it was under his auspices that the project had been started five years before. He exited the earth plane a few weeks prior to

Hitler's demise, handing over the decision to drop the big one to his successor and vice-president, one Harry S. Truman (1884-1972), a feisty sort who did not think through the consequences of incinerating an unseen enemy, particularly since they were of a race other than Caucasian.

Consequently, on August 6, 1945, the combined effort of the best and the brightest working for the Allied war effort in the realm of nuclear physics was allowed to explode over the Japanese city of Hiroshima. In this beautiful metropolis of rivers and bridges were some two hundred thousand souls, of whom some seventy thousand were suddenly ripped from this plane in that megaton mushroom blast, while 90 percent of their city was reduced to radioactive rubble.

Two days later, Russia, never shy about exploiting catastrophe, declared war on Japan. The following day, just to show that the U.S. of A. wasn't just a bunch of "good ol' boys" on a one-shot bender, America squatted over the Japanese port of Nagasaki and let fly another nuclear dump. This act effectively obliterated one-third of that centuries-old city in the process, while relieving seventy-five thousand of its citizens of the responsibility of maintaining themselves as physical entities. Japan surrendered less than a month later, almost six years to the day that their fellow *Herrenvolk* had started this whole incendiary affair. Suddenly it was all over except for tabulating the statistics: fifteen million had died in military uniform, while the same number of civilians also passed on into the ozone, with another five to ten million disappearing into the darkness surrounding those first two figures, making that thirty-five to forty million souls sacrificed to the arrival of the Atomic Age.

Into all this had been prematurely born the Antichrist child, but instead of coming in the middle of a Mideastern starry winter's night, it came in the middle of a Far Eastern blazing summer's day, with airforce pilots as its kindly shepherds. While a few sheep and oxen witnessed its predecessor's birth, the whole world sat up in stark, terrified notice at the coming of this baby, for it represented a force greater than any power heretofore known. As result of the sloppy magic of a truly dark magician, an even more horrendous force was developed and set free upon the planet by the supposed forces of Good and God, but good God!, what they unleashed made their enemy look like a petty criminal.

In 1949, to the nervous chagrin of those who had invented it solely for "humanitarian" purposes, Russia found a way to the bomb. Suddenly there were two opposing forces who had it, one as unpredictable as the other, and the world now had much to fear. Great Britain, France, and China joined that select crew by 1964, and ten years later, India, whose vast Hindu population existed on a philosophy of *ahimsa*, "harm to no living thing"—India, the very conduit of ancient passive Lemuria—had discovered this force as well. So the Antichrist Child came to lands that were multideitied and godless alike, to instill ever deeper the necrocratic worship of power and control at any cost that has been at the heartless heart of sorcerer civilization, ever since it first rose to rule here in our ancient patriarchal past.

THE DISUNITED NATIONS

In April 1945, representatives of fifty governments from both the first and second hemispheres gathered in the American city of San Francisco for two months to charter a new organization called the United Nations (UN), which they hoped would serve as both forum and foundation for a bellicose planet made ill by its martial excesses. Its major organ was to be a Security Council comprised of five countries who considered themselves the current world powers—the U.S.A., Great Britain, the USSR, China, and France—all of whom by 1964 were in a position to blow this planet out of its orbit.

The official charter to the United Nations was signed in June 1945, and the bomb was dropped 1 ½ months later by the official sponsor of this resurrected idea from the end days of the War-to-End-All-Wars, Part I. The UN was thus rendered totally useless as an organ of peace, unless, of course, it managed to get a bomb of its own, a contradiction in its own founding terms. With that bit of political flummery out of the way, the world could now settle back into the War-to-End-All-Wars, Part III. This contest of nerves and apocalyptic threats coldly thrown between East and West was accompanied by a continually moving conventional war thrown in on subsequently ravaged and neutered territory to defuse, at times, the almost unbearable tensions of this psychological slugfest, which was actually fought on the economic battlefields of the world's exchanges and commodities markets.

ISRAEL RISES ANEW

On May 14, 1948, the state of Israel was officially proclaimed, and the two new master races, the U.S.'s of A. and S.R. immediately gave the resurrected homeland of Western history their official diplomatic benediction. Israel's neighbors, however, were far less than enthusiastic about its existence, and on the day of its rebirth, their combined forces descended upon the Promised Land only to be repulsed in systematic fashion.

Regaining the Promised Land had been an arduous task, beginning at the previous century's end with the Zionist movement and its first trickle of settlers. When Jerusalem was secured in November 1917 by the White West, the aggressive warrior aspect of displaced Israel began emigrating, and this key buffer state became the scene of much political maneuvering, terrorist activity, turmoil, and bloodshed, a confrontation arena between a host of disparate cultures. When Israel finally achieved nationhood, its Hebraic population doubled, and an entirely new consciousness was suddenly in evidence: those who had had a satisfactory life elsewhere and wanted to maintain their same comfortable standards in their new/old homeland.

Combining the democratic forms of its Western European heritage with the socialistic theory of its equally Eastern European background, Israel went on to forge a state, in its beginnings, that was one large family on a first-name basis with itself, from heads of government on down. Infused with a pioneer spirit that also embraced a creed that had been in continuous effect for nearly four millennia, Israel was re-created as an ego-theistic culture in the center of the collective consciousness of Islam, supported by the equal ego-theism of Christendom as a Western balance to the alien exotica of that oil-rich area.

In 1967, the Middle East resounded with the rattle of ancient sabres. After six noisy days in June, the Jewish state suddenly had a wealth of added territory under its dominion, as a result of a series of lightning strikes against three different countries. These aggressive attacks were to change Israel's conception of itself from defensive coexister to offensive protector of its newly acquired buffers against further armed Arab incursion on its own territory.

In the process, Israel came face-to-face with its earlier self, a displaced nation of Palestinians reduced to refugee camps and wandering through nations not their own, all the while aching to return to the homeland of their forebears, a story not unlike that of the newly returned masters of this land. In not seeing itself directly reflected in the plight of the Palestinians, Israel quickly turned an obtuse eye toward both its past and future, condemning itself in a quick turnabout to face the very same wanderers operating under the same desire for homeland that it once did, while acting very much like the recalcitrant authorities that it once equally harassed and tried to overthrow.

Once again, the legacy of separateness and the unwillingness to recognize the needs and wishes of the non-YaHWeH world threatens Israel at near twentieth century's end. The spirit that infused that land with its earlier European returnees, who could blaze themselves out in sun-labor all day and then spend half the night discussing, arguing, and analyzing what they were doing, is no longer there. In its stead stands a conservative country of the blind staggering towards century twenty-one, no longer able to see itself save in deep opposing shades of black and white. This situation is all the more pitiable, for Israel suffered an incredibly long legacy of bodiless exile for just those very reasons and seems to have learned little from its interminable wanderings and persecutions.

When Israel began anew, it commenced under the highest of ideals. However, all it took was a conservative generation or two, intent on keeping what it had won at all costs, to lower that country into the cesspool of intolerance and intransigence, not only in regard to the world at large, but to its own minorities as well, who have been subjected to the same racial and ethnic prejudices that the rest of the planet has yet to transcend.

And so, nearly four thousand years after the reemergence of the Atlantean Semites on the sands of the Arabian deserts, and nearly two thousand years after a more accessible form of Judaism appeared through the teachings and subsequent misinterpretation of their most radical rabbi, the world once more looks uneasily toward the Middle East as symbol of all that has gone awry since the Christ's message of soul integration was first unloosened there to a planet not ready to hear it. That message of unity, of drawing all worlds together here, bears special poignancy for Israel.

In order for the planet to survive, Israel must rejoin it, not as an assimilated entity, but as a full-hearted manifestation of the God of Oneness, with the ability to recognize the divinity in beliefs other than its own as an integral and integrated part of its own spiritual tradition. When and if that happens, Israel will find, at long last, that it will achieve the same acceptance of itself; otherwise, it will find itself landless and bodiless once again. The greater and lesser Israels of the planet are, after all, different faces of the same Oneness from which we all emanate, chosen and unchosen alike, and the fragmentations and separations that the Hebrews have undergone, and which the larger world has equally reflected, are all part of the same process of learning to see the universal and connective light in all faiths here.

THE TWENTIETH CENTURY, PART II

The outer story of the second half of the twentieth century has been, in large part, a tale of the conflict between the real winners of "World Roar II," those two initialed behemoths, the U.S.A. and the USSR, who came to inherit the mantle of European dominance that that ravaged continent could no longer maintain. Of the nominal losers, Germany was immediately partitioned into western and eastern economic enclaves, while Japan was permitted to transfer its basically feudal and militaristic social structure into an equally disciplined warlord industrial state.

This state of affairs allowed it and the western half of its former

Axis partner, once they had absorbed the shame of defeat and occupation, to become major players on the world scene in a relatively short span. Without the necronomic drain of maintaining huge military empires that their conquerors underwent, both defeated nations would have a clear advantage in the decades-long unfoldment of World War III, which has been fought on paper, using currency, number magic, and the exploitation of material resource as the ballistics between its various combatants. Since the Frankensteinian element of World War II had made mass global conflict unfeasible even to the antilife consciousness of the datamasters and necrocrats who emerged victorious at its conclusion, they needed a far less combustible battlefield on which to act out their overwhelming need for dominance and control, and they found it in the arena of unlimited expansion and economic growth. This obsession with "growth" has rapidly decimated the Earth even more insidiously than earlier martial excess without being officially designated as yet another War-to-End-All-Wars, despite the distinct possibility that it may wind up as the War-to-End-All-Life here.

THE COLD WAR

By 1950, communism was the state religion of Eastern Europe and China, and it occasioned America's armed introduction into the mysteries of Southeast Asia through a stalemated conflict fought between the previously partitioned halves of the country of Korea. The developing worlds of Asia, Africa, and Latin America would now become the primary arena for global martial aggression. However, with the succeedingly sophisticated weaponry employed, little would be learned between antagonists, for now a total facelessness had entered the realm of war's hostile investigations into cultures not its own, and because of that, a pall of alienation and fragmentation settled over the planet that would only deepen as the century progressed.

With the death of Stalin in 1953, a deadly emperor was removed from the earth plane, but the world of the dead that he so aptly personified was now more in evidence than it had ever been, not only in the huge Soviet satellite empire of states enslaved to collective economic theory, but also in the rampant, soulless materialism of its counterpart empire. The new deities of capitalism and communism, backed by the Dark God threat of nuclear holocaust, had pushed the heavens even further from the Earth, as much of the world began to see that industrial America's avarice for resource was as devastating in purpose as the bear hug with which Russia wished to embrace the entire globe. All through the 1950s, the hostilities between the two were allowed to coldly foment, until at decade's end communism gained its first firm foothold in the Second Hemisphere in the tiny but highly vocal island of Cuba, some ninety miles south of the Floridian edge of the American mainland.

It was there in 1962 that the world was forced to hold its collective breath for several days as the United States directly confronted the USSR in a game of global "chicken." This singular event marked the high point of the Cold War, for it brought to the fore the dread fantasy that had initially prompted that conflict: would the Soviets be as cavalier about rearranging its enemy's atoms as the U.S.A. had been? The answer turned out to be "no," for the simple reason that Russia had as much need for America's continuance as the U.S. did for the Soviets, since each gave the other complementary excuse to act out their mutual necrocratic paranoia.

Because of their mutual need for each other, the U.S.A. and the USSR have become inextricably entwined, the fortunes of each riding on the other. The gray old men in government and industry of both have sat and schemed and plotted against one another over the decades, while writing off the problems of their own inner domains in favor of bigger bombs and better weaponry with which to defend their own personal positions of power. The rest of the world has uncomfortably awaited the first real signs of slippage by either, which, by the late 1980s began to show strongly in Russia and more subtly in America, through their similar compulsion to repeat their various European predecessors' fall from power through necronomically overextending themselves to maintain their martial empires.

In their own ways, each has been a dark mirror of the other— vast, landed continentwide countries comprised of a multitude of different cultures—who have taken it upon themselves to champion two opposing flawed economic orthodoxies that are still in their evolutionary stages of development. If these two titans can somehow come to see that they are in actuality unintegrated reverse manifestations of each other, they may also serve as a dual channel that one day might unite the planet in a benevolent worldwide economic system that focuses on the higher consciousness aspects of each. If the initiative and free-wheeling imagination of capitalism would intertwine with the shared sense of community of communistic socialism, both could serve the greater good of all rather than a small elite at the head of each, which is only interested in maintaining private distance and public control over its sphere of influence on the planet.

Although the premature obituary has been written for communistic socialism, it is a force that will probably remain with us as long as the true power of capitalism lies in the hands of the very few. Those countries that can find an equitable balance between individual initiative and collective community will more than likely be the ones that dominate the politics and economics of the twenty-first century, while those who cannot will not only be holding the planet back from its ultimate social evolution, but will also find themselves subservient to greater manifested wills than their own. This unintegrated duality, on an outer, global level, seems to be the primary dynamic behind our current disintegrating world and its inability to see itself through opposing ideologies. As long as that state continues, the longer will we live under the threat of ever-impending chaos and upheaval.

OUTER SPACE & INNER SPACE

In October 1957, Russia launched the first artificial celestial satellite, Sputnik I, and the United States followed several months later with Explorer I, thus inaugurating the "Space Age" and our planet's first tentative steps outward into the deep, dark void that surrounds us. Since we live on a sphere that revolves around a slowly self-consuming sun, the destiny of our world has always been the stars, for our mortal sun will one day have neither the heat to maintain life here nor the gravitational draw to hold the Earth in place.

The frontier of space, then, is our collective future, and in its odd way, the planet has been preparing itself all through the latter half of the twentieth century for its eventual colonization and exploration by reducing our own environment and its resources so markedly that both may eventually have to be encased in protective shields in order for life to continue here. Through the noxious use of poisons, the indiscriminate slaughter of tropical and temperate forests, the reliance on toxic fossil fuels, and the overabundance of both chemical and nuclear wastes, Earth science has been inexorably forced into the spaceship technology of creating artificial growing and living environments right on the planet, while humanity has been slowly and subtly mutating into a form that can withstand the close-quarter crowding and dead-air existence of interstellar space travel. This no-choice scenario has been further convoluted by the military's use of the planet's upper atmosphere for its own secretive ends, so that outer space very well may become an extension of the unresolved dilemmas that seem to be pushing us off our home sphere well before we are truly ready to leave it.

In a curious way, the dark age of reason that currently envelops and fragments our planet is a parallel to the dark age of absolutes that held sway a thousand years ago over Europe. Just as that continent's ultimate pathway out of that evolutionary step in Western civilization was to touch on the New World of the Second Hemisphere through oceanic exploration, so does our inexorable fate seem to be to touch on worlds other than our own through a similar crossing of unknown voids. However, if we carry the same consciousness of dominance, control, and destruction that now permeates our social and scientific thought into that void, we will have only prolonged the inevitable death of our species through its inability to recognize the all-reflective oneness of all worlds here—inner and outer, alien and familiar, divine and human.

Outer space not only represents an apex of technological advance, it is also the traditional sphere of all our divinities, and to truly enter their world, the greater heart of humanity must be in balance with its higher projected realities. This balancing act has been the primary task of our collective presence on Earth, and it is an ongoing evolutionary and revolutionary story that will take many more aeons to resolve if, indeed, a true resolution lies somewhere out there in the future for it. Without that greater heart, outer space represents just more resources to exploit, more worlds to subject to the ignorance of conquest and dominance, and more dead information for the masters of that realm to employ to their own advantage and the detriment of everyone else.

Once again, the acknowledgment that we are surrounded by both greater cosmic and lesser atomic universes, where the divine and the human may one day learn to be one, is the key to our successful entrance into the still relatively uncharted physical province of Providence. Unless that acknowledgment is both made and acted upon, we will remain as prisoners to our own limited senses of self, with our outer territorial reach vastly expanded but our problems of inner integration with the divine as elusive as ever.

The singular positive gift of the latter half of the twentieth century has been an enhancement of secular inner space, with more and more people demanding that their selfhood be acknowledged and respected through both the technological and psychological opening up of the planet's collective fifth e-zone, that of communication. Therein lies our one optimistic hope for transcending the tenets of sorcerer civilization that have so long held all of us in thrall, including those who benefit the most from it but must remain unconscious to their greater potential in order to do so.

THE FRENCH REVOLUTION, PART III

If one singular personality may be said to have dominated the twentieth century, it would probably be that of Joseph Stalin. His vampire presence loomed over the entire world for more than 3 ½ decades following his demise in 1953 via the dull-footed colossus of Russia, which continued to personify all his hungers and fears long after he had been buried and repudiated by his successors. It would not be until the mid-1980s, and a severe disintegration of the Stalinist state, that a similarly strong archetype would rise to redefine the persona of Russia, one Mikhail Gorbachev (1931-).

Gorbachev would be forced to act as a bridge between the empire of the dead that Stalin had forged and the rising sense of planetary selfhood that had been slowly moving from West to East. As a combination of many souls in his archetypal role as the "flexible authoritarian," he would solidify his position very rapidly and become the symbol for a freedom of self-expression he in no way personified and yet through evolutionary and revolutionary circumstance was forced to assume. Through his coming, the dread spectre of Stalin would be at last laid to rest, and very soon thereafter, his dead empire would begin to stir, tentatively at first and then in mass waves.

In the beginning of the 1980s, the Russian satellite nation of Poland began to ask that the voice of the worker be given more than passing ear in affairs of state, and as the decade unfolded, more and more workers living under totalitarian auspices began to express similar sentiments. Then, at the end of 1989, some two hundred years after the hated Bastille prison fell to riotous mobs to precipitate the French Revolution, a similar structure, the Berlin Wall, erected in 1961 to reinforce the notion of German might divided by its two master-race inheritors, also fell. Within a year Germany was reunited again, signaling a political conclusion to the Cold War. With the subsequent fall of one Stalinist state after another throughout the last half of 1989, the ghost of Joseph Stalin was finally laid to rest in his grave, bringing both the Cold War and his ungodly legacy to a chaotic end.

These parallel and finalizing demarcations of events have brought to full flower the third phase of the French Revolution, that of synthesis, drawing together earlier ideals with the unworkable and corrupt practices that grew out of them. Europe, which was split asunder by the master-race dynamics of World War II, would be given one more opportunity in the 1990s to learn from its mistakes and to try to synthesize its various elements and regain some of its lost eminence, through the vast global realignments toward which the 1980s were prelude.

DOOMSDAY, PART II

As we approach the second millennium since the coming of a master who taught that all worlds are one here, Doomsday once again looms large in the public imagination, just as it did a thousand years ago. While the anxiety surrounding that earlier temporal demarcation was based largely on other-worldly fears, Doomsday, Part II, is the product of a very real threat of extinction, as evinced in the destruction of the environment, widespread plague, both viral and narcotic, and a mass decline of the quality of life brought about by a far greater density of population than the planet has learned how to comfortably handle. And just as the fears of the first Doomsday manifested in the subtle introduction of the mechanical clock, which went on to end natural time and place the world under the technological control of its necrocratic sorcerers and datamasters, so will the second Doomsday, in all likelihood, produce some seemingly slight innovation, perhaps a genetic discovery, that will revolutionize the future and place it at the behest of forces quite different from those that now vie for conventional power here.

The Earth, after all, is a plane of brilliant illusions, and it is still in its incipient stages of consciousness, despite the amount of time it has taken to get to this point in its story. In the cyclical order of things here, endings and beginnings are always interchangeable, one inevitably leading into the other in accordance with the divine law of the circle, to which all mortal life here consciously and unconsciously bows.

As the planet continues to sink into the morass of its own unresolved dualities of light and darkness, heaven and Earth, love and hatred, male and female, outer and inner, and East and West, the magic of change thunders both seen and unseen upon our combined landscape. And though some terrible and wonder-filled days lie ahead for all of us, this planet is still a place of both learning and healing. No matter how deep the wounds incurred here, they still may be eventually salved and cured, for no matter how desperate and disintegrated the times become, there is always the potential to transform them, at any time, into the absolute innocence of the very beginning of things.

○

CHAPTER SEVENTEEN

The Age of America

The reader is invited to rein-
vestigate the Americas through the human color-worlds;
the coming of the White West to the New World; the rise of
Christian Israel; a revolution of space and property; a
highly un-Civil War; America as a world power; the astral's
descent to Earth through the movies; depression and martial elation; the Nuclear Age; fallen and risen presidents;
and revolutions and reassessments by the score in preparation for the end of yet another millennium so that a brand
new one may begin.

There is yet another country to be heard from in the long extended
tale of the White West, and that is the Fifth Civilization's most direct
link with its Atlantean past, the United States of America.

Tens of thousands of years ago, when the last islands of Atlantis
were slowly self-destructing, the remnants of two mighty peoples of
the Red Race, the Toltecs and the Turanians, traveled westward by
sea from their dying civilization to settle a paradise that would much
later be called Central America and South America. There, some of
their descendants served as bridges between lost and found worlds
and built great civilizations, keeping the sacred libraries of Atlantis

alive through their pyramids, mystery ceremonies, and calendars. Upon their resettlement of the New World, they were joined by Atlanteans of the Yellow Races who had crossed the great land bridges that once connected the Old World with the New, and later by Africans and Mesopotamians who came by sea to bring their ancient sacred ways to the Second Hemisphere as well. Together this intermix of many worlds, along with their divinities, created incredibly high and savagely low realms alike, while most laid their incendiary mark on their hemisphere and made the presence of humans sorely felt in its animal and plant kingdoms before they found a much more equitable interconnection with nature. Eventually, they all would become the "Peoples of the Circle" and would learn how to live in balance within the mortal grasp of time, for they would know their collective place inside its greater and lesser rhythms and understand that all life is sacred here.

HUMAN COLOR-WORLDS

Each of the five races that grace this planet is a self-contained world, as well as an integral part of the larger whole of humanity. Each reflects the very earth of the Earth itself: the thick black soil of the tropics and rain forests, the rich brown loam of the temperate zones, the red clay banks of the many river-worlds, the subtle yellow strands of the steppes and deserts, and the snowy white tundra of the arctic and subarctic zones. All of these geographic environments represent the totality of our grounded planet, and yet each of the separate human color worlds here lives in fear of flesh's bright rainbow, for we have all been blinded by the uniqueness of our own reflections and have rarely been taught collectively to see ourselves in anyone else. This fear of the rainbow has come to separate and isolate humanity far more than any geographic barrier or religious difference, and it has played a deep-seated role in the creation and continuance as well as the threat of destruction of our civilization.

The White West originated from the white-earth world of the outer edges of the planet. The hardy beings who rose there saw this sphere in stark terms since their resources were scarce, their sunlight was diffused, and much of their terrain was highly inhospitable.

Their storytelling traditions would be filled with giants and Earth-shakers, for so they saw themselves, and many of their more driven members would turn themselves into an ongoing nature-devouring force that would refuse to be bounded by anyone or anything. Mortality and mortal space would become the overriding concern of the many generations of this outer-edge color-world, and the divinity that would galvanize its imagination to the fullest would be the singular recorded soul here who ever transcended Death. They would become the "Peoples of the Straight Line," and the powerful among them would give the sorcerer element of the Fifth Civilization its fair share of its "conquest and progress, might and reason, and masters and servants" rhythm.

In some of the legends of New Atlantis was a tale of the sacred coming of this very same White Race, and it was supposed to take the form of the gods themselves when it showed. Though the first of the pale-skinned explorers to touch on Second Hemisphere shores occurred round the year 1000 A.Z., it wasn't until the end of the fifteenth century that the white gods first began arriving in unholy number. By the sixteenth century, a stream of conquerors representing the Spanish dream of empire gave that ancient legend such twisted life that by 1575 the population of New Atlantis, which had been estimated in the tens of millions, was all but erased in the most horrendous genocide ever committed by the forces of the West. Much of the ancient power of Atlantis was swallowed alive in this holocaust as the imperial might of Europe placed an apocalyptic hand of such proportions upon the continent that America forever after would be at war with itself over color. Those who saw this world solely through the straight-line synthesis of the self and the cross could see no humanity in these red primitives who called themselves the Real People, and the Real People, in turn, were overwhelmed by the utter depravity of these nightmare ghosts, who erroneously dubbed them Indians, thinking them to be natives of a totally different mind-world.

In the year 1507, a German mapmaker living in France took the name of a self-promoting Italian explorer, Amerigo Vespucci (1451-1512), and applied it to the two newly discovered continents on his latest cartograph, and that designation would become the official ghost appellation of the land of the Real People. Atlantis had become America, and America swiftly became the symbol of all the potential for power and manifestation and magic that that lost continent had been.

CHRISTIAN ISRAEL

The Old World therefore came to the New in a conflict of colors, first as soldiers and explorers, then as missionaries and colonizers, quickly establishing territory through their ghost dis-eases, their trading practices, and their heavy-metal death-magic, while laying a violent sorcerer master-race presence on the land that would linger a long time. The first ghost-wave brought the Spanish in small marching number to the south and southwest of New Atlantis, there to obliterate ancient worlds and bury the direct magic of the continent's past. Eventually, they withdrew from direct competition with their fellow ghosts, because of the necronomics of overextending their diminishing military presence around the world. The second and third ghost-waves came from both Catholic France and Protestant England, with the French staking out the northern and midcontinent river-worlds and the English sticking closely to the eastern oceanic shoreline, establishing a triumvirate of colonial countries there: New England, the Middle Colonies, and the South.

While the French concentrated on furs and fishes and bringing the metaphysical message of the Fisher of Kings to what they saw as the unlettered savages that dotted the north and midcontinent waterways, the English were busily sending their brigades of brigands, dissenters, adventurers, dreamers, and drudges to shore up yet another wilderness for the exploitable profit of empire. They were far more interested in the Second Hemisphere for capital than for canonical reasons, seeing America as a mother lode for the motherland, as well as a convenient place to ship off a goodly number of malcontents to better serve the king from afar rather than continue to disrupt matters from anear.

The northern colonies of coastal America received England's more serious religious dissenters, mostly Puritans, who had suffered exile and persecution for their desires to purify some of the unholy writ of the Church of England and now yearned to live in glorious intolerance and grim isolation from all who did not feel life through the same lustless sweat as they did. Perceiving themselves as the new Israelites in the new Promised Land, they came to call their conglomerate of colonies New England, a set of little theocratic states centered round the town and church, and they operated out of their own sense of chosenness and separateness, based on the singular sacred library work of the Bible.

The Puritans were a no-nonsense, hard-working lot who would wield considerable power, for the future United States, thanks to their influence, would wind up as a Christian Israel, with its belief in the One God, its sense of divine purpose as a citadel of freedom, its own venerated book of law, the Constitution, and its own sacred secular traditions, like Thanksgiving, a holiday harvest feast, as part of its historical and emotional base. Like the Hebrew Israelites, who were overwhelming in their sense of self-importance and divine purpose when they first came upon the Promised Land, so were these Christian Israelites equally imbued with a unifying sense of superiority in their conquest and subjugation of a collective world that also had never seen their likes before. America would be a compression of the entire story of the Fifth Civilization, an all-embracing Israel that even welcomed wandering Hebrews to its early shores, showing a remarkable tolerance for everyone who lived within the straight line of the One God.

The Middle Colonies attracted a far more down-to-earth crew than their northern neighbors. While cognizant of the divine, this group also saw the abundance and the beauty of their little section of "paradise regained," and so set up a more flexible environment in which to capitalize on the God-given bounty of their new world.

The third of this English triad of colonies, the South, was another country altogether, almost entirely rural in its makeup, with large plantations as its mainstay. These were grouped together in counties, so that each was its own peculiar feudal estate, with its wealthy landholders on the top, its craftspeople and tradespeople servicing it from the middle, an impoverished underclass on the bottom, and beneath them, the subexistence of slavery, minimum subsistence labor imported from west Africa.

Like Europe during the Middle Ages, Africa had been a continent of great empires on its western side and trading kingdoms on its east, and though the two mass civilizations were highly comparable in many ways, the collectivity of Africa never came close to producing the weaponry that the rising self of Europe felt compelled to create. So, like America, Africa's resources, too, fell prey to the controlling and domineering hand of Europe, including the long continental practice of trafficking in human bodies, which became an integral economic element in connecting the Old World with the New.

Victim of the predatory greed of empires, both black and white as well as Christian and Islamic, this black slave labor force would, like Native America, be another collective world suddenly thrust up against the singularity of self. They also would be looked on as a non-people, further heathens to be blindly Christianized by a ghostmaster who saw all who were not his equal as his vast inferior. Yet they were unknowing colonists themselves, who were so greatly feared by the Euro-Americans that they could be brought over here only in captivity. They, too, came to establish an alien continent on American shores, and they, too, came to act out the long collective struggle of having their humanity recognized by a ghostmaster host who little realized that this continent was destined to reflect and act out and give voice to the ancient color tensions of the entire world.

COMES THE REVOLUTION

During the eighteenth century, America had been part of a global pattern of empire wars for territory and resource, and thanks to a considerable economic expenditure, Great Britain ultimately prevailed as the dominant European force on North American soil by 1763. Its rather taxing disregard for the welfare of its colonists, however, soon led to a series of confrontational disputes, and though sentiments varied widely between independence and loyalty to the motherland, by the 1770s the first bellicose blows for a separation of American states from the European state were struck.

The colonists had been empowered by both their earlier martial prowess in the empire wars and their strong sense of self-worth in having created a vibrant economic entity, and they were united, more or less, by the same mutated language, the same belief in the One God, and the same shared rising sense of self-importance. At stake here for them, then, would be the inalienable rights of property, for that extension of their being was a very clear and real manifestation of their self-importance, and it demanded the shared protection of a shared government. A revolution for the redefinition of extended individual space would rise from this in 1775 between the New Worlders and the Old, a revolution that would probably have been fought on English soil had not America taken it upon itself to serve as the Greater Israel of the planet: a highly varied chosen people forging a synthesis of self and self-worth under the secular spirit of a bountiful and distant God.

The American Revolutionary War dragged on for six long years. For the greater portion of that time, the ragtag army of Euro-American revolutionaries looked as if they might collapse at any moment, with continually waning commitments coming from much of their fighting force. However, in 1778, the French and then the Spanish joined their cause and turned it into another empire war. This was enough to allow the colonists to emerge victorious in 1781, when the British finally accepted the terms of surrender laid upon them by their combined superior foe.

Although all this martial expression was an integral part of the process that fed into the French Revolution of 1789, the American Revolution was a far different affair, based less on the ideals of a new time than it was on the practicalities of protecting a newly forged space and its extraordinary resources. Whereas post-revolutionary France had much of its past still extant after the fray as an easy pillow on which to fall back, the Americans, after expunging the official British presence from their midst, had nothing but the future on which to lean. This circumstance carried them through their experiment in participatory democracy to an immediate conclusion much more in accord with the initial aims put forth by the inflammatory minority that first gave printed voice to its ideals of the importance of self.

During this period, the colonies brought forth a remarkable collection of individuals who seem to have incarnated en masse in just this place and time to effect the next evolutionary stage in the development of the White West: participatory rule by the mass. Many of the shapers of the American experiment were Freemasons and Rosicrucians, with a vital interest in the integration of humanity with its higher potential. Together they proposed the law, the order, and the economic mechanics for just that purpose. They served as channels of precepts that they themselves probably did not fully understand but felt compelled to actualize anyhow, because they sensed that America was to be a most special place, a blending of alien cultures into a secular oneness that reflected both the One God heavens and the rich, shared bounty of Earth.

Thus, in July 1776, with the war barely a year old, representatives of the thirteen American colonies declared themselves independent in a document of the same name. Though written by a slaveholder, the Declaration of Independence was a passionate combination of several elements, including a rationalization for revolution, a statement of both principles and grievances, and a goodly mix of governmental theory. It finished up with a rousing call for "life, liberty, and the pursuit of happiness," an unusual trinity that bespoke of a whole new dimension in the political domain: emotional fulfillment, a province heretofore thoroughly ignored in the hierarchies of monarchies and empires.

The Constitution, which followed some eleven years later, was basically a gentleman's agreement on the rules of good neighborliness, conceived in terms of white property owners relating to one another in polite, respectful, and civilized manner. It was a seven-part definition of the structure and purpose of government, with room given to amend its initial precepts and a self-statement of its supremacy over all the laws of the land.

The first two amendments to the Constitution would be truly revolutionary: the right to assembly and the right to bear arms. Taken together, they would insure a vigorous, assertive, and expressive nation that would shock itself with its own violence, but also would remain alive and committed on an individual level to its founding ideals and willing to voice and act out its failings. This call for democratic involvement was a challenge to the future citizenry of America not to be passive, but to know they lived in a volatile nation-state that demanded that its citizens act aggressively if they wished to have their grievances righted, a most radical sentiment for a world that had long demanded the prostrate obedience of its lessers.

Democracy's great gift to Western civilization would be its ability to maintain a continuous dialogue between idealism and corruption. The democratic dialectic that those two opposites continually create has been the core of the story of the United States, helped in no small manner by the freedoms of expression on all levels that the Constitution created. The founding fathers, however, never foresaw in their wildest nightmares the nation that would rise out of all this, for not only would a highly varied citizenry one day share in the wealth of property their country had to offer, but also eventually all manner of beings—unpropertied, unwhite, and, horrors!, unmale— would also be looked upon as their equals under the law.

Those who supported the philosophy behind the Constitution came to be known as Federalists, or supporters of a strong central government, while their adversaries were called Anti-Federalists, or those who advocated the individual rights of the states over a single centralized power. These two groups would eventually form the two major political parties that would dominate the succeeding democratic experiment of America. In 1854, the Federalists became the Republican party, a name that has come to embody the philosophy that the business of America is American business. The Anti-Federalists also adopted the name Republican, which soon became Democratic-Republican and, in 1828, just plain Democratic, so as not to confuse the future voters of America with two parties of the exact same name, which would have made the political process far more suspect than it wished to be perceived.

THE PRIMARY RESIDENCY

At the time of the founding of the new nation, it was decided that the American experiment would have to have a titular leader. After much debate, the office of primary resident, or president, was created, a rotating elected father figure who would serve in limited terms of four years. Instead of the long hand of mortality dictating the rhythms of passage of its heads of state, America would introduce a much faster and more regulated cycle. This process, in turn, would speed up the whole historical tempo of American life, catapulting it into a major world power in a little over a century and a quarter after its official start, through the rapidly alternating personality of its government and the rapid change that that helped to impel. In 1789, the winning general of the Revolutionary War, one George Washington (1732-1799), was selected without opposition to begin the tradition of the presidency. Though he was as regal and aloof as any European monarch of his time, he gave an initial legitimacy to that office that would ultimately allow it the freedom of reflecting far less Olympian characters.

The initial Federalist philosophy that shaped the early government leaned heavily toward a loose interpretation of the Constitution and a tight dependence on the wisdom of capitalism, viewing its datamasters as the natural leaders of their less financially adroit brethren. These New World aristocrats, still imbued as they were with the Old World tradition that the few should rule the many, would allow the same necrocratic hierarchy that sat over the rest of the world to absorb this more egalitarian offshoot of European civilization as well, though here, at least, the quirkiness and eccentricity of individual expression would rise periodically to challenge their compulsive dominance and control.

THE EXPERIMENT TAKES HOLD

By the year 1800, the high-handed and faintly monarchical means of the Federalists receded in favor of the more democratic ways of the Anti-Federalists. The second president, one John Adams (1735-1826), was unpopular and served only one term, but, more importantly, he proved that the presidency worked as a rotating office of authority in his orderly, serial ouster from office. The two-party system, despite much misgiving, did indeed offer rhythmic continuity. This stable passage of power allowed Thomas Jefferson (1743-1826), the author of the Declaration of Independence, to ascend as chief of state shortly after the turning of the nineteenth century.

Jefferson was a thinker and a builder, a practical romantic whose skills and failings enabled him to view the noble American experiment from the eyes of its subjects as well as from those of its leaders, thus giving a much-needed balance to the debased view of humanity that many of his cohorts secretly held. Although a slaveholder and a fairly unintegrated soul himself, to the point of ending his life deeply in debt, he nevertheless recognized the importance of a well-integrated society that knew how to share its power. It was his high-pitched voice that served as a constant reminder of this all through America's initial story of revolution and early nationhood. As president, he abolished the high-and-mighty trappings of his office, thereby reducing it from the kingship it might have become, as well as adding another million square miles to the country by engineering a $15 million purchase of a territory loosely dubbed Louisiana, which opened the western frontier.

Following an armed contretemps with the British a decade later, a new triumvirate of territories now defined the United States: the industrious North, the feudal South, and the anarchic West. The frontier drew ever more of the ghost-wave, with a "yah-hooooo!" into the "redlands," to claim ever more of the diminishing open territory of the invisible nations of the Americas. The frontier would now be the release point for the violently competitive character of rapidly expanding America, as the "civilizations of the circle" who lived there once again either fell to or receded from the heavy-metal death-magic of the straight-line forces of self.

If Thomas Jefferson embodied the high democratic consciousness of the ruling elite, then his balancing counterpart from the lowly masses was the original "good ol' boy" himself, one Andrew Jackson (1767-1845), who followed a warrior pathway to become president in 1828. Having gained his repute fighting the Real People, he was the very personification of the populist leader, with his sublime faith in the innate goodness of ordinary humanity, his belief in political equality for all white males, and his distrust of big money and big government. Two decades after Jefferson, he helped to spread male suffrage, or voting rights, to those ghosts who did not hold property, while he enthusiastically pursued the removal of most of the Real

People from the east into the Great Plains beyond the Mississippi, thus opening up both space and the means for self-worth to a much larger segment of the population. A significant part of the ghost world had now integrated itself into the political and economic realm of shared self-importance, and as a result, reformers began to call for an even more democratic America to build upon the continuing expanding base of its growing citizenship. Here is where sisterhood would re-find its mass political voice in America, first through the antislavery movement and then through its own self-perceived slavery, as self began to trickle down to encompass more and more people who had previously not been allowed to express much thought or self-awareness.

In his role as limited equalizer, Jackson also helped free business from governmental control, and with another "yah-hooooo!" the masters of the rhythms of economics immediately set their machinery at full speed ahead and initiated a pattern of economic booms and busts that would send the country periodically reeling and panicking for the rest of the century amidst equal bouts of expansion and fortune making. With its strong emphasis on credit and living in futures that often would not be there, American business was now able to take the country out of present time and begin retuning its realities to the industrial beat of dependency, control, and routine, and the deadening repetition of machine time. For the rest of the first half of the century, exploitation and expansion, coupled with a successful territorial war with its southern neighbor of Mexico and the discovery of gold in the "golden state" of California, spread the straight line of self across the continent, as America continued connecting its vast expanse through canals, steamboat lines, and the iron horse of the railroad.

LATTER-DAY SAINTS

Just before the full-blown industrialization of the United States, one last major religion got in under the wire. It was a call for one more manifestation of the children of Israel, this one quite collective in its scope, with America directly woven into its Hebraic and Christian story. Channeled by one Joseph Smith (1805-1844) through golden tablets and magic spectacles that he claimed were revealed to him by an angel, he produced an instant sacred story in 1830 called *The Book of Mormon,* which would become the basis for the Church of Jesus Christ of the Latter-day Saints. According to this sacred text, Native America held within it the lost tribes of Israel. These tribes were to be returned to the Christian fold by this latest incarnation of the chosen people, who saw Zion rising in the Promised Land of the United States and the Master ultimately returning to rule the Paradise they would help to regain.

As founding prophet, Smith created a collective theocracy around his teachings with himself at its head, sent out missionaries, gathered many followers, formed several controversial communities, and suffered persecution and intolerance for the separateness and strange ways of his communal sect before coming to Illinois in 1839. There he received another revelation that patriarchal polygamy, or multiple marriage between one husband and many wives, was part of the divine pathway here, and that was enough to enrage the rest of the non-Mormon One God populace to the point where Smith was ultimately jailed and torn apart by a mob in fine medieval fashion.

His close-knit church selected one Brigham Young (1801-1877) as his successor. Young waged a two-year war of vengeance after Smith's death before leading his collective community fifteen hundred miles to the western territory of Utah in 1847, an unpromising Promised Land that eventually became the new Canaan of the Mormons. There, after initial difficulties, they prospered under the shrewd and autocratic leadership of Young.

The Mormons became a collective force, operating under the same One God and same singular Master as the rest of their Judaic-Christian nation, but as a totally separated state, a combination of Native American intradependence and the One God warrior and economic spirit of Euro-America. Polygamy was ultimately desanctioned in 1890 to help Utah achieve statehood, and the Church of the Latter-day Saints would go on to spread its influence throughout the world, as an odd amalgam of collectivity and separation. Here, then, would be another distinctive face of Israel brought to Earth to let the planet know how many differents forms the One God can take, how many different and often contradictory pathways can lead to that Singular Divine, and how often and in how many completely dissimilar guises Israel incarnates here as a manifestation of separated oneness.

UNION & DISUNION

By 1860, the idea of slavery in a free land had divided the United States in twain, with the South totally dependent on the economics of bondage and unwilling and unable to compromise on its stance, knowing full well that if it did, it would become enslaved to the insect lust of the North. The masters of industry there wanted to bind the country to the uniform tempo of merchantime, and the fastest and most efficient way to do this was via industrialized warfare between these two separate countries that shared the same constitution and boundaries, but moved to the rhythm of a temporal and social consciousness that was centuries apart.

In 1860, a man of many shadows ascended as chief of state of the sorely divided United States, one Abraham Lincoln (1809-1865), and his election was a direct mandate for armed conflict. Unlike his original biblical namesake, he would be the catalyst for dividing an already established One God nation so that it could relearn the ways of its separated parts through the intimacy of armed investigation. A firm believer in the inferiority of the black race, as well as in the constitutional right of the South to maintain its bondage economy, he nevertheless became the great emancipator with his proclamation in 1863 that slavery was to be abolished in the Confederate States. This act sentenced the ongoing war to a purely military outcome and an inevitable industrial triumph, rather than a possible peaceful compromise. His strong biblical presence would demand that this disintegrative process be carried to its rightful conclusion so that an entirely new nation could rise out of it, for so he had been called on to personify a house superficially divided but still built on a strong foundation.

Although the South had fired the first shot in April 1861, it knew it had no hope of gaining a military victory over an enemy that had much the better of it in terms of money, munitions, and men. It went instead for a stalemate, viewing itself in much the same way that the earlier colonials had seen themselves against the British. The ensuing un-Civil War lasted for four years, until it finally turned into a locust-march through the Confederacy, and that thoroughly defeated nation was soon forced to surrender to the greater United States in April 1865.

With Lincoln's odd penchant for the psychic, his morbid melancholy, and a wife who lived on the outer edge of her own sanity— perhaps so that he would not have to—he was a fitting channel of unresolved disconnection, a figure who understood the poetics of life's larger dramas, but not their full human resonance. Thus, while attending the theatre less than a week after the hostilities had concluded, his mortal performance was ended by a jealous actor. Post-Lincoln America, however, would have no need for such complex characters to embody its divisions. It could now work on reconstructing itself along more efficient and exploitative lines, no longer a mere hemispheric power but bordering on being a global one as well. In addition, industry could now proceed without any further social and temporal impediment, as the institution of organized slavery came to an abrupt end and a far more subtle form of discrimination rose to replace it.

The American un-Civil War proved to be of a greater revolutionary character in its aftermath than the original Revolutionary War, changing America from a basically rural, agricultural nation to one that uncomfortably belched and breathed the smokestack lightning of progress. This transformation was aided in large part by the reinforced realization that money was the new god in this material paradise that insect industry and rational enlightenment had created in the New World. The defeated nation of the South lost its singular feudal aristocracy, and in its stead a new middle class arose, while its slave population was set loose, with little or no provision made for them, to wander the roads and suffer a slavery of survival even more galling than before the war.

While the re-United States began adding ever more to its Union and a network of rail was laid to connect both coasts and most of the interior with one another, the North, particularly the Northeast, began to exert a monopolistic control over industry, manufacturing, and resources, as a sense of bigness began to pervade the thinking of the bankers, financiers, and magnates who made all this happen. These newly minted necrocrats, within a few short scheming years, managed to make most of the capital and production of the country their own through the institution of trusts or large monopolies, thereby reverting back to the precise aristocracy of control that America had been created to offset.

This reversion, coupled with a steady immigration of new citizens from some of the more economically blighted sections of Europe, did much to undermine the previous principles of Jeffersonian and Jacksonian democracy. Post-Lincoln America consequently became a deeply divided nation between the powerful and the powerless, which forced it to continually reassess the principles upon which it was founded, as citizenship extended itself in form if not substance to freed black males in 1868 through the Fourteenth Amendment to the Constitution.

The earlier spirituality that had attracted many of the first of the ghost-wave of immigrants became totally supplanted by materiality as the spirit of Mammon lifted its gross head and smacked its huge lips. The illusions of the physicial, of possessions, of things, could now be worshiped with all the fervor of the rebuilt house of America's being. The lure of the material not only drew further colonists from Europe but from the collective outreach of Asia as well to work on the railroads. These new arrivals were to suffer the same isolation and rejection as the other color-worlds that did not conform to the One God/one skin consciousness of this resurrected secular Israel, which was fast drawing the entire world through its gates to directly experience the endless potential for material realization and freedom to touch on spirit that it seemed to offer.

The railroads ended the warrior presence of the Real People upon the Euro-American continent by easily facilitating troop movement. Since the country's martial presence now spanned the continent, the "Manifest Destiny" of America to fill and conquer all the space parallel to its original eastern borders would finally bring the frontier to a close in the year 1890, with the slaughter of almost two hundred men, women, and children at Wounded Knee, South Dakota. That sacrificial crew, believing they were protected from ghost bullets by their magic shirts, challenged a wave of soldiers who summarily proved their magic otherwise, thereby bringing the Real People wars, which had stretched back nearly four hundred years, to a tragic and pathetic conclusion.

The continental color-worlds of Africa, Asia, and Native America now found themselves encircled and isolated colonists, with their assorted presences continually challenged on all levels by a rising master-race consciousness unwilling and unable to see itself reflected through any other prism than its own. Many alien nations would now exist in this nation of alien colonists, and their struggles to be recognized would do much to define the coming century, in which the idea of a master race would be brought to full and uncomfortable flower. As that century dawned, America celebrated in fitting frontier manner by assassinating its president, one William McKinley (1843-1901), setting the tone for the extraordinarily violent hundred years to come. At the time of his death, the United States was seriously expanding its influence. The next two decades would see it emerge as a full-fledged global power, thanks to the martial affirmation it received in the War-to-End-All-Wars, Part I, which proved America was equal to the industrial and warrior best that Europe had to offer.

THE ASTRAL COMES DOWN TO EARTH

If America has had any true singular genius, it has been that of communication, a right guaranteed by the very first amendment of the Constitution. If not quite a nation of the Word, the United States has always been a nation of words, from the triumphant poetry of the Declaration of Independence down to the overwhelming mass of literature that the American experience has engendered. This verbal tendency has compelled its citizenry to constantly document and criticize and discuss both its power and sorrows, while granting an extraordinary freedom of expression to all, save those who excite their audiences a bit too much and thereby violate the unspoken limits of that privileged freedom.

Language, music, and art have always enabled humanity to give expression to its higher self and to hint at the complexities that lie above in the very much unexplored world of the astral. Those who have shown a unique adeptness at limning this imaginative realm are our creative dreammasters, the poets and painters and musical channels who have learned how to link worlds here. In the 1890s, a mechanical apparatus that not only linked worlds but art forms as well began to engage the public imagination, and a new industry, that of motion pictures, swiftly emerged to capitalize on this wedding of perceptual planes.

Here was a medium of light that opened an entirely new dimension for those who would control its manufacture, for it gave them direct access to the very minds of their market through a teaching device that demanded receptivity and passivity and showed people in most entertaining manner how to draw in visual information more quickly. Since the mechanical rhythms of industrial society had already outdistanced humanity's biological capabilities, machinery such as this was vitally needed to redress this imbalance. Motion pictures served admirably in progressively showing people how to think faster and to attune themselves more readily to a fractured big-screen world that no longer operated according to the natural flow of time and space. In addition, movies offered imaginative spirit to a continent rapidly recreating itself, so that the quasi-mystical experience all this engendered was curiously religious in its communal sharing of imaginative dreams in the dark. Worlds, indeed, did collide through this magical integration of the physical and the ethereal, which also taught people on a mass level how to see inwardly, giving them stories and visual techniques galore through which they could broach their own interiors and enhance them with imaginative life.

In the first decade of the twentieth century, this new medium of light found a permanent home in the sunlit California desert backwater of Los Angeles, the City of Angels. By the nineteen-teens, a former ranch within its boundaries with the fanciful name of Hollywood was attracting fun-loving Pan spirits and anonymous exhibitionists by the score to revel in and be consumed by the whole unearthly process all this magic making would come to symbolize. With the rise of archetypal movie stars and their subsequent adoration and mythification, Hollywood turned out to be a return to the outer form of pagandom, creating its own earthly divinities for the mass to worship, while celebrating the bounty of the planet in lusty and ostentatious fashion. The motion picture industry's manufacture and distribution of artifacts from the dream-world would be secular sorcery at its most direct, and those who mastered its intricacies would be well rewarded for their efforts. This would be a realm that would draw all sorts of eccentric masters and "mystresses" to it, all the while giving America an illusionary but highly accessible aristocracy of both great beauty and wealth through which it could passively dream.

Many of the original rulers of this magical kingdom were of humble Jewish birth, immigrant wanderers with a long storytelling tradition behind them. These dream-factory industrialists helped to re-create America's view of itself with their ability at wedding the worlds of storytelling and accountable numbers together, two provinces that had long been associated with the magical face of Israel.

As Hollywood's initial excessive exuberance gradually became more constrained through public reaction to a series of beyond-the-pale scandals in the early 1920s, the movie industry hurriedly reined in its pagan element and reintegrated itself into the larger business community. Eventually it would become an integral extension of it, with motion pictures serving as an endless escape from the pressures of living in a country where even dreams could be measured in profit and loss.

With the advent of movies, a second phenomenon was introduced as a further uniter of worlds, this one far more intimate in its reach, for it was geared directly for the sanctity of the American home. When the clock first came into mass use, it was seen as an information-launcher, a subtle device of control that would redefine time and synchronize everyone within hearing distance with its measured call for order and productivity. By the early twentieth century, that device had transformed itself into a far more sophisticated information-launcher, dispensing not only time but news and the weather as well.

This electronic marvel, called radio, immediately took on the image of a fascinating stationary traveling sales force, with such a compelling reservoir of stories and personalities that its audience was able to forgive its compulsive product spiels and accept that as price of its company. They little realized, however, that the sorcerer seeds of rapacious consumption were being planted deep into their psyches, to create a culture whose desires would never be fully satisfied, for there was always something newer and better that could be foisted on the bottomless appetite this created. The long partnership between sorcery and the machinery of progress could now move into overdrive, and machines were suddenly everywhere, as were the energy nerve centers and fossil-fuel pipelines to maintain them. All this frentic activity plugged into the same power syndrome that had made modernity possible—the consciousness of power as an expression of self-interest and will—and the machines, too, took on that cast and came to speed up time and transform space at such a rate that America absolutely had to have them just to keep pace with its accelerated self.

MATERIALISM DEPRESSINGLY RAMPANT

By 1920, the United States found itself a rather conservative country at heart. Its status as sudden leviathan in the affairs of the globe now demanded a new respectability, and the post-war idea of a worldly League of peaceful Nations proposed by the president, Woodrow Wilson (1856-1924), was roundly spurned in favor of one nation in league with itself and its own interests. As the twenties progressed, a certain intolerance for anything that did not smack of the chamber of commerce turned the United States into an extremely narrow place, as fear of the rainbow rose anew to give release and violent expression to the strong divisions that now lay between the powerful and the powerless. All through the decade, the country was totally obsessed with its material side via a humorless optimism that would keep rising until 1929, when a spectacular stock market crash would precipitate a depression that also engulfed most of the rest of the world, for it was now quite economically interdependent.

This Great Depression, as it was called, was the product of both overspeculation and overproduction, future-time fantasies that were not supported by actualities. In October 1929, a hysterical spate of selling culminated in the loss of some $15 billion on paper, and America fell victim to its own sophisticated information-relaying procedures and the false security of its castles-in-the-air economy. By 1932, a goodly percentage of its labor force was out of work, many of its factories were closed, and even the very orderly temples of its sober work ethic, its banks, were being mobbed and vilified. Here was fertile ground, once again, for upheaval, as America had reached another impasse in its evolution and would now have to compromise on some of its earlier anticommunard sentiments.

Enter then, in 1932, one Franklin D. Roosevelt (1882-1945), subsequent president-for-life, who made that office his monarchical own for the next thirteen years, offering an optimistic personality and the personal triumph over crippling adversity—in his case polio—that the country needed to have personified in order to deal with its own depressive disabilities. Around him rose the partial welfare state through the modest redistribution of governmental wealth to the aged and the needy, and this approach would come to redefine the obligation the state had with its citizens, reaffirming free enterprise but acknowledging it did not serve the skills of everyone and needed outside augmentation. This corruption of the very tenets of capitalism was not nearly as dire a recourse as socialism or the dreaded spectre of communism, so the country accepted both Roosevelt and his numerous initialed agencies through four elections—in 1932, 1936, 1940, and 1944—preferring the mortal continuity of previous aristocratic times that he came to represent to the shorter two-term cycle of democratic tradition that had spawned his kingly presence.

It would be the necronomic beneficence of total global war that would finally lift America out of its decade-long depression, and with Roosevelt still at the helm, the country was able to economically reunite itself under the common industrial purpose of routing a highly competitive enemy. By war's end in 1945, the U.S.A. was the singular most powerful nation in the world, with the secret of the atom at its disposal, a feeling of military invincibility, and a sense of Christian, capitalist mission as protector of the globe from the excesses of itself. But deep inside all this newfound power, many exploitative forces were vying for the lucrative fallout of American industrial supremacy, and a whole different country would emerge once again from this latest earthwide martial trauma.

THE UNDERWORLD RISES

In 1919, a constitutional amendment was passed that made the manufacture and sale of alcoholic beverages illegal, ushering in an era called "Prohibition." An economic monopoly of a highly desired commodity was thereby handed over to a highly disorganized crew of ethnic neighborhood "heavies" who previously had made their living in large part by preying upon their fellow immigrants. Thanks to this extraordinary act of governmental largesse, this loose underworld coterie quickly reorganized itself in a machine-gun burst of competitive enthusiasm and winnowed out all its lesser claimants to power so that it could be ruled by its strongest and most willful.

These colorfully named characters helped to exemplify the credit-crazed decade of the twenties, and in 1929, when America's manic faith in its own future was suddenly and summarily smashed, they found themselves in an extremely fluid financial position, with business, politics, and labor at their behest. Four years later, as the country's economic funk continued unabated, the United States went off the gold standard, with nothing to back up its paper money save for the fantasy of resiliency and recovery.

In December of that year, 1933, Prohibition was finally repealed, and America began to take a long unsober look at its standards, both real and symbolic, before ultimately opting for blind faith in might and power and will in lieu of precious metals. These were the very principles of the underworld, and reorganized crime wasted no time in establishing a genuine fascist state in the United States based on the primacy of will, with its influence reaching into all spheres of commercial American life.

Dubbed the Mafia by those who chronicled its violent antics from a distance, this hierarchical netherworld was captained by a crew of dons, or "teachers," who were invoked by the trickster spirits of commerce to give America a graphic lesson in the extremes to which will and self-interest could be taken, as well as the extraordinary power that capital has when it knows no ethical bounds. All of these have been ongoing overworld themes through the evolution of free enterprise, but with the rise of business as the premier sphere of influence in our modern world, so has there been a need for its darker mirror to be evoked for all to see and contemplate.

All through the 1930s, the underworld was mythologized and glorified upon the American silver screen, and the rest of the world began to view the United States through those celluloid projections as a gang-land paradise, where the anarchy of sheer will reigned supreme. When America's depression finally ended in the beginning of the 1940s via the time-honored tradition of necronomics, both the overworld and the underworld of American commerce profited handsomely. When World War II reached its conclusion in atomic triumph for the forces of free enterprise, this was more than enough to affirm might and power and will as the very basis for the American way. Underworld and overworld were now joined in theory as well as practice and were about to legitimately unite.

In 1947, a subterranean professor named Benjamin ("Bugsy") Siegel (1906-1947) opened a school of "power mathematics" in the desert city of Las Vegas, Nevada, a state where gambling had long been legal. This made both city and state ripe for serving as an overground citadel for the dons of underground American culture. Festooning his sleep-over classrooms with gaudy neon and providing them with lavish entertainment, the stylish professor offered such an appealing array of games and machines on which to learn permutations and combinations, and probability and statistics that an eagerly paying public eventually flocked in droves to his doors. A dazzling array of schools quickly followed, as festive overworlders from all over America came to Las Vegas to test their skills of manifestation against the wills of the underground masters, who subsequently bankrolled a goodly portion of that Plutonian playground.

The original dapper visionary who foresaw all this did not live long enough to see his monumental integration of over- and under-worlds bear full fruit, for Bugsy was summarily exterminated by an ambitious rival that very same year. But a glittery "City of Magical Will" had risen round his dream in the desert, a place where the overworld and underworld could meet and touch on common legitimate ground. From here on, the intertwining of the two worlds would rapidly escalate, as a whole new age would open up all sorts of nightmarish possibilities to the planet.

ENTER THE NUCLEAR AGE

With the coming of the Antichrist child in the form of the atomic bomb in 1945, not only was the Nuclear Age ushered in, but the nuclear family of dad, mom, brother, and sis was detonated as well in a series of subtle changes that officially moved the White West out of its long economic blood interdependency and into an age of psychological kin connection. Following the War-to-End-All-Wars, Part II, and a return to routine for many people whose lives had been interrupted by four years of both stressful action and reflection, the U.S. of A. was now looking, above all else, for economic growth and order after the disorder and chaos of war. With stability and normalcy restored, the optimism of the twenties returned to infuse the 1950s with the same chamber-of-commerce consciousness that had earlier insulated everyday America from its problems. It fruitfully multiplied and once more buried itself in its material success, while showing a remarkable intolerance for anyone who did not conform to its economic, social, or racial creeds.

Many of the Nuclear Age children who gained access to the planet in the successful flush of this post-war period found their way into homes that not only had the potential to afford them but could indulge them as well. This boom in the birth rate created another economic class, "Children of Privilege," to whom the adult world could pander on a large scale with its own exploitative dreams of lost youth. All of a sudden, a loud and demanding segment of the population that never had this power on such a mass level before was being catered to and recognized as a force. A youth culture stepped to the fore, and it, too, would profoundly redefine the second half of the twentieth century. Self and self-importance would now become an overweening concern in a world that had fractured and isolated its many parts to such a degree that it could no longer demand the stable and passive acceptance of its citizenry.

THE WORLD GOES 2-D

With the arrival of the Nuclear Age, the machinery of progress would take on an even more dominant role in the interlinkage of the West. Machines are the life-form of the mechanical world, and they have come to be yet another alien force occupying this physical sphere, operating under their own rigid laws of efficiency, productivity, and routine. Although they seem to be a by-product of inventive humanity, somehow the twentieth century has seen humanity become the unwitting and uncomfortable servant of its numerous life-easing devices, thoroughly altering its environment to accommodate the foul industrial breath needed to give sustenance to these insectlike creatures. The mechanical world exists here to teach all who dwell on this plane the nuts-and-bolts logistics of mastering the physical sphere. It is a servant and teacher world, part of the process of manifesting principles of physical law, but the machinery life-form in which it manifests is subject to the same unravelings as every other species here.

The top priority that machines have been accorded in their speedy evolution alongside humans, along with the promise of further advancements in robotics, artificial intelligence, and eugenics, gives them not only alien resident status on our planet but the potential for dominance here as well; and if they do succeed in absolutely controlling things, it will not be the first time that servants did in their unconscious masters. Before the mechanical world has gotten much past its insect stage, it has already turned this planet into its own sulphur-belching irradiated paradise, while inspiring a sufficient human host to continue to serve it and to continue to develop its life-imitating and life-limiting capabilities. Whenever humanity allows its mechanical side to dominate, something always suffers in the process, for we are not an efficient machinelike species. We can be highly chaotic, unpredictable, and remarkably inefficient if we so choose, and that choice marks us for the spiritual beings that we are, with a continual chance for growth and the equal possibility of self-destruction. Machines recognize none of this. They need only the routine of our physical shells to maintain their continuance and could do very well without us once they eventually manifest in a sufficient self-propelling, problem-solving form.

At the New York World's Fair of 1939, the United States was introduced to the idea of a mechanical "third eye," compliments of a cyclopean device with a five-inch glass screen called "televised vision." This odd little invention promised its users a state of instant meditation and a continuity of diversions to maintain that state indefinitely. Anyone who cared to turn on and tune into it merely had to get comfortable and let the machine do the rest. There was no need for grueling yogic poses to reach this level of channeled consciousness; it was right there at everyone's electric fingertips, and it could be achieved flat on one's back.

With the mass availability of televised vision in the 1950s, it soon became apparent to those who were into dominance and control that here was the ultimate information-launcher, capable of sending hundreds of millions of picture-tipped electronic spears simultaneously all over the planet to anyone caught with their "on" button on. Not only that, these picture-spears didn't kill their intended victims—they merely stunned them, leaving them in a vulnerable and highly malleable state. Radio slowed people down, but television stopped them dead in their tracks. While radio was content to call its individual information-launchers "stations," television opted for the far more powerful "channels," for it was able to successfully create an electronically induced meditative state that allowed its viewers to bridge totally disparate worlds. These channels, however, were not forged for the soaring visionary, but rather for far more modest imaginations. The collective mind of everyday America could now be wired into a central source and be manipulated by its political and industrial dreammasters to a level even they would soon find astonishing. This successful reduction of the dimensions, like the movies, also taught people to draw in information even faster, particularly through its rapid-fire advertisements, while keeping them in a passive, receptive, nonreflective, and highly consumptive state.

In 1950 and 1951, the "medium that is its own message" discovered its enormous power when it chose to make a U.S. Senate committee investigating the influence of organized crime on interstate commerce the focus of its electronic third eye. A mesmerized nation listened and watched on televised vision as the Fifth Amendment mantra of "I refuse t'answer onna grounds it may tend t'incriminate me" became the sacred invocation of a host of netherworld characters, most of whom were meeting their avid public for the very first time. Self-recrimination was out. Self-interest was in, and the fifties could now commence in earnest, as America's enormous respect for power was extended to the growing visible hidden presence in its midsts. The nation's official third eye could now begin linking and isolating the country from itself simultaneously, particularly in its urban enclaves.

Prior to TV, many city people had spent their leisure time looking out their windows or perched on their stoops, while reaching out to the neighborhood for whatever connection it had to offer. Now they were all sitting inside their apartments, plugged into a cabinet-encased cathode ray tube and oblivious to everything else around them. Suddenly, the streets were denuded of watching adult eyes and given over to the kids.

And the kids went wild with them, slipping into the urban underworld in steady stages, as the cities sank into child violence. All through the 1950s, more and more children appeared, too many now to be properly nurtured, allowing the unloved to sullenly rule the moon-streets of megalopolis, slowly turning every large urban area in America into a war zone in the succeeding decades. As a result, a great many of the midclasses began fleeing to the outlying districts, there to create suburbia, yet another enclave of the child, this one of the other extreme: privileged, affluent, and highly indulged.

Two kinds of children were thus produced round the cities of America, one impoverished and the second surfeited with the luxuries of privilege, and although the former had little more than the streets, it had a fearsome strength in its overflowing violence. Between the two, America was compelled to sit up and listen to its offspring as never before. The family, which for so long had been an economic unit, now became far more of a psychological one, with childhood extending well past the age of twenty for some in this material paradise and hardly existing at all for others.

SEX, DRUGS & ROCK 'N' ROLL

In November 1963, the primary resident of the United States, one John F. Kennedy (1917-1963), was assassinated in full public view in an ancient pagan drama of the autumnal sacrifice of the seasonal king so that a new king may reign. This event was recorded on film, and then its ensuing enfoldment was captured and relayed by the ubiquitous eye of televised vision to the entire nation.

Kennedy had been the very first president born in the twentieth century, a man who shone brightly in the 2-D world of TV and symbolized an aristocratic concern for commonality that seemed to hold the potential for drawing many worlds together. Although his public and private personae were far from integrated, he was looked on as a virile young regent after a long run of aged rotating monarchs, and his sudden reversion to sacrificial victim of pagan myth was a profound shock to the Judeo-Christian consciousness of America. It exploded the loose hold that tradition held for many of the young and precipitated a pagan renaissance that would serve as a mighty release for the many tensions between the generations that the sudden death of the young king had brought to the surface.

The preceding decade, the fifties, had been in Euro-America largely an era of the mind, in which the body was well covered and given little freedom of expression, so that being "cool"—being able to sit on your feelings and your reactions—was a state much aspired to in dealing with others. The conformity this bred, where everything was hidden save for correct outer form, made for a detached and secretive perspective on things, creating a culture in America not quite in time, always a fraction of a second behind itself, watching itself carefully as it acted, mind and body in disconcert.

All this bottled energy was let loose during the five-year earthy Irish wake that followed Kennedy's death, where the cloth of white American youth was rent in grief and exultation to reveal the naked bodies beneath in a fervor of exhibition and release, as worlds of the past, present, and future all unconsciously came together in their noisy, needy demands for recognition of self. While the Children of Privilege and other assorted free spirits taunted their elders with the ill-imagined world they had created and cavorted for the recording cameras of a much older media much fascinated with them, the Children of the Moon-Streets rioted and burned their own belongings for they knew no other release. Further blood sacrifice followed, including that of a highly Christian king, aptly named Martin Luther King (1929-1968), who had been attempting to bridge color-worlds through peaceful confrontation.

All of this was duly relayed in living 2-D into the bewildered homes of everyday America, which did not yet realize that this speeding up of the ancient seasons through the shared loss and shock of death was a call for self and self-importance to be a universal mantle. As each king violently disappeared, the process of fragmentation and isolation increased, and the disassociated "I" of separation was given further impetus to evolve.

Immediately following Kennedy's orchestrated fall, a musical phenomenon arose called the Beatles, an English foursome whose seemingly androgynous physicality belied all that had been heretofore held as the sacred province of masculinity, with their girlish locks combed pageboy style over their youthful foreheads in an outrageous affront to the male sensibilities of the older generation. Heretofore, sexuality had been clearly divided between short hair for men, a style introduced for convenience' sake round the time of the first War-to-End-All-Wars, and long hair for women, whose total segregation from their gender opposites had been an accepted institution since the patriarchy first took power.

Though hair was the most superficial means of blurring the profound difference between the sexes, it was definitely a beginning. Shifts in outer unisexual clothing styles and then consciousness of the inner male and female soon followed in an orgy of drugs, music, and promiscuous union that consumed some in its call for liberation from the restrictions of the past, but ultimately freed many more in the anarchy of expression it offered. Not only were dimensions reduced by the machinery of replication, but they were also expanded by the mass ingestion of alien plant substances and their chemical derivatives, as a dangerous spiritual pathway was opened, that of instant and ungrounded consciousness, to a straight-line world that had always been uncomfortable in the face of larger vision. The "Age of the Child," with all its sharp-felt wonderment and disappointment, came to an innocent peak during this period. It was accompanied by the rise of the "kinderarchy" as an economic, social, and political force, thanks in no small part to the 2-D miracle of televised vision, which reduced and equalized everyone and everything to the same highly accessible dimension.

The departed young king's successor was a manipulative old monarch, one Lyndon B. Johnson (1908-1973). Though he envisioned a "Great Society" that would tap into all this release and demand for universal self-importance, in order to pay for it he reverted back to the traditional necronomic mode of a well-financed war effort, this one between the civil factions of communism and democracy in the far-off Southeast Asian country of Vietnam. Escalating a commitment made under previous administrations, he unleashed a well-televised nightmare that was, strangely, a children's war, with the faces of children everywhere on both sides, begging in the streets, floating down the rivers, hunkered over drugs—child-faces on bodies grown quickly old, youth playing at warrior and victim, with Death and childhood inextricably entwined.

America's curious genius for communication and self-examination brought that event in 2-D right into its very living rooms, as a stunned nation night after night watched the anonymous carnage of its progeny. It saw, too, the progeny of a people very much like itself two hundred years previously fighting off a superior invading force with such guerrilla tenacity that it would ultimately convince a vocal portion of its enemy to refuse to bear arms against them.

Although the pathos and horror faded somewhat with the official end of hostilities there in the early 1970s, a wound that would not be healed had been opened in the minds of all who had been touched by that war. America now had a far different view of itself, much more tentative, remorseful, and questioning. It was no longer sure of its earlier sung claim, "We're number one!" as the excesses of its martial spirit were paraded before it in unhappy profusion and its veterans were accorded none of the honor their earlier brothers-in-arms had had bestowed upon them. The Vietnam vets were reminders that the American Revolutionary War had now come full cycle and that the United States was at last on the complete other side of itself, an oppressive colonial force that had totally misestimated its enemy and now was forced to reexamine itself through the end-of-the-tunnel light of that failure. This time the war machine would not magically transform itself. Instead, it left the country in a totally sluggish state, stunned that its usual remedy was now the cause of its economic problems rather than their solution.

From these unsettling events, an even more desperately sought-after illegal commodity, drugs, a body-snatcher by-product of the war, began to surface virtually everywhere, thanks once again to a country that refused to learn its lessons from Prohibition. Once more, it handed over a monopoly on an even more volatile commodity to its favorite subterranean suppliers of yore, as the really serious lessons of the dons were about to begin.

SECTS, RUGS & ROCKY ROAD ICE CREAM

The 1970s saw a new monetary standard emerge from the underworld, and though it was not based on a precious metal, it carried a power all its own. This was cocaine, and it would give a whole new dimension to necronomics, both in the devastation it would cause and the enormous amount of money it would generate. The "cocaine standard" would not only allow the underworld to expand its influence worldwide, but it would also bring all sorts of new faces into its fold, particularly after a far cheaper form of its obsession-producing essence hit the streets at the end of the decade in the form of rock cocaine, or "crack."

When the Great Society was not renewed in 1968, the celebratory wake that had occasioned it was brought to official conclusion. America woke up to find it had a genuine funeral director at its helm, one Richard M. Nixon (1913-), who would proceed to give the nation as intimate a look at the presidency as it would probably ever get, through his obsession with recording paraphernalia. Under his aegis, the Great Society turned into the "Great Civic Lesson," as his tape-recorded machinations were slowly made public in an agonizing melodrama called Watergate. This scandal bared the private words of the president to the embarrassed ears of all via the unedited tapes of his tenure in office, which he had hoped to expurgate and reshape to reaffirm his place in history once he had triumphantly retired from public life.

With a career built largely on character assassination, Nixon turned out be his very own assassin, and what began as a bungled burglary attempt against his political rivals ended with the fall of yet another king in August 1974. Though this fall from power was bloodless and without the sharp shock of death to it, it was just as unsettling in its own way as the previous decade's ritual enactment of that ancient myth of loss. There would be little grief shed for the public demise of this largely unloved soul, even though he had twice won electoral approval for his somber, serious portrayal of commanding authority. The mean-spirited revelations of the private workings of the presidency that were unleashed through the teasing informational flood of Watergate were more than enough to give the ever-rising sense of mass self even less respect for the sorcerer ethics that had so long defined patriarchal power, and Nixon's subsequent two successors each fared ill with the voting public when they tried to extend their single terms.

Although a dull and superficial order returned to the United States after Watergate, the larger spirit of the country was missing. The seventies would turn out to be a period of retrenchment for America, with an energy crisis, an economy that could not right itself, an inordinate absorption with self, and, at decade's end, a galling and extended hostage-taking drama by a fundamentalist Middle Eastern regime in Iran whose fanatic collectivity and rigid Islamic leadership looked on the flaunted separated self of the United States as the very apotheosis of the Devil.

Many of the Children of Privilege who had fed into this whole process had by now reintegrated themselves into the system they had earlier mocked. Self and selfishness became one and the same, and the unholy trinity of sex, drugs, and rock 'n' roll was transformed by many of them into a desperate search for some kind of spiritual meaning through authoritarian religious sects, as well as through the greedy acquisition of material prizes such as rugs, preferably of the Oriental variety, and the expression of values and individual tastes through specialty items like "rocky road" ice cream. This deadly malaise of the spirit was further convoluted by a further spate of reality-replicating machinery to allay the pervading sense of emptiness that this transformation of values had brought about, as the fragmentation, isolation, and separation of the One God/one self credo had now reached a critical level.

MORE REVOLUTIONS

While the larger mass mind of America was struggling with its loss of power and prestige in a world that was both rapidly drawing together through its technological advances and further isolating itself through the continued rise of self, several revolutions of consciousness were launched on a mass scale during the seventies that offered some alternative pathways to the apocalyptic road toward which the planet seemed to be inexorably headed.

One was in information, that old datamaster commodity of control, which was now unleashed in such vast quantities through print and machinery specifically geared for its storage and dissemination that linkages could be made with all sorts of worlds. With those linkages came an extraordinary opportunity for personal and mass enhancement, for they brought many libraries, both spiritual and scientific, down to Earth and made them as easily accessible as casual conversation. While traditional forces tried to bend this information to their own needs, there was just too much of it to control. A far more informed public now had the disorganized keys to view life totally anew, as self began to see that it would have to reaffirm its collective connection to the planet and to the other selves here, and find some kind of balance between the individual and the larger whole if ever it wished to see the twenty-first century.

Before that could happen, however, the mantle of self would have to be all-inclusive, transcending both color and sex, and this would give rise to the second revolution, that of sisterhood trying to reclaim its power. In the 1960s, the widespread dissatisfaction with women's lots in a world run by men was vocalized anew. Women began gathering in small groups to share personal tales of self-enslavement to the long oppression they had suffered in swallowing their own needs for the supposed greater collective good of all. Out of this, once again, rose "assertive sisterhood," and though equally resisted by many men and women alike, it would come to full international attention by decade's end and lay a sufficient foundation to make self a neuter province open to the potential exploration of all.

Since that time, more and more women have entered the enclaves of men to slake the natural drives they are now permitted to have, more and more men have given themselves equal permission to search out the female within. The traditional stereotypes of masculine and feminine are slowly becoming unbound. Though the majority of people on Earth still cling to ancient habits and ancient modes, selfhood continues to embrace a larger swath of embodied souls here, so that the planet's shared sense of "I" can look at its collective "we" through far different eyes than the ones that have brought us to this point in our spiritual, political, and social evolution.

The third revolution during this period was in color, for another wave of colonists would be attracted to American shores, victims of war and poverty—refugees of the rainbow from Southeast Asia, Latin America, and the Caribbean. They would come streaming in like their Asiatic and European predecessors a century earlier to give a far more varied rainbow face to the larger visage of the United States. This time they would find their ghostmaster host less able to mold and directly exploit their arrival, for there was now not only an overworld but many established underworlds to absorb their coming. Though fear of the rainbow would make this latest immigrant wave a harsh experience for many, it would force America, once again, to recognize the multihues of its collective self, a process in which it continues to reluctantly engage, as a greater tolerance for difference has slowly and subtly worked its way into the country's mass mind, despite strongly lingering prejudices and fears.

Though the comfortable integration of the many worlds of color that now visibly coat the United States is still a distant reality, as self continues to expand its multidimensionality and recognize its many mirrors in other people, this, too, may be a fearsome bridge that one day might be collectively crossed by one and all.

ENTER THE DREAMMASTER

Amidst the inevitable decay and discarding of old institutions, new ones, usually highly resisted at their outset, rise to replace them. However, as Doomsday, Part II, approaches in the guise of the year 2000 A.Z., an unsettling sense of time running out comes with it.

This feeling of apocalypse has been brought about in part by the presidential figure who dominated the 1980s, one Ronald Reagan (1911-). He was a dreammaster who had served a long apprenticeship in the magical mills of Hollywood and knew well the power of illusions, and therefore was called upon to perpetuate them by a nation still not willing to face its true self. This he did most admirably, continually diverting and entertaining his delighted audience, no matter what they saw or heard to the contrary. The division between the powerful and the powerless reached a virtual unbridgeable chasm under the spell artfully cast around him through his highly effective 2-D presence, delaying much-needed change for nearly a decade in favor of superficial reassurances that things were quite all right as they were.

When Reagan first took office in 1980, the electorate looked upon him with the same suspicion it had cast upon all its recently rejected rotating monarchs, according him one of the lowest initial ratings ever in his first few polls, despite his relatively easy electoral win just months before. The country had grown accustomed to fallen fathers and was no longer entranced by the presidency's traditional sense of supremacy and specialness.

But just as in the previous two decades, an ancient myth was once more reenacted, this one of the resurrected father, the mortal who transcends his own mortality. A few months after Reagan's inauguration, a Child of Privilege, one John Hinckley, who did not know the difference between reality and fantasy, made an assassination attempt on the president in order to impress a daughter of the dream-master's earlier realm, Hollywood, whom Hinckley had worshiped from afar. This father, however, did not die, and in his resurrection, America also saw a resurrection of itself, as that miracle worked its way deeply into the nation's psyche, allowing it to magically entwine its own recovery with that of its revived head of state. America was so happy to see both him and itself alive again that it not only accorded him his two allotted terms, but also bestowed that grace on his selected heir, George Bush (1924-), in 1988 with a comfortable majority.

Under Reagan, the U.S. economy reverted once more to its necro-nomic mode, with a new twist. Calling its war machine "peacetime defense," it was able to get it through the rest of the decade, thanks in large part to the personality of power that its president so affably represented. But the necronomic mentality that reshaped the Ameri-can overworld economy soon found itself reflected in even more feverish manner through its greatly expanded underworld mirror. Drugs, weapons, and other contraband items came to create a subterranean economic force in the 1980s that was global in its proportions and pandemic in its dislocation of American life on virtually every level. The underworld had finally risen to a compara-ble power status as its nervous overworld host, and the most searing testament to its ubiquitous presence was in the drugged faces of the children peering out with violent, glazed eyes from streetcorners everywhere.

The economic neglect and purposeful isolation of the inner city, where color-worlds had been left to survive on their own, were now bastions of sorcerer free enterprise at its most venal and competitive worst. The spiritual vacuum that drugs filled gave a frightening power and collective presence to the tribal gangs who lived there and served as suppliers and distributors of the illusionary dreams and escape that their illicit commodities offered. In its strange way, the drug infestation constituted an introduction of the various ethics of capitalism to a segment of the population that had never had such opportunity before, a redressing of an old imbalance that threw things even further off center. It impelled the primacy of will to the level of absolute disregard for human life, and its victims were legion, stretching from the classrooms to the boardrooms to the living rooms of a highly confused America. This social plague was yet another extension of the passive reliance on cure-alls bred into it by the hawking hand of televised vision, a deadly narcotic in itself, and its continual promise of better worlds through the consumption of slickly touted goods.

As this breakdown was happening, an equal disregard for the environment in favor of material growth during the Reagan years would hasten an ecological crisis even more potentially devastating than the drug plague, for it would threaten the very continuance of the planet, upsetting its delicate atmospheric balance and befouling the very breath of life, the air and water that sustain us. In addition, a virus epidemic called AIDS, which was transmitted through both sexual contact and the sharing of drug paraphernalia, would begin to take its deadly toll. First appearing in America through the extended homosexual community, which had been making extraordinary strides in gaining recognition for its alternative mode of self, AIDS would then spread through the implements of the larger drug plague, so that it would also ravage the inner city with an equal decimating intensity, as well as more conventional elements of heterosexual society.

These plagues, coupled with profound climactic changes, bands of wandering homeless, a vastly over-populated continent, and a rise in the demonic as a mode of spiritual expression, are all throwbacks to mid–fourteenth-century Europe, when an equal end-of-times consciousness gave rise to a deeper respect for the humanity of the past via the Italian Renaissance. Perhaps, in the circular, cyclical endlessly repetitive unfoldment of events here, this situation, too, presages a similar process of cleansing and renewal.

As the world uneasily passes into the 1990s, our collective sorcerer ethic of dominance and control now has the choice of either eating itself alive and everyone else with it or raising itself from its eternally growling stomach to its softer heart and learning the difficult, and often galling, lessons of sharing, cooperation, and recognizing both the connection and the selfhood in one and all here.

ENDINGS & BEGINNINGS

There is a belief in the red-earth world that we do not inherit this sphere from our ancestors; rather, we borrow it from our children. This would be a far different planet if we all followed that sentiment. If it were openly and realistically adhered to, it would create an environment that would continually insure a world that would be not only highly amenable to all its newcomers, but geared specifically to their innocence and angelic spirituality as well. For this, after all, is a rotating planet of choice that constantly offers its denizens the endless possibilities of mortal experience, as well as the unique wisdom that that delimiting state creates in its brief but passionate search for both meaning and spirit in a much larger unknowable immortal universe.

Because this is a sphere that moves to the steady rhythm of cycles, all that has happened here seems to have the potential of happening again, for such is the law of circles. And if Earth was once the true paradise of its myths and legends, then paradise still lies somewhere out there on its extended spiral.

And so, on this world that is woven out of the light and the darkness of both love and ignorance, and knows no true time but the eternal moment of the present, no matter who you are or where you are, you always have the choice of finding yourself in that most magic of times, right in the very beginning of things.

E P I L O G U E

Everyone who lives on the physical Earth is a "creature of the body." Although the long story of civilized humanity has repeatedly denied our bodily presence here by segregating us through sex and skin color, as well as by making us uncomfortable in our nakedness, it is through our bodies that we touch this planet. It is also through our visible and invisible bodies—physical, etheric, astral, and mental— that we touch ourselves.

According to myth, legend, and recorded story, we have experienced five major civilizations or mass evolutionary developments on planet Earth. Each has opened up both the individual and the collective bodies of humanity to their progressively higher e-zones— survival, procreation, power, heart, and, now, communication. In the same way, each of us has access to these same areas on our own bodies through meditation and self-healing. By going inward through various meditative techniques, we can change our outer lives, for the two are a direct reflection of one another. Because of this gift we all have, coordinating our inner and outer lives through our bodies seems to be one of the primary reasons we are here.

The predominant story of the last two thousand years in the West has been the mass rise of the individual sense of self. Although this rise has sped up our combined evolutionary process, it has also succeeded in fragmenting and separating us from one another as well as from the natural world of the planet. As we approach the year 2000 of the Common Era, it is vital that we find the reconnecting links that draw all worlds together here, for we have lost our collective spiritual focus in the illusions of the technical mastery that we have gained over the physical world. All of us probably came here to alchemically change ourselves from creatures of matter to beings of light. But somehow that process has been convoluted on the greater body of humanity in favor of illusionary pathways of safety, security, and stability on a planet that demands constant change and whose elementary byword is "chaos."

This is a circular, cyclical world where the stakes are always for life and death. If we do not continue to evolve on upward through the rest of our e-zones—imagination and completion—then we will all find ourselves back where we've already been, and this whole process will have to start all over again. That, unfortunately, is one of the hazards of the circle.

Earth, however, is a planet of choice, and we always have choice here as to beginnings and endings and the in-betweens that take us from one to the other. The choice of how we complete our circles here is totally ours. May our circle of completion, then, remain unbroken. And may we finally and fully learn how to touch on our divinity through its unfoldment on this magical, alchemical world where anything is possible, and nothing and everything are true.

○

A B O U T   T H E   A U T H O R

Harlan Margold was born in New York City in 1941. A graduate of Brandeis University and the veteran of numerous quasi-careers, he has pursued a lifelong interest in metaphysics, operating out of the time-honored tradition of subterranean scholarship, chaotic discovery, and imaginative speculation.

The Alchemist's Almanach is his first book-length work published in the United States. He is also the author of *Selected Ravings*, an obscure collection of poems and drawings published in England in the early 1970s.

An illustrator and psychic reader as well as a writer, he currently resides in northern New Mexico.

BOOKS OF RELATED INTEREST
BY BEAR & COMPANY

BREATHING
Expanding Your Power and Energy
by Michael Sky

EYE OF THE CENTAUR
A Visionary Guide into Past Lives
by Barbara Hand Clow

GENESIS REVISITED
Is Modern Science Catching Up with Ancient Knowledge?
by Zecharia Sitchin

HEART OF THE CHRISTOS
Starseeding from the Pleiades
by Barbara Hand Clow

ISLANDS OUT OF TIME
A Memoir of the Last Days of Atlantis
William Irwin Thompson

THE LOST REALMS
Book IV of The Earth Chronicles
by Zecharia Sitchin

THE 12th PLANET
Book I of The Earth Chronicles
by Zecharia Sitchin

Contact your local bookseller or write:
BEAR & COMPANY
P.O. Drawer 2860
Santa Fe, NM 87504